The Complete

Manual of

Sports

Science

The Complete Manual of

Sports Science

A practical guide to applied sports science

Wilf Paish

A & C Black • London

Published in 1998 by
A & C Black (Publishers) Ltd
35 Bedford Row, London WC1R 4JH

Formerly published in 1991
as *Training for Peak Performance*

ISBN 0 7136 4854 6

A CIP catalogue record for this book
is available from the British Library.

Acknowledgements
Cover photographs courtesy of Sporting Pictures (UK) Ltd,
except for the image of the cricketer which is courtesy of Action-Plus.
Line diagrams by Ron Dixon and Jean Ashley.

Typeset in Palatino
Printed and bound in Great Britain by Hillman Printers Ltd, Frome, Somerset.

Other books of interest from A & C Black

The Complete Guide to Sports Nutrition (Second edition)
by Anita Bean
This highly successful book will show you how improved nutrition can help to enhance performance, boost energy levels, achieve faster and better training gains, and reach higher competitive standards. (ISBN 0-7136-4388-9)

The Complete Guide to Strength Training
by Anita Bean
Draws together the latest scientifically-proven ways of increasing strength using highly effective training methods and optimal nutrition. (ISBN 0-7136-4389-7)

Soccer Coaching and Team Management (Second edition)
by Malcolm Cook
In drawing on 30 years of experience, as well as on numerous interviews with many top-class coaches and managers, the author sets out clear and commonsense guidelines for aspiring coaches and team managers. A unique insight into this increasingly high-profile field. (ISBN 0-7136-4458-3)

Soccer Training (Fifth edition)
by Nick Whitehead and Malcolm Cook
This book brings together over 60 games and drills aimed at developing specific soccer skills, games and drills that have been used and recommended by some of the world's top soccer coaches. (ISBN 0-7136-4748-5)

Sports Training Principles (Third edition)
by Frank W. Dick
An acknowledged classic in its field, this is a comprehensive reservoir of information essential to preparing people for achievement in sport.
(ISBN 0-7136-4149-5)

Total Rugby (Fourth edition)
by Jim Greenwood
One of rugby's most seminal coaching manuals. Total rugby is the antithesis of play-safe rugby. Total rugby is an open, ebullient game in which every player is encouraged to show what he can do as attacker, defender and supporting player. Total rugby is all about well-judged risk-taking. (ISBN 0-7136-4545-8)

Contents

"Wilf Paish and I go back more years than I care to remember. However, the years have done nothing to diminish his enthusiasm for sport in general and his desire to constantly widen his horizons. I have always valued his specialist advice regarding the preparation of footballers for competition because he has always managed to translate theory into practice, moreover practice which can be understood by the layman. *The Complete Manual of Sports Science* is a very informative read."

Howard Wilkinson, Technical Director, The Football Association

"Sport at the highest level requires an understanding of sports science support services which covers exercise physiology, nutrition, psychology and biomechanics. Unfortunately the world of the sports scientist is often too clogged with scientific terminology for the general public to understand. Wilf Paish's knowledge in the sports science areas underlying athletic performance is outstanding. *The Complete Manual of Sports Science* will be a major contribution to any sports library."

Kevin Hickey, Technical Director, British Olympic Association

"Wilf Paish is one of the great coaches in British sport, with a wealth of experience and expertise to share. One of his greatest strengths is his ability to communicate with athletes and players in easily understood terms. All coaches need to understand clearly the vital role sports science plays in support of their coaching: they will all benefit from Wilf's clarity of thought and expression."

**Geoff Cooke OBE, former Chief Executive,
National Coaching Foundation**

"Just what the doctor ordered! *The Complete Manual of Sports Science* shows how the latest research findings can help the coach and athlete, and in language everyone can understand."

Ed Fox, Publisher, Track & Field News

"Any list of mine giving the world's leading sports coaches would always include the name of Wilf Paish. He is unique in that he has coached successfully not only in a wide variety of sports but also at every level of ability. Wilf has always possessed a remarkable capacity to link theory with practice and to communicate clearly and directly with both coach and athlete. *The Complete Manual of Sports Science* is another demonstration of his rare ability to translate scientific complexities into practical programmes which can be understood and effectively delivered to the athlete by the coach."

Tom McNab, international coach

Preface

This book started its life as *Training for Peak Performance*, published back
in 1991. At the time I felt that there was a need to translate the
volumes of sports training research, which exist mainly in university
libraries, into a form that would be accessible to both athletes and
coaches. For sports people involved in practical performance, time is
always at a premium. Reading through numerous journals in the hope
of gaining the odd snippet of valuable information would be time wasted
for such people (even assuming that they had access to this literature).
Most of this information is directed at the sports science student.

Feedback from those who read *Training for Peak Performance* persuaded
me to believe that the potential readership would be greater if it could
be modified to become an inherently practical manual of sports science,
very much a publication for those who work at the sharp edge of sport,
producing performers at a high level. *The Complete Manual of Sports
Science* is the result.

Much of the information in the manual is in its original form, updated
where necessary in the light of recent research. There are additional
chapters aimed at encouraging the reader to become aware of the
specific nature of the basic training components, to view the aspect
of skill through the eyes of the biomechanist, and to become a realist
in the debate relating to nature versus nurture.

Wilf Paish

Introduction

Most books devoted to sports training are aimed at improving the novice's level up to that of an average performer. This is in line with the contemporary philosophy of sport-for-all, mass participation at a level that most people will enjoy. Indeed, it is true to say that for this level one can 'play to get fit'. But what about that elite group of people who wish to achieve peak performance, and who wish to 'get fit to play'? Those people who aspire to top-level international status, who commit three or four hours each day, for seven days a week and for 52 weeks of the year, towards training for peak performance? This elite group is unique and requires very special attention as far as their training routines are concerned.

Many people involved in sport would not accept that there is a need to treat the ambitious sportsperson differently or that training programmes vary in terms of content as well as quality. This dated philosophy is usually supported by ex-internationals who say, 'We didn't do this in my day.' However, sport is now both a political tool and a thriving business in which massive cash rewards await those who are successful. Television has turned our top sportsmen and women into superstars; they have become household names, an accolade previously only bestowed upon pop and film stars. All participants in sport, certainly at international level, are encouraged to try to reach the top and to stake their claims to the financial fortunes on offer. Sportsmen and women, the world over, train harder and seek the advice of coaches, trainers and other support agencies.

This philosophy might be alien to many people involved with sport, as it does tend to promote the win-at-all-cost idea, in extreme cases leading competitors to resort to performance-enhancing drugs. But society has changed, and will continue to change, and the days of the true amateur in sport have gone, probably never to return.

Any competitor striving for the highest possible goal is going to start by asking the question, 'What are the factors necessary for peak performance?' This whole book is, in a sense, the answer to that question, but in very basic terms one must *assemble the right people, in the right place, at the right time*. What does this mean in practice?

First are the 'right people'. Top of the list is the performer. He or she must have proven ability, the capacity for training, good health and, above all else, the desire to succeed. There are many people with the natural ability, but who lack the necessary commitment; those prepared to sacrifice many of the pleasures of this world, in their pursuit of excellence, are those who will be successful.

In modern sport, it is unlikely that anyone will make the grade by 'ploughing a lone furrow'. It is team work that will produce the champions of the future and most aspirants require a team of support people such as a coach, trainer, sports scientist, and paramedics.

The coach or trainer must have very special abilities: to inspire and to motivate the performer to increased levels of training, to act as a support when things go wrong, and to guide the performer back on to the road to success.

When injured, the average performer would not object too violently to taking a rest period. To the elite performer such a demand would be unreal, hence the need for good medical support, offering instant diagnosis and treatment. All too frequently, performers are taken out of their sport prematurely, by not having access to injury diagnosis and treatment. Hence the sports doctor ranks very highly on this list of the 'right people'. Sometimes medical specialists should be included; for example, it is not unusual for athletes and soccer players to be forced to rest because of their failure to seek the advice of a chiropodist. Those who wish to aspire to peak performance cannot afford to allow any stone to be unturned, since under that 'stone' might rest their key to success.

The concept of the right place might not be so obvious. It is no longer possible to produce peak performance with, for example, only a grass pitch to train on. To achieve success at the highest level, one needs a conditioning room, a gymnasium, a weight-training room, and an injury treatment room. It makes work much easier, and cuts travel time, if all of these facilities exist at the same venue.

Finally, what is the 'right time'? The correct time of the day and the year for training both make an impact upon success at the highest level. For many, the right time of the day frequently means the only time of the day. For those who have to support themselves with other work, the evening might be the only time available to train, but there is very strong evidence that this is not the ideal time for the greatest adaptation to training to take place. The body is often tired at the end of a day, especially when the pressure of work has been physically and mentally demanding. For most people, the most beneficial time to train is the middle of the day.

Have we arrived at the time when all who wish to compete at the highest possible level need to work full-time in their sport? Many elite performers who recognise this possibility have secured sponsors, or generous employers who turn a blind eye to the hours spent training. Some athletes manage to exist on part-time employment, while others have negotiated flexi-time, where they can be released at the most suitable time of the day, to do their training. This unsatisfactory situation might force a number of nations to consider their current philosophy of elitism in sport, and make the necessary changes to the rules. Not only is mid-day the best time physiologically for most people to train, but if those training at a peak level could use the facilities at this time it would relieve the pressure on them when the general public wants to use them in the early evening. However, individual variations have to be considered, as some sportspeople train better in the early morning, and others in the late evening. Studying the individual's biorhythm to establish the best time of the day, and the best time of the month, could be the way to inject the highest training loads, so making adaptation more efficient.

These circumstances are in outline those felt to be correct for elite levels of performance. This manual is devoted to a scientific analysis of what is necessary to help produce performers of the highest calibre. While it is aimed at the coach and the performer, together with those who wish to study sports science at any level, it should also be of value to parents, trainers, administrators, journalists and other media representatives, etc., indeed anyone who wishes to be made aware of what science can offer modern sport.

Training theory

A patient discharged from hospital will be declared 'fit'. A top-class soccer player failing a fitness test on the eve of a game is declared 'unfit'. Yet in the true context of the meaning of the term, the two people are poles apart and the soccer player is in a vastly superior physical state to the invalid. Fitness is *relative*.

Similarly, a world-class sprinter, who is not familiar with swimming, could have great difficulty in swimming the length of a pool. Fitness is also *specific*.

Fitness is relative to the individual at any period in time. The elite performer recognises how fitness is continuous, and the factors that influence its level and cause a state of flux. One frequently hears that the elite runner isn't racing fit. While all of the components of fitness might have been conditioned correctly, a few carefully selected races are required to hone fully the competitive edge, to produce what is recognised as total fitness. Anyone associated with preparing individuals or teams for competition also becomes well aware of its specificity. The fitness demands required to last a full game of soccer are very different from those placed on the marathon runner. Even within a sport, specificity is relevant, such as in the difference between the rugby forward and the rugby back, or a wide receiver and a running back in American football.

The coach who wishes to progress towards peak performance must be aware of both relative and specific fitness, and recognise the demands that a change in either can have upon the physical structure of the body. Those involved with the promotion of fitness also recognise that while fitness is specific, there are a number of general principles that contribute towards the total meaning of the term 'fitness'. So what is general fitness? How is it promoted? How does one recognise the various levels of fitness? The one certain factor is that the person who wishes to achieve peak performance must have a higher level of fitness than the less ambitious competitor.

Components of fitness

Sports scientists recognise that general fitness has a number of components, frequently termed the **'S' factors: speed, strength, stamina, suppleness and skill**. The contribution that each makes towards total fitness, and the methods used to train each of the components, will be discussed in detail later. For the time being it is sufficient to identify them. They do not exist in isolation, as the development of one will influence the development of another, in what is known as **cross-component effects**. Each sport calls for a greater or lesser degree of each component, and for different cross-component effects.

Sport training theory has developed much of its own terminology, some of which might not be found in standard dictionaries, but which nevertheless is now universally accepted. Furthermore, like any other science, it has prompted its own laws, principles and systems that are now recognised throughout the world by sports scientists, educated in the individual sciences of physiology, psychology, biomechanics and training theory.

Most sports training techniques involve an understanding of the **overload** principle, in association with the **intermittent work theory** and the principle of adaptation. While this statement might sound like jargon, a total understanding of what is involved must be appreciated by anyone involved in peak performance.

Overload, adaptation and intermittent work theory

In overload one attempts to overload the physiological structure of the body, so causing it a degree of stress, and even a partial breakdown. Nature's reaction is to overcompensate, by giving the body enhanced powers of resistance to the specific stress.

A good example of this is when one trains for strength. An **overload resistance** is used to stress the muscle, causing the protein fibres to break down. In the adaptive, rebuilding process, the fibres grow stronger and can then cope with an identical stress later on. The muscles are subjected to greater stresses in progressive stages, with the adaptation process also being progressive. This principle applies to all of the physiological systems of the body, which are stressed during training. However, should the stressing agent (training load) be too severe, a breakdown of the system follows, and adaptation will not take place. Hence, the stress must be applied progressively, at the correct level of intensity. Herein lies the skill of devising the individual training programme.

To provide the correct level of stress, and so encourage adaptation, the stressor must be applied in gradually increasing levels, allowing a period for the system to recover before a further application of stress. In other words, the body is called upon to act intermittently. It is subjected to an **effort task** and then allowed partially to recover before it is submitted again to a similar effort task. For example, in a running training programme, an athlete might be set the task of 6 x 200m, each leg in 28 seconds, with 2 minutes recovery between each. If the same task was to be set as 1,200m (6 x 200m) in 2 minutes 48 seconds (6 x 28 seconds), only a good, accomplished middle distance runner would be capable of achieving it. However, by breaking it down into smaller tasks, and allowing a recovery period between each leg, most good sportsmen and women manage. Breaking the total down into smaller periods of effort, with a period for recovery, in this way is known as the **intermittent work principle.**

The training dose, to promote the stress, is known as the effort, or the **loading**. The load, or effort, can be intensive, with a high degree of stress over a relatively short period of time. The intensity of the above programme is the 28-second effort period, and the two minutes allowed for recovery. The intensity can be changed by varying either, or both, of the two variables. For example, a very high level of stress would be produced by reducing both to 26 seconds of effort and 1½ minutes recovery.

A different type of stress can be placed on the body by reducing the intensity of the effort and increasing the amount, or volume, of the work done. Here, the training variable is known as the **extent of effort**. In the specified schedule, the extent is represented by the 6 x 200m. Both the number of repetitions, i.e. six, and the duration of the effort, i.e. 200m, can be increased, or decreased. By carefully varying the extent and the intensity of effort, one can create a specific training effect and adaptation. These effects will be fully reviewed later.

If the intensity of the stressing agent is too low, adaptation will not be effective. The skilful coach knows how to manipulate the training variables to ensure maximum adaptation, while at the same time looking for symptoms of stress which will prevent adaptation.

Peaking

The manipulation of the training variables introduces us to **peaking**. While the concept has only recently been highlighted in training manuals, the art of peaking has been with the performer for a very long time. The coach or player involved with individual sports like track and field athletics, gymnastics, swimming or boxing has a much easier task than the person involved with team sports. For example, with the Olympic Games it is possible for an individual to experience a number of carefully planned sub-peaks and reach a climax at the Games final. However the team-sport performer must try to perform at a peak for a number of successive weeks and months, over the extended period of time of the sport's season. Nevertheless, even with these sports, the basic principles of peaking must be adopted during the out-of-season conditioning phase.

There are obstacles to this approach to peaking, particularly in the popular professional sports. The professional cricketer or baseball player might be required by contract to play most days of the week during the summer months, and then maybe to go on off-season tour or play exhibition matches. A worse situation is experienced in soccer, where a very long season might be followed by international matches. Playing the game for most of the 52 weeks of the year isn't conducive to peak performance. The body requires time to recover, both physically and mentally, to recharge the physical accumulators and to improve the 'S' factors, which can even deteriorate during a competitive season.

Rest

Rest must be an integral part of training for elite performers. Unfortunately, many athletes – in particular marathon runners and weightlifters – become obsessed with their training. The idea of taking a rest, for even a single day, produces a guilt complex. There is a very sound physiological reason for this. The act of physical exertion upsets the delicate balance of certain hormones in the body. Upsetting this balance can create a euphoric or a depressive state; it can change personalities and even promote violent behaviour. Frequently mood swings are dramatic.

Anyone associated with elitism in sport must be aware of this state. There are many tell tale symptoms which will indicate that a period of rest is necessary. It is an indication that the adaptive mechanism is failing.

Hence I insist that a total rest day is included in any weekly schedule, with an extended rest period when a specific situation makes such a demand.

Planning the year

A planned approach to a year of training and competition is a prerequisite for peak performance. It has to be carefully thought out, following extensive discussion with the athletes, and then well documented.

The full-time professional is only concerned with one factor: the period of the year when competition takes place. The elite amateur, who has also to work for a living, has other factors to consider, such as the time available for training, the availability of facilities, and training partners. However, the overriding factor is always the will to succeed. Where there is the will there is always the way.

The method by which the components of fitness are phased into the year is commonly known as **periodisation**. If there is only one peak required then one follows a single periodised year, but you can plan for more than one peak, such as in a double, or multi-periodised year. Two examples of typical training plans are given below.

Example 1

Year plan for a summer-based competitive season. The months are for the northern hemisphere; those in the southern hemisphere should start in March.

◆ September ◆

Period of active recovery. This is the month when holidays should be taken, and recreation activities not normally practised during the training period enjoyed. The performer is starved of their chosen sport, producing a 'hungry' athlete when the true training starts.

◆ October/November ◆

Period of endurance emphasis. Endurance forms the foundation of all training. The emphasis is on stamina, but do not ignore the remaining 'S' factors. For example, in a single week there might be one session devoted to speed, strength, suppleness and skill and six sessions devoted to endurance training. It is the extent of training that dominates this phase of the year. Even when the performer is working with weights the emphasis is on strength endurance, where the number of repetitions remains high and the poundage low.

It is a very tiring time, but the performer should adapt readily to the increasing work loads. Rest days are essential and it is far better to train several times in one day, in order to get a complete rest on another day, than to train once or twice every day. A four-day cycle produces the best results: *day 1*: light training; *days 2 and 3*: very hard training; *day 4*: rest.

◆ December/January ◆

Period of gross strength emphasis. During this phase the performer aims to increase strength levels appreciably by using the accepted forms of progressive resistance training (PRT). Here the extent of training is reduced and the intensity increased. Again, it must be stressed that the other fitness components are not ignored. A sensible ratio is two units of strength to one of the other components.

◆ February/March ◆

Period for developing specific strength and power. Here the coach must look at the specific demands of the sport, and carefully use selected weight training exercises – pulleys, springs, harnesses, weighted balls, etc. – to encourage the performer to use the muscles in the way they might be used during the practice of the sport, except that resistance is now applied. Further details of the methods for developing specific strength, and power, will be found in chapter 4.

◆ April/Early May ◆

Period during which the emphasis is placed upon the skill development of the sport. A period for generally speeding up all movements, so that they can closely resemble the precise movements used in the sport. It is fairly certain that this period will also encroach upon the early competitions. These must be phased into the normal training routine.

◆ Late May/August ◆

Period for competition. All of the 'S' factors must still be stimulated in training. However, the emphasis will be on retention rather than improvement. The 'S' factors will regress if not stimulated, but even a single session per week is enough to keep the system 'topped up'.

Example 2

Year plan for a winter-based competitive season. The months given are, again, for the northern hemisphere.

March	Period of active recovery, or late season games
April	Endurance emphasis, or active recovery
May	Gross strength emphasis, or endurance emphasis
June	Specific strength/power emphasis, or general strength emphasis to include all aspects of strength
July	Skill, event preparation period
Aug–March	Competition period

The above phasing allows for clubs that are still playing at the end of March, and for those that finish in early March.

Most other countries in the world, where there is a temperate climate the whole year round, allow the climate to dictate their competitive period. If applied in Britain, sports such as rugby and soccer might take a break period during late December, January and early February. In this case there would be two seasons and the need to double periodise.

In terms of double periodisation the two-monthly cycle is reduced to one, so only one month is devoted to the development of endurance, with the other factors following on in the sequence already described. In multi-periodisation it is possible to reduce a phase to just one week, providing the sportsperson is already very fit and has spent a number of years following a single periodised year.

Cyclic terminology

The various phases of training involved with periodisation have been labelled using pseudo-scientific terminology, the precise origin of which now seems rather obscure. While the terms might not be of any direct relevance, an appreciation of those used will certainly help further reading or research.

The macro cycle

This is an extended period in the training scheme. For example, in the first training plan illustrated earlier in this chapter, the period October to March would form a macro cycle of general conditioning.

The messo cycle

This is a lesser period of training than the macro cycle. Using the same year plan, the period October to November would compose a messo cycle of endurance training.

The micro cycle

This is the smallest unit used in the terminology. In most situations this period represents a week and is often so determined for convenience sake. However, there is evidence to suggest that a four-day micro cycle is the best to bring about an adaptive response, but with certain sports and certain individuals one is forced into adopting a weekly training programme to fit in with the availability of facilities. At times tradition also forces a weekly routine – for example, rugby league has a tradition of team training on Tuesdays and Thursdays. Certain other sports might only be able to book an indoor facility, such as a gymnasium, at a set time each week. However, the full-time professional is not faced with these problems.

With the information in this chapter the coach and player are equipped to prepare the day-to-day routine. Both must also be able to judge critically the efficacy of a training method, making evaluations throughout each of the training cycles. For example, there is little point in entering a training cycle designed to promote strength, if at the end of it one doesn't emerge stronger. Therefore, an accurate measurement of strength levels must be made before, during and at the end of a cycle, to make sure development takes place. Evaluation is covered fully in chapter 11.

The 'S' factors in recovery

When one of the 'S' factors is not trained, it returns to its pre-trained state over a period of time. The rate of regression depends upon the 'S' factor component, and upon the individual. However, in general terms, strength regresses the quickest and skill the slowest. Hence, these factors must be kept in mind during the rehabilitation period following any injury.

The sequence for phasing in the 'S' factors is critical. The sequence following on from the period devoted to recovery at the end of the competitive season is: stamina, strength, power and specific strength, speed, skill.

Stretching

Suppleness or mobility is maintained during each phase, particularly during the gross strength phase. Extra muscle bulk might result from this stage of training, bringing with it a decreased range of movement, hence the need for stretching exercises. Stretching exercises should form part of each warm-up routine and, in some cases, full sessions can be devoted to them.

TOTAL FITNESS

The capacity to cope with the extreme demands of sport

Speed (reaction)
The endowed and promoted speed of limb movement

Stamina (endurance)
The endowed and promoted capacity to withstand the fatigue promoted by repetitive limb movement

Skill
The endowed and trained co-ordination of limb movement that produces skill

Strength
The promoted strength of the individual muscles facilitating the efficient movement of limbs

Suppleness (flexibility)
The endowed and trained capacity of the body to extend the effective range and efficiency of any limb movement

Power
Strength applied with speed

Psychology
The trained and endowed quality whereby the mind sets the level of concentration necessary to permit the other qualities to be developed to their full

Development of speed

Speed is more a product of nature than nurture. A person is born with muscles capable of working at speed. Some people in sport term such muscles as **fast twitch**, although the true sports scientist refers to them as **fast glycolytic**. This means that, when the muscle is called upon to work at maximum capacity, the muscle fibres use the basic energy-giving substance quickly. Hence their capacity for work of a sustained nature is very limited – probably in the region of 30–40 seconds for a major muscle group. Fast-acting fibres also have to receive a special nerve impulse which is probably more refined in some people than others, so promoting the natural gift of speed.

Well before a person has reached a level where they wish to achieve peak performance, it will be apparent to them whether or not they have this gift. It is certainly evident in children of 8–10 years old, and at this age they have frequently already indicated their natural ability in any of the speed/power-based sports, such as major ball games and track and field athletics. Teachers and coaches are all very well aware that most sports are looking for the same basic speed skill. All too frequently, the best soccer player is the best athlete, basketball player, and so on, and most sports are competing to attract the same person. This endowed quality is not, though, necessary for endurance-based sports, such as middle- and long-distance running or distance skiing, or for strength-based sports such as weightlifting and bodybuilding.

While most people involved in sports training accept that speed is a quality you are either born with or not, it does not mean that it isn't trainable. A person is born with an ultimate speed potential and only by planned training can this potential be fully realised, although the performer must also be encouraged to adopt the approach that one is never likely to achieve the ultimate potential. At any stage in a player's career he or she must always function in the belief that they can produce faster movements. Indeed, this is a basic philosophy of all involved in sport – the ultimate performance is always 'just around the corner'.

The primacy of leg speed

There is a large cross-component effect in speed. If one becomes stronger, more powerful and more flexible this will almost certainly enhance speed potential. This is particularly the case with the basic skill of running at peak speed, in other words sprinting. While speed movements of other limbs are critical in some sports, the ability to sprint is a key feature of most. Admittedly, speed might only be called for over a few strides, as in soccer, hockey, basketball, or even to get into position to play a shot on the tennis court; nevertheless leg speed is a crucial factor in every foot contact sport. It will be used to change the tempo of running, or the direction of running, both ploys that effective performers use to arrive one step ahead of their opposition.

These movements call for the muscles to work in a powerful way; the terms **explode** or **explosive muscle** action are frequently used in this context. The explosive action calls for the performer to take advantage of the **elastic** quality of the muscle, which is the term most likely to be used by the sports scientist.

The mechanics of sprinting

In terms of pure physics, power is the rate at which work is done. It introduces both a force and a time factor. The bigger the force and/or the shorter the time interval, the greater the power factor. In simple terms the performer needs to exert the maximum force over the shortest possible period of time. In recent years better understanding of power and its development has enabled those in the power-based sports to perform at a significantly higher level.

Sprinting is full-effort running, requiring an instant supply of glycogen, which will last for about 30–40 seconds. After this period the supplies of energy for this type of work are depleted, the muscle becomes fatigued and the level of activity must be reduced.

In terms of biomechanics, sprinting is the product of leg speed (cadence) and stride length. Several variables affect the ability to sprint (*see* the summary chart on page 22). All but the endowed ability factor are trainable, and will respond to purposeful training. An improvement in any of the variables, without an associated deterioration in any of the others, will result in a faster sprinter.

Improving sprint speeds

Very few people, other than those directly influenced by, or involved with, the sprinters from track and field athletics will spend a significant time in trying to improve this ability. A number of very successful clubs and individuals have employed sprint coaches to improve this vital quality. For example, Boris Becker employed Frank Dick, then head coach of British athletics, to work on his speed and agility about the tennis court.

Not all of the trainable factors exist as isolated components of speed. For example, training designed to concentrate upon skill will have an effect upon relaxation; training for strength could have an adverse effect upon flexibility. Indeed, the performer must be made aware of the tremendous cross-component effect of all the 'S' factors.

Initially, the trainer, or the person being trained, should consider motivation as a prime factor in improving sprinting. The best way is to place a group of performers in a competitive situation over a distance of about 50m, and have them race the distance six to ten times, with a period allowed for total recovery. To increase the competition, the winner of each race is given a penalty handicap of one metre.

Other routines that develop speed involve allowing the athlete to experience greater running speed than he or she would unassisted. They include sprinting fast down a slight decline with gravity aiding leg speed; or being towed by a cycle, or a motor cycle (care must be exercised), with a harness or yoke. (Both have been used to good effect in the former Soviet Union, in helping the 1972 Olympic champion, Valeri Borzov.) Other ideas which have been used in sprinting and speed roller skating include running in the slipstream created by a motorised vehicle.

Another method is to use an elastic running harness, in one of two ways. The first is to anchor a 20m (65ft) length of heavy duty, stranded, elastic cable, usually by having a partner hold it (*see* fig. 1). The elastic is then stretched to its maximum capacity at which point the athlete sprints in a straight line towards the anchor point. (Speed pulley systems are now available. The power of a partner, linked by a pulley system, permits greater acceleration by helping to overcome the inertia of the body.)

The second method is to improvise a stationary running machine out of identical elastic strands (*see* fig. 2). The elastic is secured to the shoe and then put under stretch, when it is pulled towards the floor by the stretch of the elastic. It works in an opposite way to the harness, through resistance, as the thigh muscles have to pick up the leg against the resistance of the elastic which pulls it back.

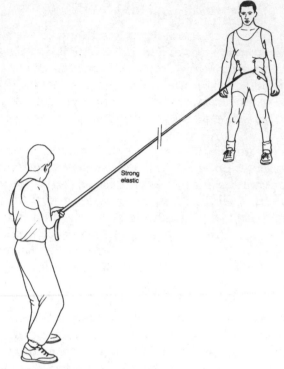

Strong
elastic

Fig. 1 Elastic running harness

Webbing belt

Elastic foot loop

Nylon rope

Fig. 2 Stationary running machine. A webbing belt is fastened around the athlete's waist. It is secured to two eight-metre lengths of nylon rope, with the free end terminating in an elastic foot loop made from stranded trampoline elastic. Each rope is passed over a wall bar at hip height and under the lowest wall bar before being secured to the runner's feet. The runner leans forward to put the rope under tension and runs on the spot on a rubber mat

Speed and speed endurance

It should be emphasised that when attempting to improve the capacity to sprint, the intermittent work principle must be used, allowing sufficient time for the active muscles to recover before a further bout of activity. Several minutes are necessary for full recovery, even for short sprints. When full recovery is not allowed, the session will develop into one that trains a specific aspect of endurance, so defeating the initial aim of speed development.

Many coaches, particularly those from team games, confuse speed and speed endurance. While both are necessary for success, the two components cannot be trained at the same time. The biology of energy supply is against it.

One of the major obstacles in attempting to develop speed in the northern hemisphere winter is the weather. Too frequently, players have to keep on the move to remain warm, so encouraging the development of endurance rather than speed. For this reason many temperate-climate sprinters spend much of their year in warmer countries where the sunshine not only makes fast running comfortable, but also stimulates the pineal gland. This gland has a depressing effect upon the hormone melatonin, which, in turn, has a beneficial effect upon muscle speed and power. Artificial full spectrum lighting can also promote this effect.

Many trainers are also guilty of trying to instil in their players what can be termed the 'nasty medicine syndrome': 'It's not doing you any good unless it hurts.' Pure sprinting sessions seldom hurt, whereas speed endurance sessions will always be uncomfortable when done correctly.

The skill of sprinting

As already stated, the skill of being able to sprint is inborn. There is a great deal of difference between individuals, since the skill is influenced by limb length, flexibility, the ability to relax, and the ability to co-ordinate the muscles involved to produce a harmonious speed movement. The coach must have a model sprinter in his mind's eye, towards which skill training is directed. The aim is to produce a relaxed, almost effortless, fast-flowing movement, of which the stopwatch is the final judge.

It is very difficult to practise the skills of sprinting as a series of isolated movements, since by essence it is a 'whole' movement. However, sprint drills, which are movements practised at a slower tempo, will help to condition the muscles involved with sprinting and should positively influence the movement itself. However, movements practised in slow motion will almost certainly follow a different pattern of nerve stimulation to the muscles than those when full speed is achieved.

Despite this, sprint drills have a very definite place in the training programme for all sportsmen and women. They help with endurance training effect, skill training and prevention of injury. Certainly, they form an ideal warm-up routine prior to more strenuous activities, such as full-effort sprinting. The ideal sequence of drills, especially for players of the major games is:

(1) high knee running, fast cadence, 30 foot strikes per 25m, 10 x 25m recovery jog backwards (can be performed in waves of running)
(2) high skips, emphasising ankle flexion, 30 foot strikes per 25m, 10 x 25m recovery jog backwards
(3) heel flicking to touch buttocks, exaggerated forward lean, 30 foot strikes per 25m, 10 x 25m recovery normal jog
(4) giant strides, 15–20 foot strikes per 25m, 10 x 25m recovery normal jog.

There is a host of other running drills from a coach's repertoire that can be used to isolate a specific part of sprinting technique. These include drills to promote relaxation, such as an attempt to relax the neck, arm and shoulder muscles, while running fast. Here a contrasting technique can produce a significant effect, whereby the athlete first tenses the upper limb muscles and then attempts to relax them during speed running.

Relaxation

Relaxation is an essential feature of sprinting, but is most difficult to appreciate. One frequently hears a coach shouting at a performer to relax, but what does it mean? Total relaxation would call for a performer to crumple in a heap on the floor. A degree of tension must be present in the body, certainly in the postural muscles. What the coach is, in fact, looking for is a harmonious interplay of muscles, involving co-ordination between the **agonists** (those muscles executing the movement) and the **antagonists** (those capable of producing the opposite movement). This level of co-ordination can only be achieved by controlled practice, which familiarises the body with the movement it is called upon to perform.

Another way of helping to appreciate relaxation is to practise certain contrasting movements, for example, running with complete tension in the upper body, followed immediately by experiencing its opposite. Certain movements can be performed against a resistance of a spring or a rope pulley and then subsequently performed without a resistance.

Mobility of joints

Coaches describe the extent of movement about a joint or series of joints in terms of mobility, flexibility or suppleness. Suppleness has a mechanical effect upon speed, in that it can provide an increased range through which the force acts, thus improving the physical factors of **work** and **impulse**. The performer can only exert a force while the driving leg is in contact with the ground. By increasing the flexibility of the thigh, knee and ankle joint, the contact time can be increased, so giving a longer propulsive phase and stride length. However, one does not want too long a contact time, so the sprinter is searching for the correct compromise between contact time and stride length, and the top-class sprinter is the one who can exert the greatest force in the shortest possible time.

To sprint quickly, one is looking for a great range of movement in each of the joints of the lower limbs, that is the ankle, knee and hip. As the upper limbs keep the balance of the body, they have to be synchronised with the legs, hence a similar long-ranging movement must also follow. The ankle joint is of particular importance in the sprinting movement, yet it is frequently ignored during flexibility training. The methods for training flexibility will be fully discussed in chapter 6.

Strength and stamina

The other factors influencing speed are best depicted by placing them in a triangle.

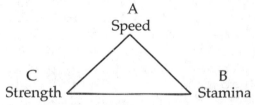

The side A—B represents the various forms of **speed endurance**, required by many major games players. A soccer player might be called upon to sprint the full length of a pitch, and a few moments later sprint again to cover or regain possession. In this situation, the energy reserves to fuel sprinting become very depleted, and only energy to sustain an emergency movement remains. However, the reserves of energy can be improved by well-designed training, so that more energy can be made available once the adaptive response has taken place.

The coach has two systems available to produce this stressed situation. One is to keep the period of effort short with an equally short recovery, and the other is to make the period of effort longer with a recovery period up to ten times the duration of the effort. An example is three sets of 6 x 60m back-to-back (shuttle) with five minutes rest between sets. The sprint over the 60m must be fast. The performer must concentrate on maximum effort, although, due to fatigue, the last sprint will be much slower than the first in each set. The term back-to-back is used to indicate that there isn't a rest between each run, there being only time to slow down and turn in the opposite direction before completing each subsequent run in the block. There has to be a recovery of at least five minutes between each block of six repetitions, otherwise the session will not produce the desired physiological effect.

The line A—C on the triangle represents the various areas of **power** – probably the most significant area for any sportsperson to develop (*see* chapter 4). Line B—C represents the area of **strength endurance**, which will be fully explained in chapter 5.

However, it is essential to emphasise that the immediate effect that any resistance training has upon speed is to slow down the movement. For example, in weight training, even if the movement is done quickly, it cannot be done as quickly as the same movement without weights. Hence the performer is relying upon the cross-component effect which extra strength might have to improve the driving force.

Using balls in resistance training

A number of world-class sprinters, for example Alan Wells, the 1980 Olympic 100 metres champion, have used a boxer's speed ball to help their development of speed. While it is very difficult to identify any immediate effect which this type of training might have upon speed, ultimately there could be a co-ordination skill effect, and also one upon local muscular endurance. To keep the ball moving at speed is a very specialised skill, and a lot of practice is required to master the arm movements involved. This skill could have a beneficial effect upon any of the sports involved in striking skills such as squash, tennis or baseball, and also upon a number of the skills used by the martial artist.

World-class javelin throwers have used highly inflated basketballs in their training, standing about one metre away from a wall and pushing the basketball very quickly at the wall on each successive rebound. Performed with the arms above the head or at chest level, this exercise has a very definite part to play as a speed activity, when used in the immediate interval between exercises, such as a bench press, where a very heavy resistance is used. The theory is that the resistance stimulates the slower, stronger fibres of the muscle, while the fast ball work exercises the muscle's fast fibres. Like the speed ball, the basketball rebound drill requires practice, but, once mastered, there is an obvious beneficial speed/skill factor involved. These skills are again a good example of the kind of avenue the elite performer must explore, as an apparently unlikely routine might turn out to give him or her that extra edge.

Other resistance techniques

Hill sprints and harness running have now become quite firm favourites with sportsmen and women who wish to develop speed, in particular for sprinting movements. The immediate effect of both activities is to slow the person down, since the incline, and the harness partner, provide a resistance that will retard movements. It follows, therefore, that any effect upon speed is through the force and range of movement factors.

To summarise, speed can only be experienced when the movements are performed in a resistance-free medium. The performer is, therefore, looking at activities that will aid the sprinting movement, such as running downwind, running downhill, elastic harness running or speed towing. Most other activities, related to sprinting, will be taking advantage of a cross-component effect.

All aquatic skills, such as swimming, rowing, etc., are certain to be slower because of the restrictive force of the fluid. Hence it is advisable to use similar movements, produced freely without the resistance of the water. The medicine ball activities described for throwing should have a carry over effect when training in water.

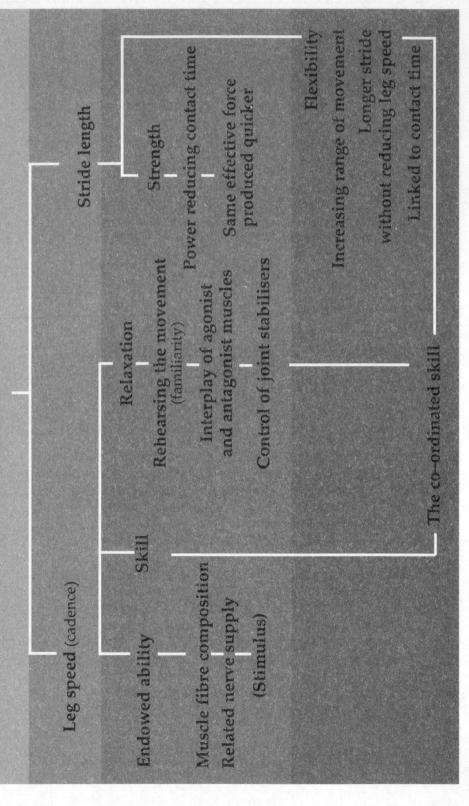

RUNNING SPEED

Leg speed (cadence)

Stride length

Endowed ability

Skill

Muscle fibre composition
Related nerve supply
(Stimulus)

Relaxation

Rehearsing the movement
(familiarity)

Interplay of agonist
and antagonist muscles

Control of joint stabilisers

Strength

Power reducing contact time

Same effective force
produced quicker

Flexibility

Increasing range of movement

Longer stride
without reducing leg speed

Linked to contact time

The co-ordinated skill

Development of strength

The development of strength, and associated power, has almost certainly been the greatest factor to enhance modern sport techniques and performance. But it is not a new concern. Theories of the best way to build up strength date back at least to ancient Greek times, when Milo reputedly carried a bull calf every day from the day it was born until it was fully grown. As the bull grew and became heavier, Milo's strength levels improved to compensate, in a form of early progressive resistance training (PRT).

Unfortunately, the subject is prone to fads. Many of the books on strength have been written by ex-weightlifters, or bodybuilders, and put forward personal views that do little to dispel the myths, but at times highlight the fads.

However, more recently the coach has gained access to reputable research statistics, which must now form the base for any approach to strength training. The 'vogue' performer will always have a significant effect upon training ideas, thus giving a degree of subjectivity to what is fast becoming a scientific field, however, the good coach must always seek the reason why rather than blindly mimicking the supposed schedules of the world-record holder. Their success might be due to a hereditary factor rather than a pet training method.

Types of strength

Specialists identify certain specific and well-defined areas of strength.

The first is frequently termed **gross** or **pure** strength. The strength used by the weightlifter is closely related to this. Scientists describe it as an ability to exert a single, peak contraction. However, such a situation never occurs in pure form in sport, as the more frequently a resistance can be overcome, the closer the activity moves to the area of strength endurance as, for example, required by a mountaineer.

The second area is frequently referred to as **elastic** strength. This calls for the elastic component of the muscle to be used. This is also known as **explosive** strength (though 'elastic' is generally preferred now), suggesting that the muscle's energy could be channelled into an explosive movement, like a jump or a bound. Both 'explosive' and 'elastic' help to convey the term the physicist would recognise as 'power' or 'impulse', introducing the idea of force being applied relative to time. In the case of the jumping activity, the time would relate to 'contact' time, the period when the feet are in contact with the ground while the force is applied. Here the impulse can be the same in two situations – a large force for a short period of time, or a lesser force for a longer period. Development of this elastic strength has brought with it a new term, yet to find its way into a standard English dictionary: **plyometrics** (*see* chapter 4).

The remaining type is frequently termed **specific** strength, that is strength developed by using pulleys, weights, etc., in a way related to the specific skill of the performer. It is sometimes developed by **transfer of training**, when there is a transfer between two related skill movements that are not identical. Here one tries to use a resistance activity that employs a similar muscular pattern to a skill used by the performer in competition. Because a resistance is applied to the muscle, it is made to work differently, and this affects the specificity of the activity. However, it is generally accepted that there is likely to be a greater transfer between skills using a similar muscular pattern of movement.

Specific strength is probably the most fascinating area for study. Modern sport techniques lend themselves to experimentation and improvisation. Almost weekly one hears of a new exercise machine designed to exploit the specificity of strength.

Muscle movements

Strength-training theory is now recognised as an integral part of general training theory, and has its own related terms, the main ones being **isotonic**, **isometric** and more recently **isokinetic**.

Isotonics

Isotonic refers to the visible action taking place during the strength-promoting movement. The muscle shortens while the origin and insertion of the muscle get closer together. Most direct strengthening movements are isotonic.

Isometrics

An isometric contraction is one in which tension is created in the muscle without any visible movement. A typical example is where a muscle exerts a force against an immovable object. This system was exploited by Charles Atlas, and was advertised in boys' papers directly following the Second World War. His principle was dynamic tension: for example, when the right arm pulls or pushes against the left, tension is produced in each muscle group, yet control is exerted to prevent movement.

The levers of the body are positioned such that one group of muscles causes extension and another group flexion. No effective movement would follow if both the flexor and extensor muscles were made to contract at one and the same time. Hence, the nerves supplying the muscles cause one group to act while the other group relaxes. The pure physiologist refers to this as 'reciprocal innervation' or 'inhibition'. However, when controlled movement is required, there are two other groups of muscles known as **fixators** and **synergists** which hold limbs in certain positions to prevent unwanted movements. These muscles act isometrically to hold limbs steady, such as in keeping the trunk in an erect posture while the leg muscles move in running.

So, for harmonious movement, muscles are frequently contracting, relaxing, working isometrically and isotonically in a pattern controlled by the nervous system of the body. The coach who wishes to understand the control of human movement should read one of the standard works on pure physiology.

Isokinetics

Isokinetic refers to a movement where the tension created by the muscle is constant. Traditional exercises create varying tension: for example, where a resistance is pushed vertically from the chest, as in the straight press with a weight, a considerably greater force is required to overcome the inertia of the weight, and set it moving from the chest than is required to keep it moving to the extent of the arms. Hence, the tension created in the muscles varies throughout the exercise. With a true isokinetic machine, such as the Cybex, the machine automatically provides a constant resistance. This is important for the sportsman or woman who might need to exert a larger force through the outer ranges, however most standard pieces of equipment have better capacity to permit development of strength in the inner ranges of movement. Isolation and concentration techniques can also be used to develop a muscle group that needs to be strong throughout its entire range of movement.

Weight training

An exercise dose, in weight training, is frequently related to what is known as the one repetition maximum, that is the maximum resistance a performer can move for one repetition only, representing 100 per cent intensity. The extent of training is then varied by using a lower percentage of this maximum. For example, training techniques involving repetitions of 80–99 per cent maximum will be designed to promote gross strength. In such a case the extent or total number of repetitions will, essentially, be low. A technique involving 50 per cent or less of one's maximum is likely to be used for strength endurance, calling for extensive training using a greater total number of repetitions.

To be most effective, the intermittent work principle should be used with repetitions grouped together in sets, to permit the muscles to recover. In weight training, various 'systems', originating with early weightlifters and bodybuilders, are used for different levels of strength: the simple system, combination system, super and tri sets, and the pyramid system. These systems, essentially designed by performers to develop a specific response, provide methods suitable for the novice through to the advanced lifter who requires massive levels of strength. They also lend themselves to be exploited by specific sports, due to the different types of strength each system is designed to promote.

Weight training offers the individual the most effective way of taking advantage of the PRT techniques mentioned earlier. A person training with weights soon experiences the fact that a resistance, which was originally hard to overcome, becomes easier as the training period progresses. The level of resistance is therefore increased gradually to keep pace with the improved levels of strength resulting from the body adapting to the training regime. This is achieved by adding weighted discs to the lifting bars, or increasing the weights in the 'stack' system.

Resistance techniques

All too frequently the term 'resistance techniques' is used synonymously with weight training, but iron discs and weights are just one form of resistance that can be used and the various forms of resistance should be differentiated. Admittedly, weights might offer the most suitable, and convenient, form of resistance for developing gross strength, but there are other forms of resistance that can be equally effective in developing other areas of strength. For example, bodyweight can be used as a resistance in circuit training.

A greater resistance can be made effective by changing the efficiency of a body lever system, as in the contrasting press-ups in figs 3 and 4. Resistance can be provided by a partner, as illustrated in figs 5, 6 and 7. Other forms of resistance used currently include springs, elastics, pneumatic cylinders and electromagnets.

Knowing the magnitude of the resistance can be a great help. Weight training, with its associated 'stack' machines, has this advantage over most other forms of resistance training, as it is quick and inexpensive to label a weight with its resistance in pounds or kilograms. This lets the performer see the degree of his or her improvement as well as facilitating progressive resistance techniques.

Fig. 3 Extended press-ups   *Fig. 4 Press-ups with arms widely spaced*

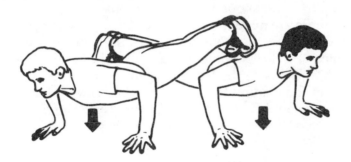

Fig. 5 Using a partner to increase resistance, both active

Fig. 6 Using a partner to increase resistance, one active

Fig. 7 *Using a partner to increase resistance, inclined sit-ups*

The simple system

As the name suggests, this is the programme for the novice lifter until both skill and strength levels are adequate to transfer to a more demanding system. Many performers in sports where strength isn't of a high priority might be well advised to stay with this system throughout their competitive career, changing the extent and intensity of loading to bring about a specific response.

While there are many possible variations to the simple system, it is recommended that all should initially follow an eight-item schedule, performing 3 x 8 repetitions of each exercise. Once the athlete has become familiar with the techniques, a more ambitious system or a variation in the loading techniques can be contemplated.

The coach should select eight different, easy exercises, designed to promote strength in all of the main muscle groups.

Simple system schedule (*see* illustrations on page 29)

(1) Seated press (fig. 8).
(2) Sit-ups (fig. 9).
(3) Leg press or straddle dead lift (figs 10 and 11).
(4) Seated French press (fig. 12).
(5) Back hyperextension (fig. 13).
(6) Straddle split squat (fig. 14).
(7) Bench press (fig. 15).
(8) Leg curls (fig. 16).

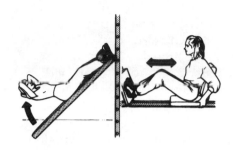

Fig. 8 Seated press   *Fig. 9 Sit-ups*   *Fig. 10 Leg press*

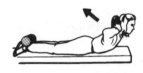

Fig. 11 Straddle dead lift   *Fig. 12 Seated French press*   *Fig. 13 Back hyperextension*

Fig. 14 Straddle split squat   *Fig. 15 Bench press*   *Fig. 16 Leg curls*

These exercises have been chosen for their safety, the simplicity of performance, and to offer a variety of lifts to promote general strength. The lifts break down into three arm exercises, three leg exercises and two exercises suitable for the muscles of the trunk. The sequence of lifts also helps to promote quicker recovery, in that each main muscle group is exercised in turn; thus an arm exercise is always followed by one designed to promote strength in either the trunk or the legs.

The simple system does not call for a circuit type rotation of the lifts. Exercise 1 should be completed in full before starting exercise 2.

The first thing the coach must do is to teach the performer the correct way to perform the exercises. This is made simpler on a multigym machine as they usually force the lifter into the correct lifting position with 'stops' to prevent gravity taking over. Where free weights are used, the coach unfamiliar with safe lifting techniques should enlist the help of an experienced lifter. With weight training the vulnerable area is the spine, hence the crucial rule is 'straight back lifting at all times', when working against gravity *and* when controlling the weight aided by gravity.

In the ideal situation, the novice should train in a group of three, two people acting as 'spotters' while one is exercising. This situation has a further merit in that recovery can be taken while partners are exercising, allowing muscular energy to be replaced before depleting it again. When exercising alone, an adequate period should be allowed for recovery between each set and each group.

However, there are many safety aspects that are beyond the scope of this text, and the coach should either enlist the help of a specialist weight trainer, or study a manual devoted to weightlifting, such as the one produced by the British Amateur Weight Lifters Association. Their coaches are also available to offer advice.

The simple system uses the widely accepted progressive resistance training techniques. The coach should establish the eight repetition maximum for the major lifts listed in the schedule, except for the two trunk exercises which should be performed initially without a weight for the 3 x 8 repetitions. The intensity can then be increased by using a weight and/or inclined board (*see* fig. 9).

In the ideal situation, the first series of eight repetitions should not produce a great deal of stress; the second series should be very hard to complete; while with the third series the performer might only be able to perform six repetitions before the energy system is depleted, rendering the muscle incapable of work. Within a week or so of training, all three series become possible, giving the coach the cue to increase the resistance and the cycle of adaptation takes place again.

The simple system can be used for developing strength endurance by increasing the extent, i.e. to 3 x 10 or even 3 x 20 repetitions of each lift.

It can also be used for developing gross strength by reducing the extent to as little as 3 x 2 or 5 x 2 repetitions, but at the same time increasing the intensity of loading, that is, the magnitude of the resistance.

The combination system

This system is ideal for promoting strength endurance as might be needed by the canoeist, oarsman, mountaineer, distance skier, distance runner, fencer, boxer, wrestler or judo player.

The system is identical to the simple system in that one should use a similar rotation of exercises for an identical number of repetitions, again using the eight repetition maximum loading point and increasing the resistance loading using the PRT techniques. The difference is in the method of recovery between the various lifts.

Using the same eight-item schedule as for the simple system, lifts 1 and 2 are combined, as are 3 and 4, 5 and 6, and finally 7 and 8. Taking lifts 1 and 2 as the example, the performer does one set of eight repetitions of lift 1 and immediately progresses to lift 2, performing the stipulated eight repetitions then immediately returning to lift 1, then back to lift 2 until a total of 3 x 8 repetitions, on both lifts, have been completed. With the combination system, the only recovery time which the first muscle group receives is while the second group is exercising. A greater endurance factor can be developed by increasing the extent of training. This system is not ideal for gross strength development.

'Super set' or 'tri set'

Further progression of the intensity factor can be experienced by using the 'super set' or 'tri set' techniques. These methods were originated by bodybuilders, using what they termed a blitzing method. These systems should *not* be used by the novice because they place a high level of stress on the muscles. They are suitable for the mountaineer, combat sportsperson and the paddler/oarsman experienced in lifting. Sportsmen and women also requiring gross strength frequently use these systems during the endurance-promoting phase of the year plan.

The super set is identical to the combination system in every aspect, except in the grouping of the exercises. The two arm exercises are grouped together, without a recovery, as the coach pairs extension and flexor muscles from the same group.

A six-item schedule could be as follows.

(1) Seated press – 3 x 7 reps.
(2) French press – 3 x 8 reps.
(3) Sit-ups – 3 x 8 reps.
(4) Back hyperextension – 3 x 8 reps.
(5) Straddle dead lift – 3 x 8 reps.
(6) Straddle split squat – 3 x 8 reps.

The tri set system is identical to the super set, except that three lifts, all from the same basic muscle group, are used in rotation, without recovery, until a total of 3 x 8 repetitions has been completed for all three lifts. An example of the tri set system schedule might be as follows.

(1) Seated press.
(2) French press.
(3) Bench press.
(4) Sit-ups.
(5) Back hyperextension.
(6) Leg raise (fig. 17).
(7) Straddle dead lift.
(8) Leg curls.
(9) Straddle split squat.

Fig. 17 Leg raise hanging from wall bars

These systems all use the basic, simple system for progression. However, a greater endurance stress can be placed on the muscles by varying time rather than the number of repetitions. For example, each lift could be performed for a period of 15 seconds, 30 seconds or

even one minute. Again this is an advanced system, only really suitable for very experienced performers. The total time duration can be
related to a specific sport – for example, analysis might indicate that
a soccer player sprints quickly for a total of 8 minutes during an
entire game, and this could be represented by 8 x 1 minute or 16 x 30
seconds sets, with a suitable recovery interval.

The pyramid system

The person who wishes to develop optimum levels of gross strength
often uses a system related to pyramid loading. With this method, a lift
is selected and the performer does five repetitions at what is estimated
to be the five repetition maximum. This is invariably between 85 and
90 per cent of the best recorded for the particular lift. The weight is
then increased and four repetitions are performed; the sequence is
repeated so that the resistance is increased and the repetition is
decreased by one. Once the single repetition is reached, the resistance
level is increased and a single repetition is performed until the resistance becomes such that further movement becomes impossible. This
point is recorded, for future reference, as a guide to performance
levels.

The proficient lifter will always keep a record of the weights lifted.
This will be in the form of the personal best effort for a particular lift,
or the total weight lifted during a training period. Documentation of
this sort is important for the elite performer, since the keeping of
written records can help to avoid past mistakes (*see* chapter 11).

Children

Although a woman's body does not have the same strength potential
as a man's, due to the influence of the male sex hormone upon
strength, there is no reason at all why women should not strength
train. The belief that they should not train in this way has retarded
their development in certain sports by a decade or more.

In some sports, notably swimming and gymnastics, elite performers can be fairly young, especially in the women's sports. However,
there are good reasons why the pre-pubescent child should not
become involved in the advanced development of strength levels.

During childhood, growth takes place in the long bones. Once
adulthood is reached, growth stops and the end plates of the bone are
sealed. Strength training has an effect not only upon the muscles but
also on the muscle tendons and ligaments surrounding a joint. It
tends to increase muscle bulk, placing tendons under a degree of
extra stretch. There is also some evidence to suggest that strength
training reduces the elasticity of the ligaments and tendons to a

certain degree. This could put an extra strain, and stretch, on a joint that is still growing, which might make the joint less efficient once growth has stopped.

Drugs

There is very strong evidence to suggest that greater levels of strength can be achieved through hormone therapy, and at most major championships testing procedures are used to detect the use of artificial hormones, frequently referred to as anabolic agents. Their use is illegal, and they can produce damaging side effects.

Phasing and exploiting weight training

The coach must also be aware that in sport muscles have to work concentrically (towards the central point) and eccentrically (away from the central point). Strength can be developed by using both types of movements, but unfortunately conventional strength-training techniques tend to favour one or the other. This is particularly the case with weight training where the performer tends to allow the weight to return to the starting position through gravity, and exerts tension on the pushing phase only. The coach must seek methods whereby strength can be developed throughout the total range and phase of each movement. Some ideas are given in the next chapter.

Like most components of fitness, strength must be phased relative to the period of competition and the competition itself. In the first situation one is looking at the year plan. Following the post-competition recovery phase, strength endurance is required. Here the coach exploits the extensive methods of weight training, using the systems that are more likely to produce it. This phase is followed by the gross strength promoting phase, where intensive methods are used and those systems most likely to promote gross strength development are exploited. This is followed by the all-important power/specific strength development phase, detailed in the next chapter. During the competition phase, one is looking to keep the status quo, maintaining the levels of strength built up during the off-season. In most situations, just one session per week devoted to strength should retain the levels necessary. But, as with most aspects of fitness, when not stimulated the system reverts back to its pre-trained state, the regression rate for strength being fairly rapid.

Strength training tends to produce quite extreme levels of muscle fatigue, so requiring a longer period of time for recovery. Strength training sessions must therefore be kept as far away from a competition as possible. In most sports major matches take place at weekends, hence Monday or Tuesday is best for this activity. As most elite per-formers will need to train several times a day, it might be advisable to use what is known as the 'split' routine; that is, to exercise the legs one day and the arms the following day, so enabling a second training session to take place without the ill effects of total fatigue that might be produced by the full weight training session. Such a method is probably most beneficial during the pre-competition period, where there is a necessity to place a greater emphasis on skill and speed.

The physiology of strength

The physiological process whereby the body adapts to the stress placed upon it is an extremely complicated one. The act of strength training causes a breakdown in the actual protein content of the muscle. In other words, the status quo (**homeostasis**) has been disturbed, and the response of the body is to return the muscle to its normal state. This involves the intricate action of hormones and enzymes, mapped out in the summary chart at the end of this and the following chapter.

For a muscle to **hypertrophy** (become bigger/stronger) there must be a stimulus together with the availability of protein and the growth hormone. The stimulus is the participation in strength training exer-cises such as shifting a heavy weight (weight training). This evokes a **catabolic** (breakdown) action which in turn mobilises energy reserves.

The whole process is considerably influenced by the stimulation of the endocrine system, in particular the adrenal glands. The produc-tion of cortisol is inhibited while the production of testosterone (the male sex hormone) is stimulated. Muscle hypertrophy, hence strength gain, is directly proportional to a high ratio of testosterone to cortisol.

It is the physiological effects of this ratio that has encouraged sportsmen and women who are interested in making massive gains in strength to cheat by taking preparations which contain testos-terone, or which promote its production. This group of drugs is known as the anabolic androgens. Another group of drugs favoured by some is the Beta 2 agonists, such as clanbuterol, which are thought to reduce levels of cortisol.

Much of the available information on the physiological adaptation resulting from high-intensity strength training is influenced by relatively recent research work, some of which is contradictory. In very basic terms it involves the intricate action of the endocrine sys-tem and the various hormones the system produces. The main hor-mones are those produced by the anterior lobe of the pituitary gland, chiefly the growth hormone somatotrophine. The anterior lobe of the pituitary gland produces gonadotrophines which stimulate the gonads (testis) to produce testosterone, the male sex hormone. This aspect of hormonal activity ensures the correct relationship with protein and the growth hormone.

At the same time, the stimulus of weight training helps to reduce fat levels by using them as a form of energy. The hormone stimulation could produce an excess level of testosterone (androgens) which the body would convert to oestrogen via the aromatising enzyme. A classic example of heavy anabolic steroid use is the male developing breasts, where fatty tissue is deposited in the nipple area. The chart at the end of this chapter attempts to give a very simplistic interpretation of the main physiological changes that take place following very intensive weight training.

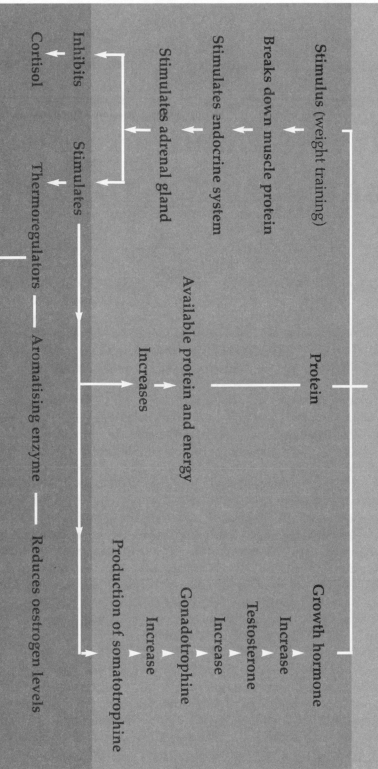

MUSCLE HYPERTROPHY
(strength gains)

Stimulus (weight training)

Breaks down muscle protein

Stimulates endocrine system

Stimulates adrenal gland

Inhibits

Cortisol

Stimulates

Thermoregulators

Reduces fat

Aromatising enzyme — Reduces oestrogen levels

Available protein and energy

Increases

Protein

Production of somatotrophine

Gonadotrophine

Increase

Testosterone

Increase

Growth hormone

Increase

Development of power and specific strength

Strength alone will not assure success in any sport. It is **usable strength** that is the key, the strength which can be applied to the body to make it move faster, change speed, change the direction of body movements, put a greater speed into a club or racket head, or make the pull on an oar faster and longer. Hence, while strength is a dominant factor one must also call upon skill, mobility and speed.

At times a sport calls for the blend of speed and strength which can be defined as **power**. At other times one requires a strength factor, applied throughout the range of a specific movement, that is termed **specific strength**. Frequently, it is difficult to distinguish between the two because of the cross-component effect, so they are combined in this chapter.

Specific strength has to be developed to achieve top performances. It has been shown by use of film that it is possible, through training, to increase the release speed of a javelin by over 30km p/h (20 mph). In many respects, javelin throwing is similar to bowling in cricket or pitching in baseball. If the fast bowler or pitcher could improve his release speed by 30km p/h (20 mph) while maintaining accuracy, then it would make it much harder for the batsman/batter. Likewise, through specific training the triple jumper can add over 12 per cent to his or her sprinting speed and vertical jumping ability. A 12 per cent increase in speed will greatly enhance performance in almost any sport.

However, there is one very major difference between the track and field athlete and the team games player. The elite javelin thrower is more than happy to spend only about 10 per cent of training time throwing a javelin, the other 90 per cent being devoted to developing qualities such as strength, speed and mobility. The suggestion to a cricket or baseball star that only 10 per cent of the training time should be devoted to using bat and ball would not be received very well. They have to be convinced of the benefit they can gain from improving their power.

Leg power

Leg power is essential in most sports, and can be developed by bounding, depth jumping, medicine ball work (which, of course, also enhances arm power), or resistance running.

Bounding

Three different techniques, all of which were evolved for specific purposes, are recommended.

The jumps decathlon

This system was developed initially to help the winter training of top-class jumpers. It provides an incentive to keep the effort levels high through the stimulus of both indirect and direct competition, and at the same time provides variety.

There are ten different jumping activities, each measured and then converted to points (*see* page 40). Hence, progress can be followed in terms of an improvement in any of the ten events or in the points total for all ten events, or in a stipulated number of events such as a jumps pentathlon. By converting distances to points, it is also possible to compare one athlete with another, adding the further incentive of direct competition.

Selected items from the jumps decathlon are used during the winter conditioning phases for those who compete during the summer, and vice-versa for those who need to peak during the winter. When used as conditioning exercises, the distances should not be measured because this is time-consuming. During the endurance phase of training the performer should be encouraged to do ten repetitions for each event. In the strength-promoting phase the number can be reduced to three, with the performer wearing a weighted jacket or belt. During the power phase, five repetitions can be used, encouraging the performer to leap beyond a grid line marked on the floor. The competitive incentive can be introduced monthly by keeping a measured and accurate record.

There is a skill factor involved in the activity, but it can be rapidly mastered by most people. There are also a number of safety factors that should be observed. First, the performer should use good quality training shoes, with a wedge pattern heel. Secondly, a good surface is essential. Thin foam mats, soft grass, etc. form an ideal landing area. If too soft, the landing will be unstable; if too hard, heels might be bruised, and even leg and back pains caused. The athlete must be encouraged to land flat-footed, since a toe landing produces instability and places a strain on the ankle joint.

Motivation plays a key role in the jumps. While the competitive element of the activities is a factor in itself, words of encouragement from the coach can do much to improve levels of effort.

The vertical columns 1–10 indicate the type of jump. For example, column 2 is for the standing vertical jump, i.e. a hop, followed by a step, followed by a jump to land on two legs. The starting leg should toe a scratch line with the flat of the foot contacting the floor. A jump of 8.00m scores 67 points, which is read out from the first vertical column.

	1 Stand long jump (m)	2 Stand triple jump (m)	3 2 hops step & jump (m)	4 2 hops 2 steps & jump (m)	5 2 hops 2 steps 2 jumps (m)	6 5 spring jumps (m)	7 Stand 4 hops & jump (m)	8 Run 4 hops & jump (m)	9 25 metre hop (secs)	10 5 stride long jump (m)
100	3.73	10.51	13.00	15.54	19.15	17.06	17.67	23.77	2.7	7.28
99	–	10.43	12.90	15.46	18.99	16.91	17.52	23.62	–	–
98	3.65	10.36	12.80	15.39	18.84	16.76	17.37	23.46	2.8	–
97	–	10.28	12.69	15.31	18.69	16.61	17.22	23.31	–	7.26
96	3.58	10.21	12.59	15.08	18.54	16.45	17.06	23.16	3.0	–
95	–	10.13	12.49	15.01	18.38	16.40	16.96	23.01	–	–
94	3.50	10.05	12.39	14.88	18.23	16.25	16.86	22.85	3.1	7.23
93	–	9.98	12.39	14.78	18.08	16.15	16.76	22.70	–	–
92	3.42	9.90	12.19	14.68	17.93	16.00	16.61	22.55	3.2	–
91	–	9.82	12.09	14.57	17.77	15.84	16.45	22.34	–	7.21
90	3.35	9.75	11.98	14.47	17.62	15.79	16.35	21.99	3.3	–
89	–	9.98	11.88	14.37	17.47	15.64	16.25	21.79	–	–
88	3.27	9.60	11.78	14.27	17.32	15.54	16.15	21.64	3.4	7.18
87	–	9.52	11.68	14.17	17.17	15.39	16.00	21.48	–	–
86	3.20	9.44	11.58	14.07	17.01	15.23	15.84	21.33	3.5	–
85	–	9.37	11.48	13.96	16.91	15.18	15.74	21.18	–	7.16
84	3.12	9.29	11.37	13.86	16.76	15.03	15.64	21.03	3.6	–
83	–	9.22	11.27	13.76	16.66	14.93	15.54	20.80	3.7	7.13
82	3.04	9.14	11.17	13.66	16.50	14.83	15.44	20.65	3.8	–
81	–	9.06	11.07	13.56	16.35	14.68	15.34	20.42	3.9	7.11
80	2.97	8.99	10.97	13.46	16.20	14.57	15.23	20.26	4.0	–
79	–	8.91	10.87	13.36	16.10	14.42	15.08	20.11	4.2	7.08
78	2.89	8.83	10.76	13.25	16.00	14.32	14.93	19.96	4.3	–
77	–	8.76	10.66	13.15	15.84	14.22	14.83	19.81	4.4	7.06
76	2.81	8.68	10.56	13.05	15.69	14.07	14.73	19.58	4.5	7.03
75	–	8.61	10.46	12.95	15.54	13.96	14.63	19.43	4.6	7.01
74	2.74	8.53	10.36	12.85	15.39	13.86	14.47	19.20	4.7	6.95
73	2.69	8.45	10.26	12.75	15.23	13.71	14.32	19.04	4.8	6.90
72	2.66	8.38	10.15	12.64	15.13	13.61	14.22	18.89	4.9	6.85
71	2.64	8.30	10.05	12.49	15.03	13.51	14.12	18.74	5.0	6.80
70	2.61	8.22	9.95	12.42	14.88	13.41	14.02	18.59	5.0	6.80
69	2.59	8.15	9.85	12.34	14.73	13.25	13.86	18.44	5.2	6.70
68	2.56	8.07	9.75	12.19	14.63	13.10	13.71	18.28	5.4	6.62
67	2.53	8.00	9.65	12.09	14.47	13.00	13.61	18.13	5.5	6.55
66	2.51	7.92	9.55	11.98	14.32	12.90	13.51	17.98	5.6	6.47
65	2.48	7.84	9.44	11.88	14.22	12.80	13.41	17.75	5.7	6.40
64	2.46	7.77	9.34	11.78	14.07	12.69	13.30	17.60	5.8	6.32
63	2.43	7.69	9.24	11.68	13.96	12.59	13.20	17.37	5.9	6.24
62	2.41	7.61	9.14	11.58	13.81	12.49	13.10	17.22	6.0	6.17
61	2.38	7.54	9.04	11.48	13.71	12.34	12.95	17.06	6.1	6.09
60	2.36	7.46	8.94	11.37	13.56	12.19	12.80	16.91	6.2	6.01

	1 Stand long jump (m)	2 Stand triple jump (m)	3 2 hops step & jump (m)	4 2 hops 2 steps & jump (m)	5 2 hops 2 steps 2 jumps (m)	6 5 spring jumps (m)	7 Stand 4 hops & jump (m)	8 Run 4 hops & jump (m)	9 25 metre hop (secs)	10 5 stride long jump (m)
59	2.33	7.39	8.83	11.27	13.41	12.03	12.64	16.76	6.3	5.94
58	2.31	7.31	8.73	11.17	13.25	11.88	12.49	16.53	6.5	5.86
57	2.28	7.23	8.63	11.07	13.10	11.78	12.39	16.38	6.6	5.79
56	2.26	7.16	8.53	10.97	12.95	11.68	12.29	16.15	6.7	5.71
55	2.23	7.08	8.45	10.87	12.60	11.58	12.19	16.00	6.8	5.63
54	2.20	7.01	8.38	10.76	12.64	11.48	12.09	15.84	6.9	5.56
53	2.18	6.93	8.30	10.66	12.49	11.37	11.98	15.69	7.0	5.48
52	2.15	6.85	8.22	10.56	12.34	11.27	11.58	15.54	7.1	5.41
51	2.13	6.78	8.15	10.46	12.19	11.17	11.42	15.39	7.2	5.33
50	2.10	6.70	8.07	10.36	12.03	11.07	11.27	15.23	7.3	5.25
49	2.08	6.62	8.00	10.26	11.88	10.97	11.17	15.08	7.04	5.18
48	2.05	6.55	7.92	10.15	11.73	10.87	11.07	14.93	–	5.13
47	2.03	6.47	7.84	10.05	11.58	10.76	10.97	14.78	7.05	5.07
46	2.00	6.40	7.77	9.95	11.42	10.66	10.82	14.63	–	5.02
45	1.98	6.32	7.69	9.85	11.27	10.56	10.66	14.47	7.07	4.97
44	1.95	6.24	7.61	9.75	11.17	10.46	10.51	14.32	–	4.92
43	1.93	6.17	7.54	9.65	11.07	10.36	10.36	14.17	7.08	4.87
42	1.90	6.09	7.46	9.55	10.97	10.26	10.21	14.02	–	4.82
41	1.87	6.01	7.39	9.44	10.87	10.15	10.05	13.86	7.09	4.77
40	1.85	5.94	7.31	9.34	10.76	10.05	9.90	13.71	–	4.72
39	1.82	5.86	7.23	9.24	10.66	9.95	9.75	13.56	8.00	4.67
38	1.80	5.79	7.16	9.14	10.56	9.85	9.60	13.41	–	4.62
37	1.77	5.71	7.08	9.04	10.46	9.75	9.44	13.25	8.01	4.57
36	1.75	5.63	7.01	8.94	10.36	9.65	9.34	13.10	–	4.52
35	1.72	5.56	6.93	8.83	10.26	9.55	9.24	12.95	8.02	4.47
34	1.70	5.48	6.85	8.73	10.15	9.44	9.14	12.80	–	4.41
33	1.67	5.41	6.78	8.63	10.05	9.34	9.04	12.64	8.03	4.36
32	1.65	5.33	6.70	8.53	9.95	9.24	8.94	12.49	–	4.31
31	1.62	5.25	6.62	8.43	9.85	9.14	8.83	12.34	8.04	4.26
30	1.60	5.18	6.55	8.33	9.75	9.04	8.73	12.19	–	4.21
29	1.57	5.10	6.47	8.22	9.65	8.94	8.63	12.03	8.05	4.16
28	1.54	5.02	6.40	8.12	9.55	8.83	8.53	11.88	–	4.11
27	1.52	4.95	6.32	8.02	9.44	8.73	8.43	11.73	8.06	4.06
26	1.49	4.87	6.24	7.92	9.34	8.63	8.33	11.58	–	4.01
25	1.47	4.80	6.17	7.82	9.24	8.53	8.22	11.42	8.07	3.96
24	1.44	4.72	6.09	7.72	9.14	8.43	8.12	11.27	–	3.91
23	1.42	4.64	5.99	7.61	9.04	8.33	8.02	11.12	–	3.86
22	1.39	4.57	5.89	7.51	8.94	8.22	7.92	10.97	8.09	3.80
21	1.37	4.49	5.79	7.41	8.83	8.12	7.82	10.82	–	3.75
20	1.34	4.41	5.68	7.31	8.73	8.02	7.72	10.66	–	3.70
19	1.29	4.26	5.58	7.21	8.63	7.92	7.61	10.51	9.00	3.65
18	1.26	4.19	5.48	7.11	8.53	7.82	7.51	10.36	–	3.60
17	1.24	4.11	5.38	7.01	8.43	7.72	7.41	10.21	–	3.55
16	1.21	4.03	5.28	6.90	8.33	7.61	7.31	10.05	9.01	3.50
15	1.19	3.96	5.18	6.80	8.22	7.51	7.21	9.90	–	3.45
14	1.16	3.88	5.07	6.70	8.12	7.41	7.11	9.75	–	3.40
13	1.14	3.80	4.97	6.60	8.02	7.31	7.01	9.60	9.02	3.35
12	1.11	3.73	4.87	6.50	7.92	7.21	6.90	9.44	–	3.25
11	1.09	3.65	4.77	6.40	7.82	7.11	6.80	9.29	–	3.14
10	1.06	3.58	4.67	6.29	7.72	7.01	6.70	9.14	9.03	3.04
9	1.04	3.50	4.57	6.19	7.61	6.90	6.60	8.99	–	2.94
8	1.01	3.42	4.47	6.09	7.51	6.80	6.50	8.83	–	2.84
7	0.99	3.35	4.36	5.99	7.41	6.70	6.40	8.68	9.04	2.74
6	0.96	3.27	4.26	5.89	7.31	6.60	6.29	8.53	–	2.64
5	0.93	3.20	4.16	5.79	7.21	6.50	6.19	8.38	9.05	2.53
4	0.91	3.12	4.06	5.68	7.11	6.40	6.09	8.22	–	2.43
3	0.88	3.04	3.96	5.58	7.01	6.29	5.99	8.07	–	2.33
2	0.86	2.97	3.86	5.48	6.90	6.19	5.89	7.92	–	2.23
1	0.60	2.89	3.75	5.38	6.70	6.09	5.79	7.77	9.06	2.13

Sequence bounding

Sequence bounding and endurance bounding are excellent for promoting stamina for power-based sports. They can be practised indoors, using the length of the gymnasium or sports hall (20–30m/65–100ft), or outside, using about a quarter segment of a soccer pitch or segments of a conventional athletics track.

Various sequences are followed:

(1) hop step-hop-step: continue sequence for 25m (approx. 80ft). Walk back to the starting line before repeating. Several sequences can be performed, depending on the phase of training

(2) hop hop step-hop hop step: continue sequence for 25m approx. Recovery and training dose as (1)

(3) hop step step hop step step: continue sequence for 25m approx. Recovery and training dose as (1)

(4) hop hop step step-hop hop step step: continue sequence for 25m approx. Recovery and training dose as (1).

The speed of limb movement should be emphasised rather than asking for long, rangy movements. Again there is a skill factor, but it is easily mastered, especially by gifted sportsmen and women.

Endurance bounding

Endurance bounding is a more strenuous activity and should only be used by people who have developed skill and endurance using the bounding techniques. Again, it involves a shuttle-type activity over about 25m (80ft), without any recovery period, until the stipulated sequence is complete.

A typical endurance bounding exercise is to hop out 25m on the right leg, turn round, giant strides back, turn round, hop out 25m on the left leg, turn round, giant strides back; double foot bound 25m, turn round, sprint back 25m. The total distance covered is about 150m (500ft). The coach can time the total sequence to provide extra stimulus and as a guide to improvement for future reference. The sequence should be followed by at least a three-minute recovery period before repeating. The number of repetitions will depend upon the training period in use.

This form of endurance bounding can be used as a race, where the whole group starts together, spread across the width of a pitch, and performs the movements for about 25 metres. It forms an excellent activity for team game players.

An even more strenuous form of endurance bounding can be based on the conventional athletics track. Here the 400m circuit can be divided into 8 x 50m segments. Over each 50m segment a different power movement is used without recovery, until the full 400m is complete. Again the total duration of the 400m can be recorded on a stopwatch and used for future reference.

The following sequence is tried and tested.

(1) Hop right.
(2) Hop left.
(3) Giant strides.
(4) Hop step hop step, etc.
(5) Hop hop step hop hop step, etc.
(6) Hop step step hop step step, etc.
(7) Hop hop step step hop hop step step, etc.
(8) Sprint.

Three to five repetitions, of 400m duration, spaced with a five- to eight-minute recovery, is an excellent power-based endurance session. This session certainly isn't for the faint-hearted!

Depth jumping

This method of training forms part of what in the United States has been aptly termed plyometrics, although any form of bounding follows the same basic principles. It involves the body in yielding first as it controls the downward momentum of the body, aided by gravity, and then uses the muscles to propel the body upwards or forward.

The apparatus needed is a raised platform of varying height, hence the standard gymnastics sectional vaulting box is ideal.

Initially, all movements should be performed with both feet together (*see* fig. 18). The performer starts on the platform, allowing the body to drop to the floor, and then instantly drives off from the floor to clear an elasticated bar, kept in place by the stands. The bar should be placed about one metre away from the base of the box. The height of the bar is then raised. Good performers can clear heights in excess of 1m 50cm (5ft) from a platform height of 1m (3ft). As the performer becomes familiar with the movement, the level of the platform can be raised, or the movement performed with a weighted jacket as added resistance. Experience suggests that the height of the platform should not be much more than one metre.

Fig. 19 shows how to drop down from the platform to rebound for a horizontal jump. Good performers can record distances in excess of 4m (13ft), measured from the base of the box, and a chalk line should be drawn at this distance as a target.

Fig. 20 shows the performer making a movement called 'out and out'. It involves pushing the body out from the raised platform by using a standard broad jump technique, and then propelling the body out again using a similar movement, trying to go as far as possible. All these jumps can be made landing on one leg.

Fig. 18 Depth jumping

Fig. 19 Depth jumping for distance

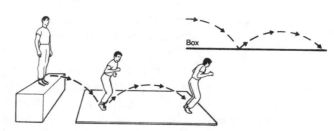

Fig. 20 Depth jumping out and out

The extent of training can be varied by increasing the number of repetitions, and its intensity can be increased by elevating the platform height and by measuring the rebound distances.

This activity certainly isn't for the pre-pubescent athlete or the athlete who hasn't developed sufficient leg strength. But for the fully grown athlete, plyometrics represents the best current method of leg training.

However, plyometrics does have its critics. Some say that it produces knee and ankle injuries, but in well over 20 years experience I have not found any evidence of this. Nevertheless, plyometrics represents an advanced form of power training that should not be contemplated by anyone who isn't already well conditioned. Certain team game players have complained that it has produced soreness and stiffness in the knees and associated muscles, but any new muscular activity will produce these symptoms, so they should be introduced gradually into the training programme, and persisted with. Well-conditioned athletes do not experience any really painful symptoms other than an initial soreness in the muscles, due to a change in the way they are made to work. This soreness wears off quite rapidly once the muscles become familiar with the way they are using energy.

Medicine ball work

Many physical educationalists see the medicine ball as a dated piece of equipment, and it is only a few practical people who are saving it from extinction. The physical education progressives looked upon it as a remnant of past theories, groups of people engaging in one-dimensional, systematised exercise as one. The medicine ball no longer fitted into their definition of free expression. Physical activity for the masses had to be enjoyable, and for all but those who wish to become elite, hard work isn't really enjoyable. So schools cast the medicine balls aside and they disappeared into the depths of store cupboards. Those who had learned to use the medicine ball became fewer as the years progressed.

To most sportspeople weight training offered a better method of strength development. But what was not appreciated was that the medicine ball could be used for the development of power and specific strength, and we now consider the medicine ball just as essential a piece of equipment as any of our multigyms. Unfortunately, it isn't quite as easy to persuade manufacturers that this is the case, and medicine balls are becoming both harder and more expensive to obtain. However, the innovative coach will be able to improvise.

The medicine ball is used in two main ways: to promote leg power, where one must enlist the aid of a very active partner; and to promote specific strength in the trunk and arm muscles.

Figs 21 and 22 show how the 'server' throws the medicine ball for the 'kicker' to return it. The kicker's movement must be very powerful and the ball must be struck with the flat sole of the foot. The distance the server is away from the kicker will depend upon the power levels of both.

Good athletes can propel a 6kg (13lb) medicine ball over 15m (50ft) with the double leg kick. With these activities both the kicker and the server get plenty of leg exercise.

Fig. 23 illustrates a way in which the leg flexor muscles can be used in a very fast, power-promoting way. The server must protect the head of the kicker by standing astride their shoulders, as shown in the illustration. The ball is rolled, with some speed, down the backs of the kicker's legs. Once the ball is felt on the heels, the kicker flicks the ball back to the server's hands.

With the methods shown in the illustrations it is ideal if both partners are active in the same sport. Recovery periods for the kicker can then be taken when the kicker and server swap roles.

Fig. 24 shows how the medicine ball can be used to promote strength and power in the hip flexor muscles. The ball is held by the kicker on the thigh of one leg, and allowed to roll down the thigh, in the direction of the knee, which is then pulled through rapidly to project the medicine ball to the partner who returns it with an identical movement. Both legs need to be exercised singly.

With these activities there is a degree of skill to master, but it is very quickly learnt. The extent of loading can be varied, according to the time of the year, by increasing the number of sets and repetitions. Initially, the performer should start with 3 x 8 repetitions, building up to as many as 3 x 20 repetitions during the endurance phase of training. The intensity of loading can be increased by changing the weight of the medicine ball, and ideally a group will have a selection of medicine balls weighing between 3–7kg (6.5–15.5lbs).

Fig. 25 shows the medicine ball being used to promote hyperextension of the back. The server must carefully throw the ball on a trajectory that will call for a large range of movement. The performer lies prone and aims to throw/push the ball from above the head.

Fig. 26 shows a way in which the medicine ball can be used to promote lateral rotation of the trunk. The thrower kneels with his back to the server and receives the ball over one shoulder, then throws it back to the server over the other. The order of the shoulders alternates to exercise both left and right rotators.

Fig. 27 shows how the ball can be used to promote abdominal strength. The legs are raised on a platform to isolate the effect of the hip flexor muscles, while the performer lies on his back. In this situation a solid wall can be used to help the server collect the rebound and assure a safe and speedy return to the thrower from a sitting position.

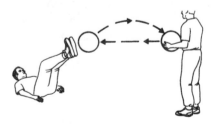

Fig. 21 Double leg kick

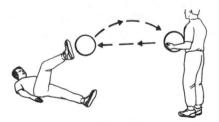

Fig. 22 Single leg kick

Fig. 23 Hock flicks

Fig. 24 Knee pick-up

Fig. 25 Back hyperextension

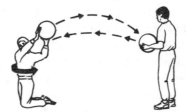

Fig. 26 Lateral twist throw

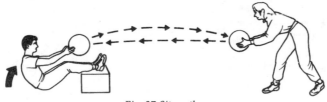

Fig. 27 Sit-up throw

Figs 28–30 show other ways in which the back muscles can be strengthened by adopting a kneeling position to isolate the legs. These exercises are also beneficial to the strength and mobility of the shoulder muscles.

Fig. 28 Double kneeling throw

Fig. 29 Single kneeling throw

Fig. 30 Standing overhead throw

Fig. 31 shows the performer exercising mainly the hip rotator muscles. The ball is thrown two-handed to a partner or against a wall. The movement is started by placing the medicine ball well behind the thrower's dominant side. The dominant leg drives the hip square to the front to put the trunk in a 'bowed' position, and at the same time the medicine ball is lifted above the head.

Fig. 32 shows how the single arm can be exercised using a small medicine or a weighted ball, leaning against an inclined bench.

The above activities also help to promote dynamic flexibility. As with all of the medicine ball activities there is a skill factor. The extent and intensity of training can be varied in the usual way.

Fig. 31 Double arm throw

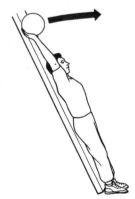

Fig. 32 Single arm throw

Throwing balls

A similar strength-training theme to that exploited by the use of the medicine ball can be explored by the use of weighted throwing balls. Throwing balls are soft so that they can be thrown against walls or into nets, and are manufactured in an assortment of weights and sizes. They are much smaller than medicine balls because they are designed to be thrown single-handed. To reduce the physical dimension of the ball, and at the same time keep the weight relatively high, the filling is usually of lead shot. They are manufactured in weights ranging from 200g to 4kg (0.5lb to 9lbs), the heavier ones being used for indoor shot putting and the lighter ones specifically designed as a training aid for javelin throwers.

Throwing balls can be used in a variety of ways to strengthen the muscles used in the various throwing actions, in particular cricket and baseball, and the various racket and bat striking actions such as those in badminton, tennis and table tennis. In the case of the striking skills, the ball is used instead of the bat and is released at an appropriate point in the arm trajectory to simulate the stroke action.

It is also possible to make weighted balls specifically for sports such as rugby or American football, by taking a cheap plastic ball and filling it with damp sand, or with a mixture of sand and lead shot. Resistance passing exercises can be performed with this improvised ball.

As far as the use of the weighted ball is concerned, the coach has to be an innovator and a master of improvisation. The coach must be capable of examining the skills involved in all aspects of the sport in question, to see how strength-promoting activities can be practised following similar movement patterns.

Using pulleys

One of the most rewarding exercises in this area of sports training is to explore the use of conventional pulley systems and resistance pulleys. Resistance pulleys, such as the Dial-Ex, are frictional devices with which the level of resistance can be varied by increasing or decreasing the frictional component of the pulley. Pulleys can be linked, by lengths of rope, to club heads, racket heads or even limbs, to promote strength in a specific movement.

Figs 33–6 show a variety of these being used in a selection of sports. In some cases, a partner provides the resistance by controlling the free end of the rope.

Fig. 35 shows the potential of tubular elastic in power training. Its resistance can be quickly exploited with both eccentric and concentric movement. The elastic can be stretched and controlled slowly back to its pre-stretched state when the resistance diminishes through the movement. Similarly the reverse movement can be performed so that the elastic is stretched gradually, in which case the resistance increases throughout the movement. The level of resistance may be changed by using different types of elastic.

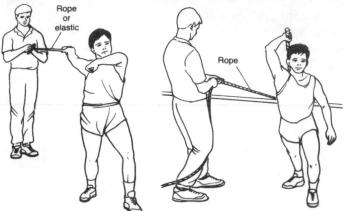

Fig. 33 Throwing action with rope. The 'throw' is made three strides away from the partner

Fig. 34 Throwing with rope over bar. The partner controls the resistance by having the rope run over a horizontal bar

Fig. 35 Standard elastic throw

Fig. 36 Throwing against rope and weight

The training possibilities in this area are almost endless, hence much must be left to the innovation of the coach to devise specialised training activities to aid the specific strength development of the chosen sport.

It is impossible to devise strength-promoting movements using any form of resistance that will be identical to the specific movements involved in the individual's sport. The aim is to find movements that might share a similar pattern, hoping that there will be a greater level of transference from the strength/power-based movement to the skill-specific movement.

Resistance running

Since running is a basic activity for most sports, making the action harder by applying a resistance is an obvious exercise.

The simplest method is to run uphill, the length and steepness of the gradient allowing the coach to vary the extent and intensity of the training programme. A more strenuous alternative is to run on soft sandhills, a method used with success by a group of Australian athletes during the mid-1950s.

When using the conventional belt harness, it must be appreciated that with this form of resistance work the intensity of the resistance must only be such to force the performer to produce a greater work load. It must not be so excessive as to radically change the running action.

An elasticated running harness was illustrated in fig. 1 (this device was used in the same way in speed training, *see* chapter 2). The elastic is placed under stretch by the forward lean of the body. The coach can improvise using elastic strands made from the sections cut from the inner tubes of car tyres: this will prove particularly useful for indoor training during inclement weather.

Wearing weighted jackets increases the intensity of resistance running exercises.

The throws decathlon

While the jumps decathlon outlined on pages 40–1 is excellent for training and evaluating leg power, there are sports which require similar power for the arms. These sports include the throwing events in track and field, swimming, rowing, bowling in cricket, pitching in baseball, and American football.

By incorporating related activities into a throws decathlon, converting distances to points and then competing against a points total as in all multi-event competitions, a greater incentive is produced (*see* pages 52–4). The competition can be direct against other team members, or against one's own score from a previous programme.

	1 Overhead backwards throw (m)	2 Kneeling putt dominant arm (m)	3 Throw through legs (m)	4 Standing Discus (m)	5 Hammer style throw (m)	6 Overhead throw-in style (m)	7 Push from chest (m)	8 Caber throw (m)	9 Kneeling non- dominant arm (m)	10 Back lying overhead throw (m)
100	22.00	14.00	6.00	30.00	30.00	20.00	20.00	25.00	12.00	10.00
99	21.78	13.86	5.94	29.70	29.70	19.80	19.80	24.75	11.88	9.90
98	21.56	13.72	5.88	29.40	29.40	19.60	19.60	24.50	11.76	9.80
97	21.34	13.58	5.82	29.10	29.10	19.40	19.40	24.25	11.64	9.70
96	21.12	13.44	5.76	28.80	28.80	19.20	19.20	24.00	11.52	9.60
95	20.90	13.30	5.70	28.50	28.50	19.00	19.00	23.75	11.40	9.50
94	20.68	13.16	5.64	28.20	28.20	18.80	18.80	23.50	11.28	9.40
93	20.46	13.02	5.58	27.90	27.90	18.60	18.60	23.25	11.16	9.30
92	20.24	12.88	5.52	27.60	27.60	18.40	18.40	23.00	11.04	9.20
91	20.02	12.74	5.46	27.30	27.30	18.20	18.20	22.75	10.92	9.10
90	19.80	12.60	5.40	27.00	27.00	18.00	18.00	22.50	10.80	9.00
89	19.58	12.46	5.34	26.70	26.70	17.80	17.80	22.25	10.68	8.90
88	19.36	12.32	5.28	26.40	26.40	17.60	17.60	22.00	10.56	8.80
87	19.14	12.18	5.22	26.10	26.10	17.40	17.40	21.75	10.44	8.70
86	18.92	12.04	5.16	25.80	25.80	17.20	17.20	21.50	10.32	8.60
85	18.70	11.90	5.10	25.50	25.50	17.00	17.00	21.25	10.20	8.50
84	18.48	11.76	5.04	25.20	25.20	16.80	16.80	21.00	10.00	8.40
83	18.26	11.62	4.98	24.90	24.90	16.60	16.60	20.75	9.96	8.30
82	18.04	11.48	4.92	24.60	24.60	16.40	16.40	20.50	9.84	8.20
81	17.82	11.34	4.86	24.30	24.30	16.20	16.20	20.25	9.72	8.10
80	17.60	11.20	4.80	24.00	24.00	16.00	16.00	20.00	9.60	8.00
79	17.38	11.06	4.74	23.70	23.70	15.80	15.80	19.75	9.48	7.90
78	17.16	10.92	4.68	23.40	23.40	15.60	15.60	19.50	9.36	7.80
77	16.94	10.78	4.62	23.10	23.10	15.40	15.40	19.25	9.24	7.70
76	16.72	10.64	4.56	22.80	22.80	15.20	15.20	19.00	9.12	7.60
75	16.50	10.50	4.50	22.50	22.50	15.00	15.00	18.75	9.00	7.50
74	16.28	10.36	4.44	22.20	22.20	14.80	14.80	18.50	8.88	7.40
73	16.06	10.22	4.38	21.90	21.90	14.60	14.60	18.25	8.76	7.30
72	15.84	10.08	4.32	21.60	21.60	14.40	14.40	18.00	8.64	7.20
71	15.62	9.94	4.25	21.30	21.30	14.20	14.20	17.75	8.52	7.10
70	15.40	9.80	4.20	21.00	21.00	14.00	14.00	17.50	8.40	7.00
69	15.18	9.66	4.14	20.70	20.70	13.80	13.80	17.25	8.28	6.90
68	14.96	9.52	4.08	20.40	20.40	13.60	13.60	17.00	8.16	6.80
67	14.74	9.38	4.02	20.10	20.10	13.40	13.40	16.75	8.04	6.70
66	14.52	9.24	3.96	19.80	19.80	13.20	13.20	16.50	7.92	6.60
65	14.30	9.10	3.90	19.50	19.50	13.00	13.00	16.25	7.80	6.50
64	14.08	8.96	3.84	19.20	19.20	12.80	12.80	16.00	7.68	6.40
63	13.86	8.82	3.78	18.90	18.90	12.60	12.60	15.75	7.56	6.30
62	13.64	8.68	3.72	18.60	18.60	12.40	12.40	15.50	7.44	6.20
61	13.42	8.54	3.66	18.30	18.30	12.20	12.20	15.25	7.32	6.10
60	13.20	8.40	3.60	18.00	18.00	12.00	12.00	15.00	7.20	6.00
59	12.98	8.26	3.54	17.70	17.70	11.80	11.80	14.75	7.08	5.90
58	12.76	8.12	3.48	17.40	17.40	11.60	11.60	14.50	6.96	5.80
57	12.54	7.98	3.42	17.10	17.10	11.40	11.40	14.25	6.84	5.70
56	12.32	7.84	3.36	16.80	16.80	11.20	11.20	14.00	6.72	5.60
55	12.10	7.70	3.30	16.50	16.50	11.00	11.00	13.75	6.60	5.50
54	11.88	7.56	3.24	16.20	16.20	10.80	10.80	13.50	6.48	5.40
53	11.66	7.42	3.18	15.90	15.90	10.60	10.60	13.25	6.36	5.30
52	11.44	7.28	3.12	15.60	15.60	10.40	10.40	13.00	6.24	5.20
51	11.22	7.14	3.06	15.30	15.30	10.20	10.20	12.75	6.12	5.10

	1 Overhead backwards throw (m)	2 Kneeling putt dominant arm (m)	3 Throw through legs (m)	4 Standing Discus (m)	5 Hammer style throw (m)	6 Overhead throw-in style (m)	7 Push from chest (m)	8 Caber throw (m)	9 Kneeling non-dominant arm (m)	10 Back lying overhead throw (m)
50	11.00	7.00	3.00	15.00	15.00	10.00	10.00	12.50	6.00	5.00
49	10.78	6.86	2.94	14.70	14.70	9.80	9.80	12.25	5.88	4.90
48	10.56	6.72	2.88	14.40	14.40	9.60	9.60	12.00	5.76	4.80
47	10.34	6.58	2.82	14.10	14.10	9.40	9.40	11.75	5.64	4.70
46	10.12	6.44	2.76	13.80	13.80	9.20	9.20	11.50	5.52	4.60
45	9.90	6.30	2.70	13.50	13.50	9.00	9.00	11.25	5.40	4.50
44	9.68	6.16	2.64	13.20	13.20	8.80	8.80	11.00	5.28	4.40
43	9.46	6.02	2.58	12.90	12.90	8.60	8.60	10.75	5.16	4.30
42	9.24	5.88	2.52	12.60	12.60	8.40	8.40	10.50	5.04	4.20
41	9.02	5.74	2.46	12.30	12.30	8.20	8.20	10.25	4.92	4.10
40	8.80	5.60	2.40	12.00	12.00	8.00	8.00	10.00	4.80	4.00
39	8.58	5.46	2.34	11.80	11.70	7.80	7.80	9.75	4.68	3.90
38	8.36	5.32	2.28	11.40	11.40	7.60	7.60	9.50	4.56	3.80
37	8.14	5.18	2.22	11.10	11.10	7.40	7.40	9.25	4.48	3.70
36	7.92	5.04	2.16	10.80	10.80	7.20	7.20	9.00	4.32	3.60
35	7.70	4.90	2.10	10.50	10.50	7.00	7.00	8.75	4.20	3.50
34	7.48	4.76	2.04	10.20	10.20	6.80	6.80	8.50	4.08	3.40
33	7.26	4.62	1.98	9.90	9.90	6.60	6.60	8.25	3.96	3.30
32	7.04	4.48	1.92	9.60	9.60	6.40	6.40	8.00	3.84	3.20
31	6.82	4.34	1.86	9.30	9.30	6.20	6.20	7.55	3.72	3.10
30	6.60	4.20	1.80	9.00	9.00	6.00	6.00	7.50	3.60	3.00
29	6.38	4.06	1.74	8.70	8.70	5.80	5.80	7.25	3.48	2.90
28	6.16	3.92	1.68	8.40	8.40	5.60	5.60	7.00	3.36	2.80
27	5.94	3.78	1.62	8.10	8.10	5.40	5.40	6.75	3.24	2.70
26	5.72	3.64	1.56	7.80	7.80	5.20	5.20	6.50	3.12	2.60
25	5.50	3.50	1.50	7.50	7.50	5.00	5.00	6.25	3.00	2.50
24	5.28	3.36	1.44	7.20	7.20	4.80	4.80	6.00	2.88	2.40
23	5.06	3.22	1.38	6.90	6.90	4.60	4.60	5.75	2.76	2.30
22	4.84	3.08	1.32	6.60	6.60	4.40	4.40	5.50	2.64	2.20
21	4.62	2.94	1.26	6.30	6.30	4.20	4.20	5.25	2.52	2.10
20	4.40	2.80	1.20	6.00	6.00	4.00	4.00	5.00	2.40	2.00
19	4.18	2.66	1.14	5.70	5.70	3.80	3.80	4.75	2.28	1.90
18	3.96	2.52	1.08	5.40	5.40	3.60	3.60	4.50	2.16	1.80
17	3.74	2.38	1.02	5.10	5.10	3.40	3.40	4.25	2.04	1.70
16	3.52	2.24	.96	4.80	4.80	3.20	3.20	4.00	1.92	1.60
15	3.30	2.10	.90	4.50	4.50	3.00	3.00	3.75	1.80	1.50
14	3.08	1.96	.84	4.20	4.20	2.80	2.80	3.50	1.68	1.40
13	2.86	1.82	.78	3.90	3.90	2.60	2.60	3.25	1.56	1.30
12	2.64	1.68	.72	3.60	3.60	2.40	2.40	3.00	1.44	1.20
11	2.42	1.54	.66	3.30	3.30	2.20	2.20	2.75	1.32	1.10
10	2.20	1.40	.60	3.00	3.00	2.00	2.00	2.50	1.20	1.00
9	1.98	1.26	.54	2.70	2.70	1.80	1.80	2.25	1.08	.90
8	1.76	1.12	.48	2.40	2.40	1.60	1.60	2.00	.96	.80
7	1.54	.98	.42	2.10	2.10	1.40	1.40	1.75	.84	.70
6	1.32	.84	.36	1.80	1.80	1.20	1.20	1.50	.72	.60
5	1.10	.70	.30	1.50	1.50	1.00	1.00	1.25	.60	.50
4	.88	.56	.24	1.20	1.20	.80	.80	1.00	.48	.40
3	.66	.42	.18	.90	.90	.60	.60	.75	.36	.30
2	.44	.28	.12	.60	.60	.40	.40	.50	.24	.20
1	.22	.14	.06	.30	.30	.20	.20	.25	.12	.10
0	0	0	0	0	0	0	0	0	0	0

(Compiled by Carnegie College students first year B.A., 1980.)

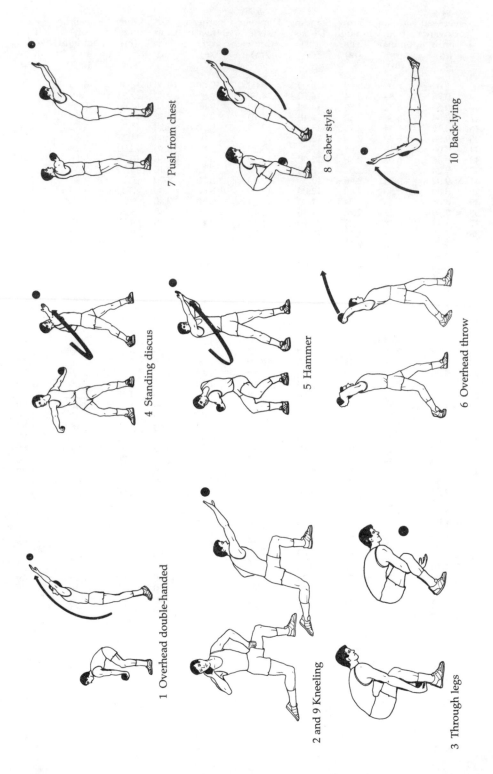

7 Push from chest

8 Caber style

10 Back-lying

4 Standing discus

5 Hammer

6 Overhead throw

1 Overhead double-handed

2 and 9 Kneeling

3 Through legs

STRENGTH

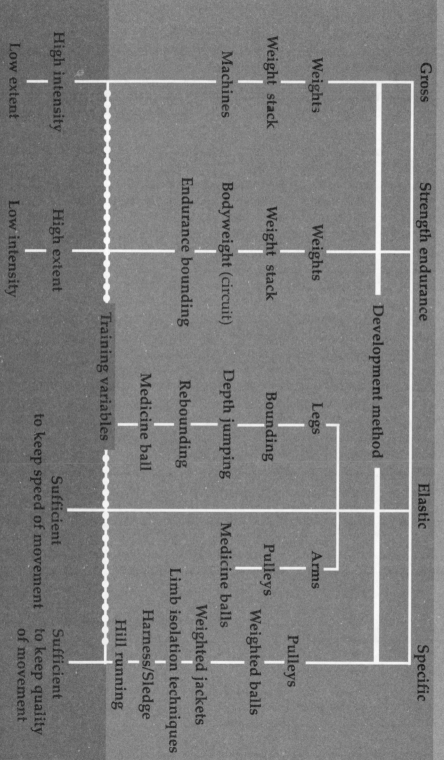

	Gross	Strength endurance	Elastic	Specific
Development method				
	Weights	Weights	Legs	Arms
	Weight stack	Weight stack	Bounding	Pulleys
	Machines	Bodyweight (circuit)	Depth jumping	Weighted jackets
		Endurance bounding	Rebounding	Limb isolation techniques
			Medicine ball	Harness/Sledge
				Hill running
			Medicine balls	Weighted balls
			Pulleys	
Training variables				
	High intensity	High extent	Sufficient to keep speed of movement	Sufficient to keep quality of movement
	Low extent	Low intensity		

Summary

- Power is a very important component of training.
- It can be especially useful when adapted to a particular sport by the use of pulleys and elastic.
- At least one power session per week should be included in a programme, increasing to two sessions during the closed season.
- Power work can be phased with the extent of the loading high during the endurance phase of training and with the intensity greater in the immediate pre-season phase.

5

Development of endurance

Endurance training lays the foundation for all other forms of training, for without endurance total fitness can never be achieved.

It is generally accepted in sports science that there are three distinct areas of endurance: cardio-vascular endurance, local muscular endurance, and anaerobic efficiency.

The heart and lungs

As the name suggests, 'cardio-vascular' refers to the functioning of the lungs in taking up oxygen and removing carbon dioxide from the body, and of the heart and circulatory system in transporting energy-providing foods and oxygen to the active tissues, and the waste products away for elimination. In order for muscles to work efficiently they must have an adequate supply of oxygen.

Exercise, or even the thought of exercise, causes the body to take certain precautionary measures to enable it to cope with the stress of needing more oxygen. There are two basic factors involved in the way the body provides oxygen for the active tissues.

The first is the rate and depth of breathing. These increase under stress, but rapidly reach a maximum level, influenced mainly by the rate at which the muscles involved in respiration can contract. As the activity of these muscles is stimulated by the response of the respiratory centre of the brain to the level of carbon dioxide in the blood, the practice of forced expiration after bouts of high level activity is unsound. It serves to decrease the rate and depth of breathing, when an increase is required to ensure that there is more oxygen available from the lungs.

The second factor is the way in which oxygen is transported to the active tissues, through the medium of special blood cells and a pigment known as haemoglobin. The more haemoglobin there is in the blood, the greater the oxygen-carrying potential. This is a key factor in endurance. Diet also has an important part to play, as the correct functioning of the haemoglobin is influenced by the presence of dietary iron. It is advisable for people involved in active sport to have frequent blood tests, so that if their iron level falls too low, they can take supplements, either in tablet form or via an injection. The absorption of iron is also influenced by vitamin C.

Red blood cells

Just prior to the 1968 Olympic Games, held at altitude in Mexico City, the world of sport started to recognise that those people born at altitude had a significant advantage in terms of the body's natural capacity to transport oxygen, and that training at altitude could enhance performance when athletes returned to sea level. When the body works in a rarefied atmosphere, it adapts by producing more red blood cells. Because of this, many of the world's leading sporting nations now invest in altitude training camps such as those at Boulder, Colorado, USA, and Font Remou in France. However, the inborn adaptive mechanisms of the native of high altitudes, both at lung and tissue level, will always remain superior to those of the trained visitor.

In an attempt to redress this imbalance, certain athletes have been known to resort to blood doping and to using the drug Erythropoietin (EPO) which stimulates the production of red blood cells. During the process of blood doping the athlete has a quantity of blood removed from the body, the packed cells are stored, and are returned to the body at a future date to co-ordinate with a major competition. The system is not without the risk of viral infection, associated with the degree of sterility in the removal, storage, and transfusion techniques.

Exercising the heart

Similar to the lungs, the heart (the driving pump behind the circulation of the blood), has two means by which to increase its output. It can increase its rate of beating, i.e. the pulse rate, and it can increase its stroke volume, i.e. the quantity of the blood expelled with each contraction. With exercise the pulse rate can increase by over five times its resting rate. However, it is generally accepted that once the exercise pulse increases much above 180 bpm, the system becomes inefficient. Also, a very low resting rate is not necessarily beneficial. Rates lower than 40 bpm are not only extremely rare but could indicate a deformity rather than a degree of efficiency.

The heart is an elastic, muscular container, thus as more blood returns to it, the more it fills, and, following the elastic principle, the more it empties, expelling more blood per stroke. This effect is known as Starlings Law. This output of blood from the heart is termed 'the minute volume' by exercise physiologists, as it is a measurement of the amount of blood pumped out by the heart in one minute.

Since the total effect is produced by contracting muscles – those involved in respiration, those involved with the heart, and those skeletal muscles doing the isotonic work – the whole system responds very well to training. The method by which this system is conditioned to undertake an extra work load is known as *aerobic* training, as it involves bodily systems dependent on air. In chemical terms, this means that there is always sufficient oxygen available to metabolise the energy-producing materials (glycogen). Hence, in this context, the word 'aerobic' refers to the way the glycogen is oxidised, producing easily excreted waste products. Unfortunately, like many words in the vocabulary, the meaning has changed and the term 'aerobics' is now used to indicate any form of exercise to music and might involve more energy systems than the 'aerobic' pathways.

There is little doubt that the best way to train the aerobic system is to run for a sustained period of time. Research indicates that a minimum period of 30 minutes is necessary for the training mechanisms to be stimulated, however, there are obviously a number of variables that influence the basic duration of the training period. One is the physical mass of the performer. The heavy rugby forward or American footballer is likely to experience greater difficulty with the duration of the effort than a lighter sportsman. The terrain will also have a significant effect, as more energy is needed over hills.

The important aspect of this type of training is that the level of exercise must remain within the person's aerobic threshold, otherwise a different, non-aerobic energy system will be trained. This threshold will vary from person to person, but the important fact remains that the exercise *must* be steady-state running. Very fit men will be at steady state at a 6–7 minutes per mile pace, and women in the region of 8–10 minutes per mile. However, these times should only serve as an approximate guide since good-class middle distance runners will be able to cope with much faster times for sustained running.

Fartlek running

Speed play, or fartlek running, was developed in Scandinavia to offer an alternative to sustained running. It is a mixture of fast striding and slow jogging over varying terrain. During this type of running the speed and distance of any fast section is determined by the individual, although they must be sufficient to increase the pulse rate to at least twice its resting rate. While fartlek running is good for variety, it lacks the standardisation of the track systems, where the speed and duration of the fast sections can be monitored, as can the duration of recovery. It must be remembered that if the run becomes too intense then another energy system will be trained, and the overall effect upon aerobic efficiency will be limited.

Interval training

Probably the most abused and misunderstood term in sport, interval training offers the degree of control lacking in sustained and fartlek running. The good sports scientist now avoids using the term and favours the more descriptive term of intermittent running.

Interval training requires a period of effort, sufficient to increase the pulse rate to about 180 bpm. Waldemar Gerschler, the German originator of the system, used distances on a track of between 150 and 300 metres. This period of effort is followed by an interval, usually of slow jogging, to allow the pulse rate to recover to about 120 bpm. Once the pulse rate is down to that level, a further period of effort begins. The system of effort, followed by the recovery interval, is continued for a period of time, or for a number of repetitions, or until the pulse rate does not return to the 120 bpm in a reasonable recovery interval. In true interval training the effort period should last about 30 seconds with the recovery period three times that of the work period, or 1½ minutes.

The theory of interval training is based on the principle of overload. The heart is made to beat fast by the effort section, but it continues to beat fast during the recovery, when there is less demand from the skeletal muscles for blood. During recovery, the bi-products of the effort are removed from the body, so allowing subsequent work to follow, without the waste products building up and having an inhibiting effect.

With interval training, the adaptation takes place during the interval and not during the effort period, making it an ideal exercise for conditioning the heart. A typical interval training session might be: 10 x 200m @ 30 secs with a 1½-minute jog recovery.

Local muscular endurance

Muscle groups can only be exercised for limited periods of time. One has only to contract a small muscle, like the flexor muscle of the first finger, to find that after a short period of continuous movement the contractions are forced to become slower, until ultimately they become impossible. This is due to the build-up of waste products in the muscle, and is a common situation in sport. The distance runner and walker, the mountaineer, the canoeist, the rower, the boxer and the fencer particularly come to mind, because of the nature of the movements they have to execute in their sport, relatively isolated muscle groups become fatigued. Their isolation also means that the exercise does not have a stimulatory effect upon the heart so efficiency is limited by the local circulation of the blood.

Circuit training offers an excellent way to improve the quality of local muscular endurance. It is frequently used by players from the major team games, since it offers a high level of physical exercise for a large group of people, without requiring any specific equipment. While a fully equipped gymnasium can offer a more sophisticated approach to this form of training, most players have little more than a grass pitch. Many world-class sportsmen and women do what is frequently termed a 'home circuit' and use common household furniture items such as a chair to perform exercises such as step-ups and dips. Press-ups, sit-ups, squat jumps, squat thrusts, star jumps and reverse press-ups all have their place in the 'open field' circuit.

There are a number of ways to organise the basic circuit. The two most common methods are illustrated on pages 66–8, together with a selection of suitable exercises. The nature of this type of training, particularly with large groups, means that the speed of one exercise, or of one individual, relative to another can create bottle-necks. The timing of each exercise, and of the recovery between the exercises and circuits, has therefore to be controlled.

The basic circuit training exercises can be further modified to provide an extra resistance, using pressure provided by a partner (*see* figs 5 and 6), or by decreasing the efficiency of the levers (*see* figs 3 and 4). However, one must not increase the resistance and decrease the number of repetitions as this will cause gross strength development instead. It must always be remembered that the purpose of circuit training is to develop local muscular endurance.

As stated at the beginning of this chapter, endurance is the foundation of total fitness. Local muscular endurance is a part of this foundation and all who wish to aspire to greater levels should include some local muscular endurance as part of their yearly training plan. It should be introduced into the scheme as part of the endurance phase of training.

Anaerobic training

At very high levels of physical stress the circulatory system cannot supply enough oxygen to fuel the activity. This forces the athlete to work in what is termed oxygen debt. The first part of this energy cycle is the same as for aerobic training, in that glycogen must be oxidised. Without sufficient oxygen lactic acid is produced in the muscles, which has an inhibiting effect upon sustained work. Once the accumulation of lactic acid becomes too great, activity has to cease. However, the body can continue to work in this condition for quite a period of time, but in order to do so the mind has to disregard fatigue. Hence, the saying, 'You're not tired, you only think you are'. Many top-class performers can force their bodies into very extreme conditions of oxygen debt, and this mental toughness often puts them on the right side of the razor's edge between defeat or victory.

Physiologically, the human body is a magnificent machine. A large proportion of the lactic acid produced by high-level exercise can be resynthesised in the liver back into glycogen. However, this is true of only about 80 per cent of the lactic acid, and the remainder accumulates in the muscle, causing a form of paralysis, that forces exercise to cease.

Not many sports take the performer into such a stressful situation. Most team sports are intermittent and during the playing time there are sufficient breaks to allow, if not full recovery, at least partial recovery, although in very important matches key players have been known to collapse into the 'legless' situation. Similarly, the racket sports player can stall play for a brief time to permit a degree of recovery, although successive, long rallies can produce a high level of fatigue. Boxing, rowing, and the middle distance events in athletics, however, are classic examples of where the bi-products of high activity force a very stressful situation. Such situations have to be recreated frequently in training so that the athlete adapts and becomes familiar with the stressful experience. However, it is difficult to reproduce the exact situation, since it requires an extremely high level of motivation, equivalent to that provided by an Olympic final, to force the body into the 'unknown'.

The precise physiology of the anaerobic system isn't fully understood, and it requires high-level research into the activity of muscle enzymes. However, this research is ongoing and fresh information is constantly forthcoming. To convert it into layman's terms, it would appear that training programmes need to prime certain aspects of anaerobic conditions, especially the resynthesis of lactic acid into a form of energy. This is done as part of what is known as the Cori cycle. The waste products become blood lactate, they then arrive at the liver and become liver glycogen. This is converted to blood glucose and is transported back to the muscles and converted to muscle glycogen.

Any training programme needs to stimulate the systems which dispose of the waste products, often well after the exercise has finished.

The acid bi-product of anaerobic work can, in the short-term, be neutralised by an alkaline, and the body has a reserve of alkaline materials which serve to buffer the blood and reduce the level of acidity. The blood buffers are stored in the kidney, mainly in the form of phosphates and bicarbonates. Research suggests that the level of these reserve alkalines can be increased by as much as 12 per cent by specific forms of anaerobic training.

Another important aspect of anaerobic training is to familiarise the body with the stressful state this level of training will produce. In other words, it is a matter of conditioning the mind to will the body to continue work, when all else is telling it to stop.

Anaerobic efficiency

The intermittent work principle is the basis of training for anaerobic efficiency. The intensity of the effort must be kept high. This in turn will have an effect upon the other training variables, forcing a reduction in the duration of the effort, and the number of repetitions of effort, and an increase in the duration of the recovery.

For example, the good-class middle-distance runner might perform one of the following sessions during the immediate pre-competition period: 6 x 300m @ 38 secs with a 5-minute recovery, or 3 x 600m @ 85 secs with an 8-minute recovery.

All of the training variables can be manipulated to bring about variety while still retaining the anaerobic training potential. The important point to remember is that the quality of the period of effort must be close to one's maximum potential (i.e. 90 per cent), for the duration of effort.

By comparison, the good-class team sport player might condition the running aspect of the game by performing the following during early season training: 6 x 300m @ 42–45 secs with a 5–8-minute recovery.

Anaerobic efficiency is primarily determined by the body's capacity to adapt to the demands placed upon the various energy systems. To date, we have only mentioned the aerobic energy system. That is the capacity of the body to produce energy from glycogen in the presence of an adequate supply of oxygen. However, if the demands of an exercise such as a short sprint or a very fast movement last for a minute or slightly more, the body is forced to produce its energy in another way.

For example, the soccer player who sprints 20m to arrive at the ball before an opponent must use energy which is already stored in the muscles. The body has the capacity to store enough energy to last for about ten seconds of high level activity. For a period in excess of this time, the body is forced to produce its energy in yet another way.

In the case of the soccer player, the energy system employed is frequently termed the 'first', and utilises a store of phosphagens in the muscles known as Adenosine Tri-Phosphate (ATP), a store that can last for about five seconds of intensive work. This part of the energy system can be improved by specific training, probably to become about 10 per cent more efficient. Once the ATP has been used, the body is left with a substance known as Adenosine Di-Phosphate (ADP). In other words, to produce energy a single phosphate has been used. The body also has a store of a substance called Phosphocreatine. If the phosphate from this substance is utilised to produce ATP, then the body can double its exercise period to about 10 seconds of intense work. Once this combined system has been expended, another energy system has to be used.

This is the type of energy used by most major team players who seldom have to work at an intense level for more than a few seconds. For example, soccer players might be asked to sprint 20m to collect a ball, and then may not be involved in any particularly active part of the game for quite a number of seconds, thus permitting the body to re-establish its reserves of energy. However, this energy system *must* be stimulated during training. The athlete should exercise at a high level for about 10 seconds followed by a recovery period of several minutes – an intermittent work plan of 10 seconds of effort, followed by four minutes of recovery, should be ideal to keep this system working efficiently.

Once this first basic store of energy is released, further ATP has to be produced by another system. This system is termed glycolysis and involves the resynthesis of the waste product lactic acid back to glycogen (*see* page 62). To detail the entire process would be beyond the scope of this practical book, however the energy systems are well documented in many of the modern texts on work physiology.

To keep the explanation simple and to give practical guidance, the ways in which this system works and responds to training can be termed aspects of speed endurance. The middle distance athlete, sprint swimmer and boxer all need to take advantage of this energy system as part of their training. It involves training at a very high intensity for periods of between 15 and 40 seconds, and at another time training for periods of between 40 and 90 seconds. Again the intermittent work principle should be used allowing a recovery period of about ten times the period of effort.

The aim of any endurance-based training scheme is:

a)   to stimulate the appropriate energy system
b)   to stimulate the appropriate excretory method necessary to eliminate or neutralise the waste products produced by such high levels of activity. This, in particular, means attempting to improve what is known as the alkaline reserve, a supply of

alkalis stored in the body which can neutralise the accumulated acid state

c) to condition a state of callousness to fatigue.

Training and recovery

Because something is good, it does not follow that more of the same thing is better. This is certainly the case with very intense training. Adaptation to the stress evoked by high levels of training follows the general pattern for adaptation that the body uses to cope with anything upsetting homeostasis. However, if the stressing agent is severe, and time is not permitted for recovery, then there will be a breakdown in the physiological functioning of the body. In other words the training becomes 'catabolic' rather than 'anabolic'.

Again the process is an extremely complicated one. Training stimulates the production of the hormone cortisol. Should the concentration of cortisol become too high then testosterone levels are reduced, making further adaptation unlikely. However, extended training past the point of fatigue will have chronic physiological as well as psychological consequences. There is evidence that the total immune system will start to break down, opening the way for repeated infections. The injury healing rate will be adversely affected, and the actual risk of injury increased, so making the 'sword' a double-edged one.

Coaches and athletes must be made aware of the symptoms of overtraining. They include frequent infections, lethargy, sleep disturbances, mood changes, stomach upsets, loss of appetite, elevated resting blood pressure, muscle pains and cramps, and weight loss, and these are just the main categories of physiological and psychological disorders following chronic fatigue.

The true answers lie in avoiding the situation in the first place, taking good spells of time away from training and competition to permit the body to recover. I repeat, rest is an integral part of training.

All aspects of endurance become quite specific once the early foundation is laid. The endurance required by the boxer, rower, or racket player is different to that necessary for the distance runner or football player. While there is a degree of common ground in training, and in the general physiological structure of the body, the individual must study carefully the specific requirements of his or her own particular sport, and if necessary discuss any problems with a work physiologist.

Chapter 8 on specificity should help to give all of those involved an insight into the changes one must make to a training programme to allow for the specific nature of the various sports.

Local muscular endurance and general fitness circuit

The circuit on pages 67–8 has been well tested with groups of outstanding people from a wide variety of sports. It is designed to develop a high level of strength endurance and cardio-vascular endurance. The best facility is a standard school-type gymnasium with wall-bars, benches and beams. It is also designed to accommodate fairly large numbers of adults.

An illustrated card approach is used with one placed at each exercise station. The stations are positioned round the gym in numerical sequence 1–12. This permits the main muscle groups to be worked in turn. Participants are given a starting number.

Two systems are illustrated: a basic repetition system and a timed system. The timed system is generally to be preferred as it avoids bottle-necks and an overall time can be accurately forecast.

The repetition system

Each participant completes three full circuits of 1–12 in direct sequence. All participants should start on an average circuit with a standard time of 40 minutes for its completion. Once this has been achieved a stiffer target should be set for subsequent training sessions. Progress can be made to the 'excellent' circuit and then by reducing the total time allowance. There must always be a strong challenge and motivation to keep the quality of work high.

The timed system

All participants start with a 30-second work period and a 30-second recovery period. Progress can be made to increase the work period and decrease the recovery period. The circuit can be done in direct sequence, or the participant can complete all three sets of work period at the one station before progressing to the next.

All circuits are repeated three times.

1   Inclined sit-ups

REP SYSTEM		TIMED SYSTEM	
		WORK	RECOVERY
AVERAGE	20	30 secs	30 secs
GOOD	40	40 secs	20 secs
EXCELLENT	60	50 secs	10 secs

2   Bench thrusts

REP SYSTEM		TIMED SYSTEM	
		WORK	RECOVERY
AVERAGE	20	30 secs	30 secs
GOOD	40	40 secs	20 secs
EXCELLENT	60	50 secs	10 secs

3   Squat thrusts

REP SYSTEM		TIMED SYSTEM	
		WORK	RECOVERY
AVERAGE	20	30 secs	30 secs
GOOD	40	40 secs	20 secs
EXCELLENT	60	50 secs	10 secs

4   Single leg steps

REP SYSTEM		TIMED SYSTEM	
		WORK	RECOVERY
AVERAGE	20	30 secs	30 secs
GOOD	40	40 secs	20 secs
EXCELLENT	60	50 secs	10 secs

5   Back hyperextension

REP SYSTEM		TIMED SYSTEM	
		WORK	RECOVERY
AVERAGE	20	30 secs	30 secs
GOOD	40	40 secs	20 secs
EXCELLENT	60	50 secs	10 secs

6   Shuttle run (length of gym)

REP SYSTEM		TIMED SYSTEM	
		WORK	RECOVERY
AVERAGE	10	30 secs	30 secs
GOOD	15	40 secs	20 secs
EXCELLENT	20	50 secs	10 secs

7   Spans

REP SYSTEM		TIMED SYSTEM	
		WORK	RECOVERY
AVERAGE	20	30 secs	30 secs
GOOD	30	40 secs	20 secs
EXCELLENT	40	50 secs	10 secs

8   Squat jumps

REP SYSTEM		TIMED SYSTEM	
		WORK	RECOVERY
AVERAGE	20	30 secs	30 secs
GOOD	40	40 secs	20 secs
EXCELLENT	60	50 secs	10 secs

9   Pull-ups (beam/bar)

REP SYSTEM		TIMED SYSTEM	
		WORK	RECOVERY
AVERAGE	5	30 secs	30 secs
GOOD	10	40 secs	20 secs
EXCELLENT	15	50 secs	10 secs

Hang in long position as arms fatigue

10   Star jumps

REP SYSTEM		TIMED SYSTEM	
		WORK	RECOVERY
AVERAGE	20	30 secs	30 secs
GOOD	40	40 secs	20 secs
EXCELLENT	60	50 secs	10 secs

11   Rocking sit-ups

REP SYSTEM		TIMED SYSTEM	
		WORK	RECOVERY
AVERAGE	20	30 secs	30 secs
GOOD	40	40 secs	20 secs
EXCELLENT	60	50 secs	10 secs

12   Press ups

REP SYSTEM		TIMED SYSTEM	
		WORK	RECOVERY
AVERAGE	20	30 secs	30 secs
GOOD	40	40 secs	20 secs
EXCELLENT	60	50 secs	10 secs

TOTAL ENDURANCE

Aerobic

- Energy with oxygen
- Oxygen transport
  - Heart
    - Minute volume
      - Pulse — Rate
      - Stroke — Output
      - Trainable
  - Gas exchange
    - External (lungs)
      - Alveoli Pressure Gradient
      - Trainable
    - Internal (tissues)
      - Tissue Pressure Gradient
      - Trainable

Running, Cycling, Swimming, Rowing etc.
Intermittent Work   Sustained 30 mins +
Pulse thresholds 120–180 B.P.M

Local muscular

- Physiological mechanisms
  - Muscle vascularity
  - Muscle energy efficiency
    - A.T.P. system
    - P.C.L.A. system
      - Enzyme efficiency
      - L.A. resynthesis
      - Acid neutralisation blood buffers
      - Excretion elimination of waste products
      - Tolerance
    - LA/02 system

Trainable
Trainable circuits
Extensive weights

Intermittent
Short/Fast 10–15 secs
4 min. recovery

Intermittent
15 secs – 90 secs
Recovery 10 : 1

Anaerobic

Development of flexibility

Flexibility is frequently ignored, yet it can considerably enhance performance if there is a systematic approach to training. All too frequently we see hockey players who lack the agility to dodge the opposition and avoid heavy tackles, and footballers who miss game after game, due to hamstring injuries sustained by the sudden stretching of muscles. Many sportsmen and women believe that it is enough merely to complete a few warm-up exercises prior to training or competing, but in fact real flexibility goes far beyond this.

Flexibility can be defined as the possible range of movement in a joint, or in a series of joints such as the spine. The type of flexibility required varies considerably from sport to sport. For example, the hurdler requires the best possible hip flexor movement, and the swimmer ankle flexibility. While some sports demand greater flexibility about one specific region, others such as gymnastics, multi-event athletics and the martial arts, require a high level of flexibility in many joints. Several sports require static or extent flexibility. However, the majority of major sports require 'dynamic' flexibility, where the joint is forced to work at a very high speed.

Natural limitations

The anatomical structure of the body, and its joints, imposes major limitations on flexibility. For example, the elbow and knee joints are termed 'hinge joints' and are only designed to move forwards and backwards, or upwards and downwards. They cannot move laterally, or with inward rotation, and injury is almost certain to result if they are pressured to do so, as when an American football player, running forwards in a straight line, is forced to the side by a vigorous tackle, and the knee joint is put under stress.

With joints such as the ankle, hip and shoulder that have a greater range of movement due to their particular construction (the shoulder joint and hip joint being ball and socket, and the ankle a modified hinge joint), the extent of flexibility is imposed by the surrounding soft tissues of tendons, ligaments, muscles and skin. With this type of joint, stability is sacrificed for flexibility.

In this way both the anatomical and the physiological function affect the degree of flexibility. With joints such as the elbow and the knee, the major imposition is bone, a non-elastic material. Any degree of flexibility is determined by the ligaments which join the bones together. An example of this can be seen in the stability of the knee joint, which is determined by the medial and lateral ligaments down the side of the knee and, internally, by the cruciate ligament. While there is a degree of elasticity in a ligament, when forced to move beyond its elastic limits a serious injury may result. It is therefore not easy to design flexibility routines to improve the range of movement about such a joint; training for joints of this nature is directed more towards the strength of the muscles that can offer even greater stability.

The anatomy of joint movement

There is likely to be a greater response to flexibility training where a joint is influenced by the physiological structure of the body, for example the hip, shoulder and ankle joints, where stability is provided by ligaments, tendons and muscles.

While only a semi-elastic material, the ligaments in these joints are slightly more elastic than those found in the elbow, or knee, for example. Here, stretching can have an influence.

Tendons connect muscle to bone and facilitate movement by applying extending, flexing or rotating forces. A tendon is considerably more elastic than a ligament, hence it is easier to injure, but it also responds more readily to training. Situated in the tendons are specialised cells known as Golgi organs which, together with stretch receptors, affect the degree of flexibility of a joint. They radiate neuro-muscular impulses which cause other muscles to function when protection, due to stress, is required.

Movement in joints is brought about by muscles shortening. The muscle responsible for the movement is the 'agonist' or 'prime mover'. For example, in the flexion of the elbow joint, the agonist is the bicep. The muscle capable of the opposite movement is the 'antagonist'. If a message went out calling for both muscles to contract, nothing would happen other than tension being created in the muscle. To cope with this there is a system known as reciprocal inhibition, or reciprocal innervation – when the bicep is creating tension, the tricep is forced to relax, so making a harmonious movement possible.

For complete efficiency in certain joints, muscles known as synergists and fixators (those preventing unwanted movements, especially where a muscle bridges a double joint, for example the hip and back joints) have to be brought into play.

Altogether it can be seen that there is an intricate nervous network causing certain muscles to contract isotonically (*see* chapter 3), others to contract isometrically, e.g. fixators, and others to relax to facilitate a controlled, efficient movement. It is towards educating this neuro-muscular control mechanism that much of the flexibility work is directed.

Muscles also have a considerable effect upon the stability and flexibility of joints. In certain situations athletes promote a considerable increase in muscle bulk by systematised strength training. In turn, this muscle bulk tends to restrict further the flexibility of a joint. Therefore, those who wish to gain muscle bulk in order to increase strength levels, would be well advised to increase the amount of flexibility training that they do.

As mentioned previously, two types of flexibility are evident: static and dynamic. Static flexibility reflects the capacity to move a joint through a great range, with the joint remaining in a static position. Much of what is done in flexibility training is directed towards this. However, certain skilled movements might call for a greater flexibility at speed, or at a specific point within the range of movement. It is important in this respect that some dynamic flexibility work should also be done. The problem associated with this type of work is in the action of the stretch reflex mechanism. When a joint extends slowly in a static position, the reflex system, which is basically protective, is not evoked. However, when a joint moves at speed, tension can increase in muscles where relaxation is required, and the stretch reflex mechanism is brought into play. Dynamic medicine ball work, outlined in chapter 4, can help to improve flexibility through its potential to educate the stretch reflex mechanism.

Biomechanics to justify flexibility training

All movements in sport cause the body to work. In pure physical terms, work = force x distance. The aim in most sports is to increase the value of work, and from this equation it can be seen that this can be achieved by improving one or more of the other variables, providing that the other does not deteriorate.

Reference has already been made to improving the force aspect of the equation by systematised weight/power training. We therefore need to examine the 'distance' aspect of the equation. The 'distance', here, refers to the range through which the force is made to act. For example, the greater the range of movement made by the fist in boxing, the more powerful the blow. The same applies to the range of movement of the tennis racket, golf club, baseball bat, cricket bat, etc. If flexibility training can increase the range through which the force acts, then the result is an increase in work with the resultant effect upon the impact force. Thus the racket, the club head, the blade of the bat or the boot on the foot, hits the ball harder if the swing is longer.

Factors affecting flexibility

Many sportsmen and women reach the top level of performance at a much earlier age than was common a few years ago. In sports such as gymnastics and swimming, this is often aided by young people's natural flexibility, and it is not until approximately 20 years of age that the innate flexibility of youth begins to decline, as the cartilaginous joints start to ossify, and stronger bones develop. Coaches should realise that the body of the young performer is not at its strongest, and is very vulnerable to injury. Excessive stretching can have a long-lasting, ill effect upon the young athlete, resulting in anatomical problems which only surface later in life, at which point it is too late to rectify them. Overstretching of the joints by the regular use of ballistic actions ought to be avoided and replaced by slow stretching.

Conversely, with the growing popularity and importance of veteran sports, many older people are still achieving elite performance. However, flexibility does decline with age. Many of the muscles and connective tissues in the body shorten and medical problems such as arthritis and rheumatism may develop. There is an increased calcification of cartilage, and of the tissues surrounding the joint. As the articular cartilage begins to wear, joints move with less ease, especially in the lower back and the knee. Degenerative conditions such as osteoarthritis may develop and many areas such as the spinal column lose elasticity and their tolerance to compression. Despite this depressing account, it is possible to retain a certain degree of flexibility, and reduce the shortening of the tissues, by stretching daily, and this should be continued beyond one's competitive life in order to maintain peak fitness.

Women are innately more flexible than men, due to their different anatomical structure and lower muscle bulk about the joints. However, a man who trains methodically for a sport requiring greater levels of flexibility can make significant improvements. High levels of flexibility can be seen, for example, in male gymnasts, dancers, ice skaters, performers of martial arts and athletes. Many of the team games played by men significantly reduce flexibility, however, for example rugby and football. Similarly, though women may be born with increased flexibility, this will almost certainly deteriorate unless regular exercise is undertaken.

Another factor affecting flexibility is temperature. A warm environment, and muscles and connective tissues which have already undergone a warm-up activity, will allow greater flexibility around the working joints.

The nature of the sport in which one specialises will often demand that greater training time is devoted to a particular component of fitness. For example, a weightlifter would spend more time on strength training, a sprinter on speed training and a rhythmic gymnast on flexibility work. However, it is important to develop all the components of fitness to a greater or lesser extent, as all contribute to the final performance. In this way, all sportsmen and women should be encouraged to spend more of their time developing the quality of flexibility.

Developing flexibility

Flexibility develops rapidly when the correct training methods are used. A distinction should be made, however, between stretching as a warm-up activity, and stretching to achieve a long-term improvement in the range of movement about a joint. Most of the easy stretching done prior to the training session or competition to familiarise muscles with impending exercise is insufficient to bring about longer-lasting flexibility benefits. Greater improvements to the range of movement will be obtained by setting aside separate flexibility sessions, within the training cycle, and working through systematic exercise routines.

Methods of stretching

Static stretching

Static stretching is a slow, stretching action, involving the placement of the antagonist muscle in a position of maximum stretch and holding the position for a set period of time. The duration of the stretch should not be less than six seconds in order to obtain a response from the Golgi tendon organs. When the limit to which the muscle can be stretched has been reached (without damage to the muscle fibres or connective tissues), it should be possible to relax the muscle while maintaining the stretch. After the stretch has been held for some time, resistance to the movement, and tension, will decrease and the muscle may be stretched further.

This method of stretching allows flexibility development without muscle soreness, because the muscle is stretched within its own extensibility limit and in a controlled manner. The muscle fibres and connective tissues are not damaged during the stretching process. The best results can be obtained by holding the exercise for up to 30 seconds, and taking a recovery period of three times the duration of the exercise between each repetition.

Ballistic stretching or dynamic flexibility

Many of the sports referred to in this book require a certain amount of dynamic flexibility to attain peak performance. In the majority of activities the joint must be taken to the maximum range of movement, at speed.

In seeking this quality, the athlete attempts to confuse the stretch receptors in the muscles by repeating quick contractions of the agonist muscle. This brings about a series of equally short stretches to the antagonist muscle. The movement required is a bouncing action, using swinging movements and gravity to stretch the tissues to their full extent. Unfortunately, these bouncing movements may exceed the extensibility limits of the tissues, thus producing a risk of injury. This form of training is not, therefore, recommended for younger athletes or anyone susceptible to injury.

Because of this risk of injury these high-force contractions of short duration are not the most effective way of developing flexibility, but many sports contain ballistic movements to which it is easy to relate these exercises, such as arm swings for the golfer, leg swings for the footballer, and back hyperextensions for the gymnast. In fact, exercises such as bouncing to touch the toes are still an integral part of the warm-up routine of many major games players, and injuries rarely happen to them unless they are fatigued. This is probably due to the fact that the stretch is within the athletes dynamic flexibility. While these exercises go some way to familiarising the body with the impending activity, they will have no real effect upon the long-term development of flexibility.

In activities such as javelin-throwing, gymnastics and high jumping, a certain amount of hyperextensibility is required about the joints. It would be impossible to achieve this range of movement by static stretching alone. Those athletes should use ballistic exercises, partners or specific apparatus in order to achieve hyperextension of the joints. However, these methods should only be employed with performers who are fully developed and well-conditioned.

Advanced stretching

Stretching can be both active and passive. Active flexibility requires the athlete to contract a muscle, or a group of muscles, about a joint, placing other muscles under stretch. During passive stretching the relaxed muscle and the connective tissue are placed under stretch by external forces, for example a partner, or specific apparatus. These principles can be applied to all stretching exercises, including a relatively recent addition to flexibility training termed 'proprioceptor neuromuscular facilitation' (PNF).

PNF is a flexibility programme initially designed to treat patients handicapped by neuro-muscular disorders. The programme works around the principle that flexibility may be increased by strengthening the agonist muscle and decreasing the resistance of the antagonists. There are two forms of PNF, active and passive (*see* figs 57–9).

Stretching routines

One of the techniques involved in flexibility training is joint isolation, when one joint is locked in an isolated position so that another joint can be stretched. A good example of this is high free-leg kicking. When the kicker is standing in the erect position, and the free leg is swung vertically upwards, the natural reaction is for the upper body to rotate backwards. While the intention might be to develop flexibility of the hip, the movement would certainly carry over to the back, with little, if any, effect upon the flexibility of either joint. But when the back is isolated by standing against a wall, the training benefit is directed towards the hip joint.

Should one put a weighted anklet on the free swinging leg, then the increased momentum of the leg plus the anklet will induce a greater range of movement. A bouncing movement, with the legs in the straddle split position, will stretch the groin area. Here, the mass of the body, aided by gravity, increases the momentum of the combination and its possible stretching effect.

Returning to the free-leg swing exercise with the back against the wall, a partner can push the free leg to a higher position beyond the horizontal. Here, the partner is being used in an active situation. Great care must be used when doing this type of work otherwise a joint can be forced beyond its elastic limit and an injury is almost certain to result.

In most forms of PNF the partner is used passively. That is, the partner holds a limb in a static position while the performer executes an isometric contraction of the isolated muscle.

Static stretching, dynamic stretching and PNF are all methods for developing long-term flexibility. It is possible to develop a routine of exercises, using any of these methods, for all of the major joints in the body (*see* figs 37–59). The routine should reflect the needs of the performer, with specific emphasis on certain joints, while providing all-round flexibility development, and should be designed at a level whereby the performer will not sustain injury.

The exercises included in the routine vary in difficulty and are placed in progressive order, with the easiest shown at the beginning.

Prior to the commencement of flexibility training it may be necessary to follow the guidelines below.

- Always perform a general warm-up before stretching, e.g. jogging.
- Start with an easy stretching programme, working all of the joints from the neck down, and finishing with seated exercises or those performed lying down.
- Always maintain a good posture.
- Do not try to cheat with the exercises. Work for individual potential.
- Place advanced stretching movements towards the end of the session.
- Do not bounce in the static stretching exercises; hold the stretch at the limit.
- Finally, when working on partner exercises ensure that the partner understands the importance of not stretching the joint too far.

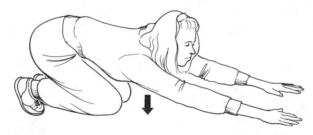

Fig. 37 Cat stretch. In a kneeling position the arms are outstretched and the head and shoulders are pushed towards the ground (3 x 10 secs)

Fig. 38 Spine. Push alternate arm and leg longitudinally, in opposite directions (3 x 10 secs)

Fig. 39 Pelvic tilt. Lying supine, with knees bent and feet flat on the floor, push hips upwards towards the head (3 x 10 secs)

Fig. 40 Hamstring. With trunk erect and head aligned naturally, stand in a wide straddle split. Bend the front leg to keep the back leg straight. Increase foot spacing on each stretch (3 x 10 secs)

Fig. 41 Quadriceps. Standing on one leg pull the free arm towards the buttocks, keeping the hollow of the back (3 x 10 secs)

Fig. 42 Calf. Lean against a wall with the front leg bent and back leg straight. Push the front knee towards the wall to stretch the calf of the rear leg (3 x 10 secs)

Fig. 43 Groin. Sitting with knees wide apart and the soles of the feet together, push the knees towards the floor with the hands (3 x 10 secs)

Fig. 44 Shoulder. Stand with a partner. Stretch the arms out to the sides with the palms upwards. The partner pulls on the arms to make the shoulder blades come closer together (3 x 10 secs)

Fig. 45 Shoulder. With a partner, stretch the arms about the head. The partner pushes under the shoulder blades at the same time stretching the arm backwards (3 x 10 secs)

Fig. 46 Back hyperextension. Lying prone with the hands under the shoulders, push to extend the arms and hyperextend the back (3 x 10 secs)

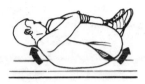

Fig. 47 Tucked back lying. Roll gently backwards and forwards on rounded back. Use foam mat for protection (3 x 20 secs)

Fig. 48 Back. Kneeling with arms straight, push the spine vertically up and down (3 x 20 secs)

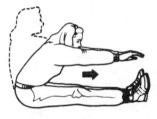

Fig. 49 Hamstring. Sit up and reach forwards, pushing head and chest towards the knees

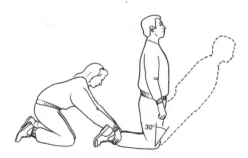

Fig. 50 Hamstring. Kneel with the trunk erect. Tilt the trunk 30 degrees forwards, holding the isometric contraction (3 x 10 secs)

Fig. 51 Trunk and hip. Sitting with arms and legs stretched open, twist trunk clockwise and anti-clockwise (3 x 20 twists)

Fig. 52 Shoulders. Lying prone, stretch out arms. Partner pulls up on arms to stretch shoulder joint. Can also do to back hyperextension (3 x 10 secs)

Fig. 53 Back and shoulders. Grasp wall bars at ear level with back to them. Allow the body to drop to full arm length. Touch bars with hips and extend legs. Push hips forwards and upwards to hold back bowed (3 x 10 secs). Highly advanced athletes can walk hands down and up bars

Fig. 54 Shoulders and back. Performer hangs from top wall bar, with a partner behind him in the front squat position high on the bars. Partner pushes performer out, away from the bars, into the 'Span' position (3 x 10 secs). (This is also a powerful squatting position for the partner. When he places his feet close to his hands it becomes more of an arm and shoulder stretching exercise.)

Fig. 55 Hips. Stand alongside a beam or box at crotch height, with one leg raised to the side to place the knee on the beam or box in the hurdle trail leg position. Push head down towards supporting knee (3 x 10 secs or 3 x 10 reps). Another exercise is to bend the supporting knee to open up the groin

Fig. 56 PNF 1. Lying supine with the partner kneeling, perform single leg raise to 30 degrees; partner supports leg on shoulder, with both hands, keeping the leg straight by preventing knee flexion. Performer forces the raised leg towards floor. The leg is stopped by the partner; hold for 10 secs. Rest 10 secs. Then raise leg to 45 degrees, subsequently to 90 degrees, with 10 secs rest in each case. Do the same for the other leg, then both legs together

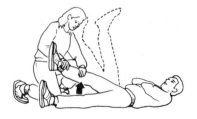

Fig. 57 PNF 2. As fig. 56, only performer tries to pull leg up against resistance of partner

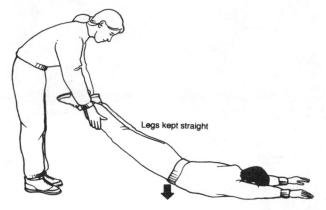

Legs kept straight

Fig. 58 PNF 3. With performer lying prone, partner takes both legs to shoulder support at 45 degrees. Performer forces down on thighs (3 x 10 secs, 10 secs rest)

Fig. 59 PNF 4. Stand against side support with one leg raised to bent hurdle position. Partner holds leg in position, while performer tries to push thigh upwards against his resistance (3 x 10 secs, 10 secs rest). A complementary exercise is for the performer to try to force the thigh towards the support leg against the partner's resistance

The long-term benefits

Time devoted to the careful thought and planning of a flexibility routine will deliver handsome rewards at a later date. Flexibility training has an advantage in that it offers two quite distinct avenues for improving potential. There is no doubt that many injuries sustained in both training and competition are the result of poor flexibility. When time is spent training for flexibility, it might reduce the time spent away from training due to injury. Hence, by reducing the risk, and often the duration of injury, it is, in fact, increasing the training time available to achieve peak fitness.

Secondly, an increase in the range of action about a joint produces an increase in total work. This can manifest itself in an increased racket, club or bat speed, which, when directed carefully, will have a dramatic effect upon the sport involved.

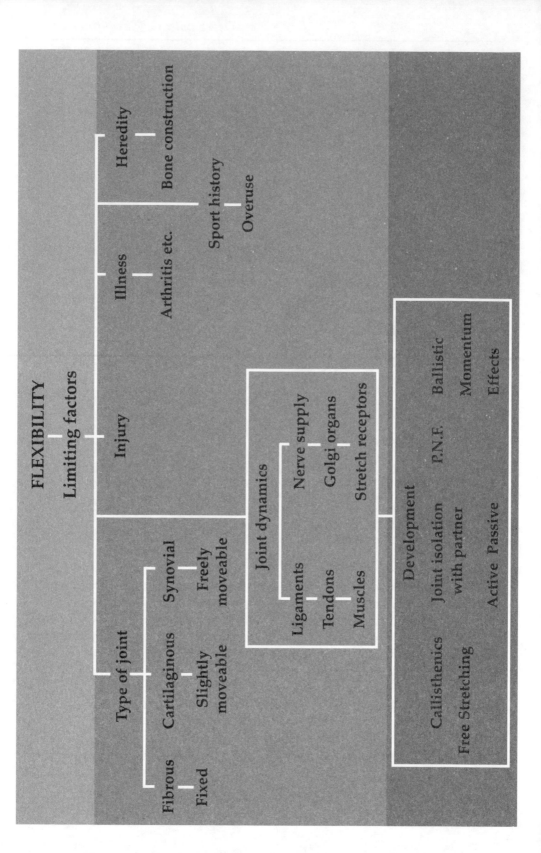

FLEXIBILITY
Limiting factors

Type of joint

Fibrous
Fixed

Cartilaginous
Slightly
moveable

Synovial
Freely
moveable

Injury

Illness

Arthritis etc.

Heredity

Bone construction

Sport history

Overuse

Joint dynamics

Ligaments

Tendons

Muscles

Nerve supply

Golgi organs

Stretch receptors

Development

Callisthenics

Free Stretching

Joint isolation
with partner

Active Passive

P.N.F.

Ballistic

Momentum

Effects

Development of skill

In order to perform most activities in life, it is necessary to learn 'skills'. Consider the skilled dentist working with a patient, the skilled driver manoeuvering a car into a parking space, or the skilled typist working at speed. Quite apart from mental and physical judgement, some skills involve the large muscle groups, and others involve small muscle groups in more intricate movements. Often, these overlap, with the distinction never being clear cut.

There is a degree of confusion over what exactly is meant by 'skill'. First, skill and technique are not the same thing. To have an efficient technique may not necessarily correlate with being skilful. A golfer with a technically perfect swing would be inefficient without a degree of accuracy, the discus thrower with the perfect turn would be inefficient without the speed and strength to propel the discus. Only in sports such as gymnastics, ice skating, diving and trampolining where points are awarded for aesthetic performance, and where subjective assessments have to be made on the quality of performance, is technique or style taken into consideration. However, a poor style can be detrimental to performance and could cause an injury when applied to a skill, for example a poor serving style in tennis could injure the elbow.

Technique, style and skill

Many sports coaches confuse technique and style, particularly in individual sports such as gymnastics, swimming, golf, athletics, tennis, etc. Technique is a fundamental that all players must possess; the movements composing a technique all comply with the laws of biomechanics, for example the way the bodyweight shifts during a golf swing, the way the leading foot goes to the ball in a forward defensive shot in cricket, the balance position of the discus thrower arriving in the centre of the circle, and the way the racket head contacts the ball in a tennis serve. Style is the way the individual interprets the skill, for example the golfer or cricketer could have an extensive or short back-lift, or the discus thrower could arrive in the balance position from a front, sidewards or backwards run. The coach must decide early on with a performer what the fundamentals of technique are and how they are going to be isolated in technique training, while at the same time allowing the individual a degree of freedom within the total movement for any personal idiosyncrasy.

Skill can also be classified as a person's reaction to the environment or to a given situation. A team player would derive little advantage from executing the perfect dodge or pass without having prior knowledge of the position of the other players. Perhaps one should include team tactics, strategies and set plays under the umbrella of skill?

Skill: innate or learned?

The late Barbara Knappe, in her work *Skill in Sport*, gave the world of physical education a sound definition of skill: 'A skill is a learned ability, to bring about pre-determined results, with the maximum degree of certainty, often with the minimum outlay of time, energy or both.'

This definition gives us the dimensions of quality and efficiency of movement, and states that skill involves both physical and mental abilities. In the definition there is a strong emphasis on learned ability, suggesting that it is neither instinctive nor reflexive, that it has not arisen as a result of a maturing process, and that skill is dependent upon practice.

A further interpretation of the definition is that the high-class performer makes complex skills appear relatively easy. Stimuli such as the Wimbledon fortnight or Open Golf tournaments on the television prompt millions of spectators out of their armchairs and into action. It is only in trying to reproduce the skills of the stars that it becomes obvious how great the level of difficulty is in many of the strokes performed. Are we impressed by grace and style when we observe skill, or is it the harmonious interplay of muscles making the movement appear efficient and effortless?

The truth is that skill is an endowed trait, refined by practice, hence returning us to the modern discussion of nature v nurture. Nature on its own will not produce the flowing movements mentioned above, but neither will nurture.

The endowed trait would appear to be a refinement of the motor section of the central nervous system. As far as skill is concerned, to take tennis as an example, this means the co-ordination of the eye, the interpretation of the information transmitted by the eye to the brain, and the subsequent co-ordination of the effector muscles to place the player in the correct position to play the shot. Ultimately it involves the way the racket head strikes the ball with speed, spin or position, to disadvantage the opponent.

Skills can be classified as 'closed skills' – sensory motor skills, often regarded as habitual reproductions of precise stereotyped movements with the minimum amount of conscious control – and 'open skills', perceptual motor skills, where movements are constantly guided and modified by the changing environment. In open skills performance is affected by the interpretation and decisions of the person executing the skill.

In the introduction to this chapter, I made attempts to define skill. The truth is, it is very difficult to define. One can see the results of skill any time a person strikes a ball with a bat for example, however, these are only the results and not the process involved in achieving them. The interpretation of the movement takes place within the body, a complicated interaction of the brain and the other components which make up the neuro-muscular system.

Applying general statements to skill is also very difficult, as it cannot be compartmentalised as the pure scientist would wish. Skill is frequently divided into two basic categories: 'simple' and 'complex' skills on the one hand, and 'open' and 'closed' skills on the other. What is a simple skill for one person could be a complex skill for another, and at what stage does a complex skill become a simple skill? Initially, bowling a cricket ball is a closed skill, however once the batsman makes a move to play the ball then the skill becomes open. The state of a pitch, and atmospheric conditions, e.g. humidity or wind, will also change the nature of a skill.

It is quite understandable that there should be a degree of confusion within a study involving the psychological as well as the physiological, thus making general consensus almost impossible. While research can be done on animals there will always remain the doubt that humans will react differently.

As regards training skills, it helps to know how the body learns skilled movements and stores them for repetition.

The physiological process of learning skills

When a skill is first learned, the movement is conscious, the interpretation takes place in the higher centre of the brain, and the subsequent result will probably be slow, ponderous, inefficient and lacking in timing. This is due to the fact that the skilled movement has to be interpreted by the upper brain, with the effector responses directed to the main muscles of the body, via the pyramidal tract of the spinal cord. Once the movement has been learned, interpretation of the stimuli moves to the lower centre (probably in the mid-brain), and impulses to create the effector muscle response are transmitted via the extra-pyramidal tract. At this point the movement becomes a conditioned reflex, frequently referred to as muscle memory. In its refined state this involves the proprioceptor nerve supply and kinesthetic sense – the awareness of the body position.

Muscle memory relies upon two important muscle sense organs called muscle spindles and Golgi tendon organs. These organs are also involved in controlling voluntary and reflex movements. Muscle spindles control the rate and magnitude of the stretch of a muscle and they relay information to the central nervous system about the number of motor units available in a movement, thus ensuring that the result is smooth and co-ordinated. The Golgi tendon organs are also related to stretch but they deal mainly with the strength of contraction. They can cause a muscle to relax if the magnitude of the stretch is so great as to cause possible injury. Hence, when the body is called upon to execute a movement, there is a subconscious involvement of the brain and the nervous system, with a whole host of receptor and effector nerves sending messages to the brain for interpretation. The subconscious linking of the various aspects of the nervous system is termed 'kinesthetic awareness'.

A good test of one's ability to interpret this sense is to stand a full arm's distance away from a wall and to make a chalk mark at shoulder height. Still standing in the same position, drop the extended arm and, with the eyes closed, attempt to draw a second line on the wall in an identical place to the first line. The degree of variation is frequently several centimetres. In this test, the body is trying to recall the degree of tension it had in the arm, shoulder and trunk muscles when the first shoulder height line was drawn.

It is information of this nature, stored in the brain and then converted into a reflex action, that permits the body to perform a skilled movement.

Relating these factors to sport, could it be that the skilled performer has a greater refinement of the nervous system? Could it be that the skilled player has a more efficient muscle memory, providing the necessary co-ordination to produce movements of the highest order, or is it the training and constant practice that refines this intricate and nervous co-ordinated exercise?

In sports such as tennis, cricket, or soccer, it is the sheer speed and power of the movements which are the hallmark of the class player. While speed of movement is almost certainly endowed, requiring fast twitch rather than slow twitch muscle fibres and a good nerve supply to these muscles, power is directly related to the magnitude of the force produced by these muscles, which is certainly a trained factor, as it is strength. However, strength alone will not produce excellence in any skilled movement. This is because, as discussed in chapter 4, strength is specific and must be related back to skill, otherwise the tennis player and weightlifter would be able to swap sports.

Model theory

Once a basic skill has been acquired, it can be refined by the advice and the personal interaction of a coach. For the initial process of learning to take place, the performer, teacher or coach, must have in mind the specific execution of a technique – in other words, a model, hence the term 'model' theory.

However, there are dangers in using the 'model' approach to the development of a technique. How can one be certain that the model to be copied is correct? Many sports players, especially cricketers, have been encouraged along blind alleys by copying a star in vogue. Too frequently, the star is aware of personal inadequacies in technique of which the player copying is not. A particular technique could, for instance, have been modified to accommodate an injury, a lack of strength or poor levels of flexibility. As a result, what the player copying is attempting to mimic could be a poor technique, developed to compensate for a weakness. When this technique is further aided by a teacher or a coach, who may also have interpreted the technique incorrectly, the possibility of error is compounded. In this situation, the performer, teacher or coach can only remedy the situation through biomechanics: the application of physics to human movement.

Perfecting a skill under the model theory today involves countless hours viewing videos and subjecting images to careful analysis, then practising the skills, under the watchful eye and guidance of a coach, until it resembles the model.

As far as learning a skill is concerned, there are three distinct areas that have to be considered. They all touch on the psychology involved, and the reader should make reference to chapter 12, where the role of the psychologist is discussed in terms of its implication on skill learning. The areas that need careful consideration are:

1) the direction of practice, its duration and the methods used for reinforcement
2) the teaching method
3) performer, teacher, coach and trainer interaction. How the various temperaments blend to produce a winning combination.

The direction of practice

It is frequently said that 'practice makes perfect'. However, if the practice is not controlled, the end result may be unsatisfactory, therefore all constructive practice sessions should be overseen by a coach or trainer. In all forms of learning the learner has a set retention period. The length of the period can vary considerably from individual to individual, but it is greatly influenced by their own motivation and the motivational methods used by the teacher. Once the retention period of the learner is exhausted, motivation levels drop and the capacity to learn diminishes. For example, a good coach will recognise when a player is becoming bored with a particular practice session, and will change the emphasis, offer a different challenge, or break for a short informal chat, all of which could restore concentration, provide new motivation and improve vigour. For example, the cricket coach could have spent a period of time emphasising the role of the arm in a fast bowling movement, to the extent where movement becomes routine and lacking in purpose. A shift of emphasis to the legs and their role in the total movement might enhance the quality of the session.

As concentration spans vary between individuals, it is impossible to lay down exact rules on training times. Guidance from the coach is needed, together with guidelines on the duration of practice. As relationships develop the coach begins to understand the athlete, and sessions can be tailored to fit his or her needs and character.

The teaching method

There are two basic methods for teaching skills, the 'whole' method, and the 'part' method, although at times there is no clearly defined line between the two. Within each of the two basic groups, the teacher will also have a whole host of practice methods.

Whether one uses the whole or part method for instruction will depend mainly upon the skill being taught, although the initial levels of skill of the learner will have a bearing. For example, in track and field athletics, the skill of hurdling is best taught by the whole method, whereas the skill of shot putting is best taught in a series of progressions. This is because in hurdling it is impossible to isolate the skill of the lead leg, since the total movement is immediately influenced by what the trail leg does. In shot-putting it is possible to isolate the action of the arm, and one can still push the shot. At a later stage the legs can be used from a static position prior to performing a complete shift.

An aspect of a skill might have to be isolated and practised separately from the full skill. For example, in shot-putting, the way in which the dominant leg produces the pushing force can be isolated and practised, before putting it back in the full shift.

Another skill that can be practised first as a part skill is heading a goal from a corner kick in soccer. The coach gently throws the ball from close range onto the head of the performer; later the ball is kicked from the correct position to the head. To perfect the skill the performer would need to head many balls into the goal, hence the coach might resort to pressure training where balls are kicked towards the header in quick succession from both the right and left sides of the field. However, this situation is quite artificial, as it only involves two or three players, none of whom have a defensive role. To place the skill closer to the true game situation there could be a 'passive' opponent, that is someone who stands in the path of the ball, between the corner kicker and the attacker. Surprisingly, even a passive performer can reduce the number of successful attempts by 50 per cent. At a later stage an active opponent can be introduced, whose aim is to try to head the ball away from the attacker. Such a situation is then close to that experienced during the game itself.

There is a danger in skill isolation and the practice of 'parts'. For example, it is quite easy for a player to become a perfectionist in an isolated part, and be unable to incorporate that part to the total skill. A tennis player can appear to be very good when practising forehand and backhand shots against a wall, but when the ball is returned from an opposing player, who disregards position and imparts spin to the ball, then the same player might be all at sea. Hence, when any skill is placed in isolation, there must be a very high transfer of training effect to the total skill itself.

Transfer of training is particularly important when skills are isolated either for strength or flexibility. For example, many heavy throwers from track and field athletics practice a weight training exercise known as the bench press, which involves the performer lying on a bench in the supine position. As the thrower always has to perform in the standing position, there isn't likely to be a positive transfer effect from the bench press to the actual throwing event. Many racket sport players insist that there is a negative transfer of training between the smash shot in badminton and the smash shot in tennis. This again returns us to specificity, and this must be kept in mind during all aspects of skill isolation techniques.

Athlete–coach–trainer interaction

Similar to a marriage, a successful coach–athlete relationship occurs when two people with a degree of compatibility learn to interact in harmony. Some partnerships gel from the first meeting, while others have to be worked at.

It is essential that in a skill-learning situation both pupil and teacher are compatible. How many potentially excellent sportspeople were put off their sport in the early stages by an unsympathetic Physical Education teacher? Skill training requires motivation and much of this has to come from the coach.

Even at the highest possible level there will always be people who have difficulty in mastering certain aspects of skills. There are those who might be termed 'slow learners'. This certainly does not suggest that they haven't the capacity to learn and ultimately become top-level performers; we are all individuals who learn skills at different rates. A common saying in sport is: 'Get them young'. There is some truth in this, but the perfection of certain skills relies upon speed and strength components, which cannot be gained at sufficient levels in youth.

While there are obviously physiological limits in skill-learning, psychological limits are more likely to 'hone the razor's edge', hence pupil motivation, and interaction between pupil and teacher, athlete and coach, are all of extreme importance in elite performance.

Using technology

The modern sports coach has many advantages that his predecessors did not, none more so than the ways in which performance techniques can be recorded, stored and replayed at a later date. Still photographs, first made available to the coach soon after the development of the camera, continue to have their place, however they lack movement. With the invention of cinematography and slow-motion projection techniques, the field of skill analysis became highly sophisticated. When this system is linked to video, digitisation and computer analysis techniques, it might appear that Utopia has been reached.

The modern coach must now take advantage of what science has to offer, and use it efficiently in skill learning. But it must be remembered that these techniques only record, store and replay data. The interpretation rests with the coach and the performer. Hence the eye of the coach, the verbal reinforcement of what the eye has seen, and the interpretation by the brain, will still remain the most powerful weapon in the learning of skills.

Skill evaluation

While the technological advances in recording data can aid the coach in both the interpretation and evaluation of skill, it still does not quite bridge the gap between theory and practice. Most performers would suggest that the century in cricket, the home run in baseball, the ace in tennis, and the scoring of a goal from a set play in soccer, are the best evaluation one could have. The feeling of satisfaction of having outwitted an opponent or done a personal best in a track and field athletics event, could suggest better, or even improved levels of skill. These are indeed the ultimate tests. However, somewhere along the road between learning the basic skill and the satisfaction of becoming a master, there exists a number of tests that might prove invaluable to future learning.

Once a skill has been learned, there must follow a further period of learning to be accurate. In this situation, evaluation using numbered targets, related to difficulty, is both a means of assessment and motivation. The skill evaluation can be made more specific by subjecting it to a degree of psychological pressure, perhaps by only nominating the target at the last moment.

There exists a list of tests that might be termed skill tests, such as the gross muscle co-ordination test and the broadjump differential (*see* chapter 11), which measure skill to a degree, but which are more reliable for measuring speed, strength or power-weight ratio. This serves to highlight further the massive cross-component effect that exists between all of the 'S' factors, skill being no exception.

In conclusion, some final words of advice. Skill is not an end in itself. It is a means to an end, the end being victory. A classic example of this is the popularity of driving ranges in golf. There is no competition to find who can hit a ball the furthest. The nearest anyone ever got to this is the old game of 'knur and spell', which is almost extinct. The real motive is to get the ball into the appropriate hole using as few strokes as possible, hence there is the problem of accuracy. Many fast cricket bowlers are indeed fast, but if the batsman does not need to protect the wicket then the value of speed is lost. There is no doubt that competition can change the nature of the performer, and hence the nature of the skill. The skill must therefore be placed into the true competition so that the player can start to understand the problems created by competitive stress, and make the necessary adaptations to the skill and skill practice. However, there is one very real danger, especially with young and inexperienced people, and that is to place the skill into competition before the 'skill base' is constant enough to permit a learning situation. All too frequently young athletes, soccer players and cricketers are encouraged to compete before a skill has become 'reflex'. This situation will not contribute to high levels of performance. Hence junior leagues, which now form part of most sport strategies, must be viewed with extreme caution. Unfortunately many aspiring young players are drawn into the 'frustrated parent syndrome'; dad would like to have won an Olympic medal but lacked the ability, resulting in his offspring being 'force fed' competition. Litigation against parents by referees who have been attacked during the course of a game is a growing problem.

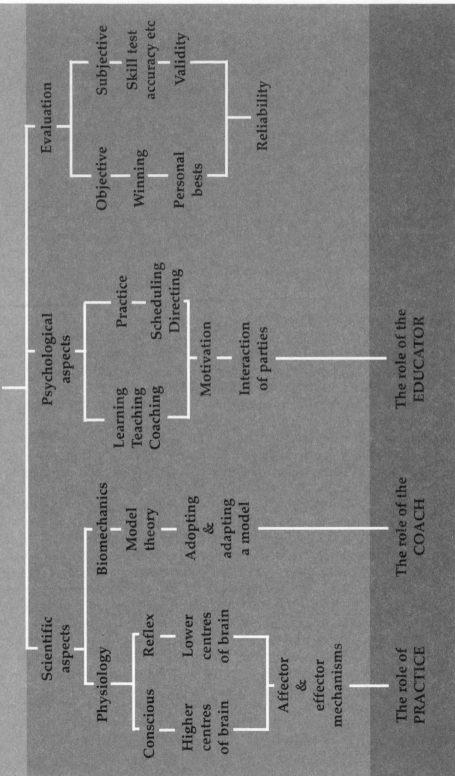

Specificity

A considerable section of this text is devoted to what is termed 'general fitness'. In most cases this refers to a general state which exists in the body whereby the heart, the lungs and the muscles function adequately to perform most tasks involved in sport. It is all part of getting fit to play, something most games players do in the period immediately before they start their competitive season. It is frequently termed pre-season training and indeed many major games players train harder during this period than at any other time during their seasonal training. It is a pre-required state on to which the more specific physical demands of individual sports are moulded.

A group of top-class soccer players were taken to the swimming baths as part of a relaxed form of training during a very highly competitive season. The following day virtually all of the players complained of extreme muscle soreness, particularly in the arm and shoulder region. Immediately prior to an Olympic Games, a group of athletes went horse riding as a relaxed form of exercise. The result was that most could not exercise the following day because of muscle soreness. While all of the athletes involved were at their 'peak' levels of fitness, they were called upon to use their muscles in a different way to that which their own sport normally demanded.

Sports scientists can now offer players and coaches far more information on this very important aspect of fitness. Classic examples can be taken from any of our major games, such as soccer, rugby and hockey. While all players are on their feet and using muscular energy for the duration of the game, the exercise only reaches what is termed an 'intensive' level for a very short period of time. A player might have to sprint flat out for probably a maximum of 30 metres, and it is usually only necessary to sustain this level of speed for about ten strides. While rugby players have been known to sprint the length of the field during the course of a game, it is always the exception rather than the rule. In the main, a period of intensive activity is followed by a period of inactivity, during which the player can recover and replenish the energy used. Players in sports of this nature seldom use anything other than energy stored in their muscles in the form of phosphagens. While the game itself will prepare the player for this specific level of fitness, the wise coach will always 'overcompensate' by preparing for the most extreme nature of any game.

During court games such as basketball, squash, tennis and badminton, the players are frequently called upon to run backwards; to move quickly to the side in a series of 'close' or 'cross-steps'; or to move rapidly in one direction and then suddenly change direction, all of which are regularly enacted in a singles tennis match. The cyclist, the 'paddler' and the rower need to fix the body in a sitting position where either the arms or the legs provide the power for locomotion. The boxer, and to a degree all combat sport athletes, have an even greater specific need. While energy is certainly used in their movements about the ring, contact blows, which can temporarily deprive an area of blood, also make extreme demands upon energy. Again, all of these specific aspects of sport must be rehearsed and planned in the training programme.

Specificity of speed

In virtually all games involving the use of a ball, golf being the main exception, speed of running is of paramount importance. The player who can get to a ball the quickest has the advantage. The running involved here is a very specific form of sprinting, related more to power than leg speed. The performance of a high powered sports car is frequently measured in terms of 0–60 in a period of seconds, this being a measurement of acceleration. This 'acceleration' is precisely what the player needs, hence a considerable part of training should be directed towards the factors that can improve this. While the power (strength) of the individual muscles is an important factor, it requires the co-ordination of several muscle groups, some of which might not appear to be involved. The term co-ordination suggests also the part played by the nervous system. The excitement of the muscle, the recruitment of the muscle fibres and the provision of the right level of energy are all integral components in this quest for speed.

With this in mind, players involved must do regular weight training, converting the strength so gained into power using forms of plyometric training. With this basic quality of power developed, the co-ordination must be rehearsed. This can only be done by sprinting at top speed. In this situation it is almost 'emergency' energy that is recruited, and there have to be incentives to promote this level of excitement during training. For example, soccer players are frequently 0.5 seconds faster over ten strides when actually chasing a ball. Placing players in a competitive situation can have similar effects upon excitation.These are all qualities which respond to carefully planned training, however the system must be stimulated frequently (i.e. several times each week) to prevent it regressing.

Speed endurance

Pure speed, in terms of the high rate at which energy is used to fuel the muscles that produce the speed of locomotion, can only last for about 8–10 seconds. After this period of very intense work, the fuel stored in the muscles is depleted. To continue working at close to maximum speed, a different form of energy must be used. This type of energy is only available for a fairly short period of time, since it involves the production of lactic acid which ultimately accumulates, paralysing the muscles and preventing them from contracting. Hence, after this period of time, about 30–40 seconds of very intense work, the player must either stop working or considerably reduce the level of activity. This level of activity is known as speed endurance.

In training for speed endurance, the player must stimulate the physiological system which creates the necessary energy. It is commonly termed the 'lactic acid' system, although the true physiological term is 'glycolysis'. It is an anaerobic process, during which the fuel glycogen is broken down to produce energy without an adequate supply of oxygen. The bi-product is lactic acid, some of which can be converted back to energy. The whole process is aided by enzymes, and these must therefore be stimulated during the training process.

In addition to the physiological process, there is a psychological process, one of 'mind over matter', that must be improved. It is a situation in which the body is trying to tell the mind that it can no longer keep up the work rate. The player must develop a callousness towards this type of fatigue, by 'willing' the body to continue. In most cases it is fulfilled by the 'emergency' form of energy which the body has available, but which is not normally brought into play.

In very simple terms, the training to develop speed endurance must involve work on the following areas: stimulation of the necessary enzyme activity; the system by which the acid state of the blood is brought back to more normal levels by the neutralising effect of the blood buffers (alkalis); the psyche of the mind to tolerate such a high level of activity.

The systems have to be trained using an 'intermittent' form of work and the principle of 'overload'. In this situation there has to be a degree of experimentation with the variables which influence the 'intermittent' work system. These include the duration of the effort period, the number of repetitions and the duration of the recovery. The intensity of the effort, however, is not a variable and must be kept close to maximum rate.

With reference to the research work undertaken in this specific field, and by experimenting with world-class athletes and major games players, I have formulated a system whereby the duration of the effort must be between 15 seconds and 40 seconds of intense activity. The number of repetitions is determined by the duration of the activity and the duration of the rest period. When the rest period is short, the total extent of training must be kept low. When the duration of the activity period is longer, the rest period must be extended, or the total extent of training has to be reduced.

By analysing a large number of games, I calculated that top-class soccer players sprint on to the ball for a total of between 350m and 720m, during the course of a game. While I admit that the variation is quite considerable, it depends upon the player, the position and the type of game. It does, however, provide us with a guide when selecting the total extent of training. Rugby and hockey players also fit into the same approximate pattern.

When working at intense levels for a period of 15–40 seconds, there needs to be a recovery period of ten times the effort period. Hence, when a player is running at peak speed for a period of 30 seconds, there must be a recovery period of 300 seconds (5 minutes).

Using guidelines I have established for the sport of track and field athletics, for distances of about 800m the extent of training should be twice that total distance. For example, the player who sprints on to the ball for a total of 700m per game, needs to sprint in training for a total distance of 1,400m. Therefore, if we took this player to do this type of work at a conventional athletics track, the ideal training schedule would be:

5 x 300m fast with a 5-minute recovery period
or
6 x 200m fast with a 3-minute recovery period.

To take full advantage of the specific nature of speed endurance, however, one must experiment with all of the variables, in particular keeping the recovery period short. Since this type of work is extremely fatiguing, it should not be done as part of any other training session. It will also require a period of rest so that the body makes a complete adaptation. Within this basic format for training, there is an almost endless variety of sessions that can be done to stimulate and promote speed endurance.

By carefully analysing sports such as basketball, sprinting, cycling and sculling, similar patterns for training can be established.

Provided one uses the guidelines listed above relating to the total extent of training and establishing the recovery period, it can be fairly certain that one is promoting speed endurance.

Certain sporting events require the performer to exercise, at almost peak rate, for close to 2 minutes. For example, the world class 800m track athlete is running extremely quickly for a period in excess of 1 minute 40 seconds. This requires the body to take advantage of yet another different energy system. This is frequently termed the 'LA/O₂' system and is the last 'exercise point' before the performer has to reduce the tempo of the activity and use an aerobic system for providing energy. To train this system the performer must exercise, at just sub maximum, for a period of between 40 and 90 seconds. The recovery period before a repeat performance should be approximately ten times the length of the effort period.

The major games player wishing to cater for every possibility might need to approach this level of speed endurance. If training was done at the track, a suitable schedule would be 3 x 600m at 100 secs, with an interval of 15 minutes. Reducing the recovery period would only force the player to run aerobically.

From experience, I can state that most major games players will be reluctant to do this type of training, however I am confident that in order to play games, and to excel, one must be prepared to do this type of work. Kicking, hitting or running with a ball might not necessarily be the best way to adapt to the physical stress placed on the body during international tournaments.

Specificity of strength

The term strength is a confusing one, and means different things to different people. However, once specificity of strength is considered, the term starts to have a more significant meaning. At one end of the spectrum is the strength required by the heavyweight Olympic weightlifter, and at the other is the strength required by the very light Olympic gymnast or the female marathon runner. The Olympic lifter has to be able to create a massive force, from the strength of the muscles, to lift the weight and also to comply with the rules. The young gymnast performing balance routines on the beam, or executing the intricate movements on the asymmetrical bars also needs muscle strength.

When the Olympic lifter almost reaches the climax of pushing the weight above the head, it might appear that only the arm muscles are working. That is because they are functioning isotonically, where the tension in the muscles creates visible movement. However, many other muscles are functioning in a different way to maintain the posture. The most obvious is the action coming from the legs. If these muscles did not keep the knee and hip joints locked, the sheer weight of the bar would force them to bend, resulting in the collapse of the whole movement. In the case of the gymnast, the muscle tension produced maintains the correct posture of the body, and the action produced by the muscle is known as an 'isometric' contraction. In both cases, tension is produced and the muscle is made to 'work', hence energy has to be used by the muscle. Research indicates that a muscle working isotonically uses considerably more energy than a muscle working isometrically. While energy is stored in the muscles, energy can also be stored in the tendons. The isotonic movement, calling for considerable tendon action, needs a specific type of conditioning to improve the tendons' energy-storing capacity.

When the development of strength is a consideration, one must differentiate between 'training' and 'practice'. While the 'S' factors respond to both training and practice, the two terms take on a different meaning when strength is the consideration. By definition, 'training' is the process of enhancing the physical and mental state of a player, while 'practice' is understood by most people involved to be the method used to perfect the technical skills. For example, the rugby player might practise a drop kick, the tennis player a back-hand drive, and both movements have a strength component. When the strength component is improved, the ball will leave the boot or the racket head with greater speed, provided the other variables, such as timing, remain constant. This equation only remains true when speed is the primary factor. At other times accuracy might be more important, and in this situation strength could be a detrimental factor.

It therefore follows that not all strength-promoting activities will enhance skill. Conversely, ignoring strength-promoting activities might prevent the player from executing a particular skill efficiently. Therefore, the development of strength must be carefully considered in the context of the skill, for example the kind of strength gained from training with barbells will only assure success in Olympic weightlifting. It is therefore most important that both a skill and its strength component are developed harmoniously so that the skill is improved.

Most participants in sports in which running is a basic activity, have managed to master the particular skill of running. To become stronger, one must also master the skill of lifting weights. When making this statement I am conscious that many forms of strength training no longer involve lifting weights, there now being elaborate lever, pulley and stack systems in existence. However, I remain adamant that to become really strong, one must lift weights, hence some time must be spent practising the correct, efficient, lifting techniques. Failure to get the correct advice could lead to permanent injury. It might, therefore, be beneficial to place a greater emphasis, for a short while, on mastering a new skill such as weightlifting in order to progress in a more sport-specific skill. There might also be a need to solicit the help of a specialist in this new field to enable the skill coach to concentrate on the specifics of the individual's sport.

To design a strength-promoting programme, the following conditions must be applied.

1) There should be a careful analysis of what the sport requires, together with a careful analysis of the skills involved. This task is fairly easy for the Olympic weightlifter and the heavy thrower, since all that they need is a single peak effort. The rower, who will be placed in a cramped, seated position will be making powerful contractions for a period of between 6–8 minutes; the canoe paddler for between 3–5 minutes. Hence it is a very specific type of strength endurance that is required. The wrestler, the rugby player in a scrum and to a degree the climber need to sustain an almost isometric contract for approximately 10 seconds.

    The individual activity must be carefully analysed by people who understand the sport and the various aspects of strength conditioning. Such an analysis is best achieved with the aid of a video camera with split second timings inserted. Experienced physiologists can wire performers up to a monitor to calculate exactly what the physiological demands are. By placing recording devices on certain key points of the body a very accurate kinesiological/biomechanical analysis can be made. It does sound like science fiction but in fact the facility is available in most elite sporting countries of the world. Furthermore, the knowledge and equipment is improving day by day.

    Only through analysis of this kind can an efficient programme be devised. However, the performer and the coach must keep the main issue in focus. Research for research sake is of very little value, and the researcher will be only too keen to have as a subject a very elite performer, since they do not follow any of the standard norms.

2) The analysis outlined above will indicate the exact nature of the specificity. Is it gross strength or strength endurance that is required? The former training requires a high intensity and a low extent system. The latter requires the opposite.

3) Is strength required throughout the whole range of movement? Is the same level of intensity required throughout the same range? For example, the weightlifter requires maximum strength to overcome the inertia of the weight and set the

weight in motion; progressively less strength is required as the momentum increases. The gymnast requires greater strength in the outer ranges of a movement, e.g. when pushing away from a piece of apparatus, or the floor. Similarly, there are instances with both the weightlifter and the gymnast when they need a greater 'pulling' strength than 'pushing' strength, and vice versa. Hence the coach must look at developing strength both eccentrically and concentrically. (*See* chapter 10.)

In summarising this aspect, the analysis must be individual specific, sport specific, event specific, and position specific (for major games players). It must also be remembered that a strength training pro-gramme can be remedial, and therefore injury specific. While it is possible to get rapid increases in strength, there might not be quite the same speedy returns as far as skill is concerned. Hence strength training must be viewed as a long term investment and must never become an end in itself other than for the Olympic weightlifter.

In this chapter it has only been my aim to highlight the specific nature of strength. It is not possible to list a specific schedule for each and every sport. In conclusion I must emphasise that the system used for promoting strength must be sport specific and that the exercises used must be as close as possible to the movement skill which the sport demands.

Specificity of endurance

We need to examine further how the body produces the energy needed for activity. In the sections on speed endurance and strength endurance I have mainly considered the anaerobic pathways of energy production using both the 'alactic acid' and 'lactic acid' systems.

When a movement is repeated more than once, the system gradu-ally moves towards the realms of endurance. The greater the extent of the effort the more it progresses towards a totally aerobic activity. There are events which demand extreme levels of aerobic efficiency, for example feats of endurance such as the popular 'comrades' marathon and the 'two oceans' marathon in South Africa, where con-tinuous activity takes place for periods in excess of four hours. There are similar long distance skiing and cycling events which last several days, such as the Tour de France. However, these events are not totally sustained since there are periods set aside for rest.

It is fairly safe to say that the limiting factor in these 'ultra' events is not the aerobic provision of energy, but the capacity to rehydrate – to drink enough of the right kind of liquid to permit the correct electrolyte balance and eat the correct type of food at the correct time. Chaffing and blistering can also prove to be a significant limiting factor. The effect of these factors can be reduced by careful preparation rather than by making any specific adaptations to a training programme.

One hears of athletes 'hitting the wall' during long distance events such as the marathon. This is a process related to the provision of energy, however once a person can train aerobically for a period in excess of two hours it is unlikely to be a limiting factor. Of course there is a skill element which I relate to 'pace judgement'. The runner who sets off too quickly in a marathon or any other ultra distance/time event is unlikely to feature well at the finishing line.

Hence as far as aerobic efficiency is concerned, there is no substitute for experience. That is the experience of building up a vast reservoir of aerobic functions, and of pace judgement, and varying climates and terrain, etc.

Specificity of flexibility

As outlined earlier, most people involved in sport only pay lip service to this important quality that can influence performance. Here I would state that the specificity of flexibility is more related to experience than any physiological function. Sport frequently recognises two distinct aspects of flexibility: 'dynamic' and 'static'. For example, the gymnast would certainly need dynamic flexibility, whereas the climber, attempting to make a different move, would require something of a less dynamic nature. Sport also recognises the extremes of limb movement influenced by 'extent' flexibility. That is the maximum range of movement (joint distortion), in any particular plane, that a joint can exhibit.

In most cases flexibility influences the work capacity of a lever or series of levers. In this case the scientific definition of work is used, i.e. the product of force and the range through which the force acts. Any improvement in extent flexibility should therefore have a significant effect upon the work potential.

Again, careful analysis of the actual range of limb movement during any skill activity should be recorded, evaluated and then considered when devising a specific training routine.

I am convinced that the role of 'specificity' is one that will, in the future, have a profound effect upon elite sporting performance.

9

Genetics

During the course of my lecturing to degree students, coaches and teachers, I frequently make the statement: 'I would have been world record holder for the discus event had I selected my parents carefully'. My parents passed on to me 'genes' which enable me to master physical skills quite easily, hence I find the skill of throwing a discus quite simple. However, the side of my family with the dominant genes are all very short, hence I have the temperament of a thrower but the physique of a marathon runner. Since a discus used in competition weighs 2 kgs, discus throwing will always remain the domain of the big, strong person. Like basketball, there is no place for the vertically challenged!

Other times I make the statement: 'You can't put in what God left out', a reference to the genetic structure a person inherits at birth. The individual becomes a conglomeration of genes from both parents. However, a particular type of gene can miss out a generation or more, and some are only passed on through the female line of heredity.

The study of genetics, even to seek a definition of a 'gene', is extremely complicated and quite beyond the scope of this text. The reason for its inclusion is to substantiate the continuing debate: 'Is the gifted sportsperson more the product of "nature" than "nurture"?', and to provide a basis for accepting what the study of sports science can offer, or, in simpler terms, what the coach/teacher/trainer can realistically hope to achieve. There is little point, as far as success in the Olympic arena is concerned, in persevering with the training of a fully grown 1.5m tall discus thrower. Likewise, it would not be productive to help a 2.2m tall gymnast.

In basic terms we are dealing with how the various proteins which make up a cell are assembled. For example, genes control the production of all enzymes. In our reading so far we have come to realise how important enzymes are in the production of the basic unit of energy which facilitates our movement potential. It is therefore safe to say that genes control our ultimate destiny as far as sport is concerned.

The study of genetics is a vast and ever-growing field of knowledge. That which was considered impossible last year becomes possible this year. Genetics is primarily studied in order to recognise the genes passed on through the breeding process, for example those genes that can cause horrendous illness, disfiguration and malformation. It also introduces the ethical problem of 'genetic engineering'. When breeding a race horse or a show dog, the breeder is attempting to arrange for the 'right' genes to be passed on, without any of the 'wrong' ones. Perhaps the supporters of the Third Reich attempted to do the same in 1930s Germany to create the Aryan race. Hitler was certainly influenced by Eugene Fischer's text on genetics: *The Principles of Human Heredity and Race Hygiene.* The text probably had an influence on the nation's determination to eradicate, according to their ideals, the less fortunate. It is hard to decide whether these experiments, and those of the earlier eugenics ('well born') movement were attempts to preserve the 'wealthy' or the 'fit'.

Probably the most successful sporting nation of recent years has been the German Democratic Republic. Those envious of their success mainly attributed it to the corrupt use of hormones, however other nations with access to the same artificial hormones failed to replicate their success. I feel that they took advantage of everything sports science had to offer, ensuring that their coaching staff were familiar with the science, to produce an athlete support structure that became the envy of the world. They maximised on their coaching potential, creating schools specialising in sport as well as general education, for example they housed in one school those with the potential to become track and field athletes. Selection was often at an early age, and took into consideration the physiques of the parents.

Research in the field seems to show that environment can influence genetic structure over a period of time. One of the main factors that determined population growth was the number of diseases which affected the children of less than a century ago. The diseases have since disappeared and with them the relevant genetic structure. It was also found that black Americans had a greater risk of high blood pressure, and hence heart disease. This was attributed to a poor diet and the fact that the community smoked more than others. But is it a case of 'chicken and egg'? Do diet and smoking affect the genetic structure, or is it the genetic structure that influences the result? It has been firmly established that genes affect intelligence, so why shouldn't they also affect blood pressure?

It is also known that genes affect haemoglobin, the oxygen carrying pigment of the blood. This being the case, perhaps the great distance runners are a result of genes or 'nature'. The tribespeople of

East Africa are born with long legs, possibly a result of the environment making it essential for them to have long legs, hence a genetic adaptation progressed with heredity? If one adds to this the effect of altitude upon the oxygen transport system, then it is no wonder that this area of Africa dominates distance running events.

Experiments which involve treating mice with the gene influencing the production of the growth hormone cause the mice to produce offspring the size of rats. Scientists have also identified the gene which influences the immune system, and hence the healing rate from injury. Will these findings reduce the use of anabolic androgens, and make physiotherapists redundant? Will the sporting stars of the future employ their own geneticist who will become part of their support organisation? The debate is almost endless, as too are the implications.

However, to bring the debate back to the current situation, the genetic make-up of an individual has a massive effect upon performance. Identical twins who at an early age had the same IQ and were then brought up in totally different environments still end up with an almost identical IQ. Frequently, I am asked to look at young female high-jumpers, whose parents and teachers are convinced that they will be world beaters. On introduction one always sees a young lady with extremely long legs and a very skinny body. Since their centre of gravity is higher than most of their peers, they are bound to jump higher even with only a modicum of technique. Add to this their strength to weight ratio and there is a great potential for producing power output ('spring'). At a later stage, however, once the genetically influenced female hormones have staked their claim, one could end up with the physique of a shot putter rather than a high-jumper. Thus, premature attempts at advanced coaching are quite futile and unproductive; a classic example of early selection without a knowledge of heredity.

At a very early age, well before the impact of the formal education environment, it is easy to pick out those who can run, kick, jump and throw with ease, as children copy adults during their play. Even as a school teacher, it was clear that the same people made up the teams for the major games. The only real exception I found was the cross country team, which seemed to attract the introvert who got pleasure from being alone, running around the countryside.

Many researchers in the field of skill learning, from the physiologist to the psychologist, have tried to identify what makes the 'natural', the person who learns physical skills easily. The physiologist will suggest that it is a result of an efficient 'muscle memory' structure incorporating all of the various stretch receptors in the muscles and tendons, and linking via the the nervous system. The psychologist would probably favour differences in opportunity. While I am convinced that the physiologist is correct, the motor system (the system co-ordinating movement) itself is the result of a set genetic structure.

While it seems certain that the destiny of the elite athlete is prescribed by genetic endowment, and in all probability the Olympic champion is a genetic 'freak', the role of opportunity must be stressed. This is the role of 'nurture'. For elitism in sport this means assembling the best people, in the best place at the best time. The best people are firstly the performer with the correct genetic make-up, followed by the coaches, together with all the other support members including the sports scientist. This immediately introduces a selection structure, that of assuring the best athletes are part of the structure. Initially this will be part of a natural process where most of the talented athletes identify themselves early on in their careers. This must then be supported by an evaluation profile compiled by the sports scientists and medical support team. There will always be people who escape the talent identification process, and there will always be exceptions to any rule, in that some athletes not deemed talented enough might make the grade. However, the whole structure must form part of a system designed to reduce the number of variables.

In respect of the best place, one is looking at the training facility and the competition venue. However, it must be made very clear that facilities alone have never produced elite performance. Rather it is the pooling of the best people and the way in which they make use of the available facilities. The best time of the day, year etc. will be determined by the make-up of the individual and that of the sport.

It is a fair statement that: 'a cart horse will never win the blue riband of the horse racing calendar'. The same applies to any aspect of human endeavour in sport. It is a philosophy that produces elitism, a desire to become a world beater. To many, the idea of determining the outcome of sport through genetic endowment would be anathema. However, to achieve success at the highest level there must be an elite philosophy. Politically it is good for a nation's sportspeople to be successful, but success does not come cheaply nor without sacrifices. Success demands commitment.

Time is of the very essence where elitism is concerned, particularly the time of the performer and the support staff. Hence, at some stage a realistic debate has to pose the question: 'Is there any point in devoting the time and expertise of the total support agencies to those who lack the necessary genetic endowment?'

Biomechanics

Biomechanics is a word which has only recently found its way into the vocabulary of those involved in the study of sport. In very simple terms it is a study relating to the laws of physics when they are applied to human movement. To fully understand biomechanics one must become familiar with a set vocabulary, particularly that associated with the dynamics aspect of physics. However, physics is a precise science and biomechanics is not. The study of physics is one relating to rigid levers, and to finite particles, whereas the levers of the body are never fully rigid and there is no finite point of the body in movement, unless we refer to the centre of gravity of the body. For example, we can state that the speed of a ball leaving a tennis racket head is 80mph, or 40m per second, a statement reflecting the general movement of the ball through the air in a set direction. However, we know that the surface of the ball might be moving faster, and even moving in a slightly different direction, as would be the case with a top spin serve, for example.

What is the purpose of studying biomechanics if it is not a precise science? The reasons have to reflect the complex structure of the human body, its available movement patterns and the limitations imposed by the nature of the science. The main value of the study, for people involved in sport, is in the analysis of skill. Is the correct skill being used? Is it the best one for that individual? Most people learn a skill by imitation. That is they copy a person they see performing a skill, or they copy a movement pattern illustrated by a teacher or a coach. This is known as the model theory. The problem is that the model could be incorrect. I would say that the best model to copy would be that of the current champion or an elite performer, and this is precisely what most young performers do. However, to support this further, I would need to examine the model to see if it is bio-mechanically correct. This can be done through an understanding of the science movement/skill. The logical extension of this would then be to examine how the model needs to be adapted to suit the physique and individual qualities of the person copying. For example they might be stronger or faster, shorter or taller, and this would call for a modification. Hence the real purpose of the study is one of 'adopting' and 'adapting'; we can adopt a technique of serving in tennis and then adapt that technique to suit our own personality. We can adopt a given make of racket and then adapt our technique to make the best of the piece of equipment. We can even use the science to justify whether or not we are using the correct weight of bat, the correct length of golf club, etc. This choice normally reflects the power of advertising rather than the scientific choice of the individual, however it would be safe to say that the advances made in modern equipment, footwear, clothing, etc. now reflect a study of biomechanics.

It is not the intention of this chapter to provide a treatise on the science of movement. That would constitute a book in itself. It is my intention to highlight the advantages to be gained from the study of biomechanics, to introduce the reader to some of the terminology, to outline the nature of the 'tools of the trade' and to stimulate further study.

In order for movement to take place the body must first apply a force. The force is produced by the muscles, creating tension, causing a lever (the joint) to distort. For example, the stationary tennis player waiting to receive a serve. The instant the visual stimulus of the approaching ball is interpreted, the body moves instinctively into a position to effect an efficient return. To move, the muscles must produce the force necessary to effect the movement. To fully understand this process we must study Newtonian physics and the laws of motion. These laws define for us what a force is. The first law tells us that a force is that which will 'disturb the state of rest of a body or change its direction of movement in a straight line'. The second law quantifies a force by stating that 'a force is equal to the amount by which the body changes its rate of speed (acceleration)'. The third law then tells us that the force must be exerted against something and that it is the reaction to the force that creates the movement, 'the reaction being equal and opposite'.

While I have only given a brief interpretation of the three laws of motion, the student needs to become familiar with all of the terms related to these laws, such as work, impulse, mass, momentum, velocity, speed, acceleration, and power. For example, take the basketball player who wishes to jump to collect a high ball. Firstly, the muscles must exert a force against the floor. This force creates what is known as an impulse which, by definition, is the product of force and time. The variables in the equation are therefore force and time. To increase the size of the impulse, i.e. make the height of the jump greater, one has the options of increasing the force of the muscles (implying better strength training) and/or increasing the time over which the force is made to act (implying improved skill/timing and improved flexibility of the joints involved in creating the action). Both justify the training of strength and flexibility. The equation also shows that the movement can offer us a compromise. Do we make the force greater and reduce the contact time, as would certainly be the case of the basketball/volleyball player jumping for a ball? Or do we make the force slightly smaller and apply it for a longer period of time, as might the high-jumper or pole-vaulter? In terms of skill this tells us how we must plant the take-off foot. The longer the contact time, the greater must be the heel to toe 'rocking' effect of the foot action against the ground. To make the resultant force greater we can use an effect known as 'transfer of momentum', whereby the jumper moves the arms and the free leg in an upward direction, thus increasing the impulse and providing greater lift.

Similarly, striking a ball with a bat involves the principle of work. Work, by definition, is the product of a force and the distance through which the force acts. In other words, it is almost the same as impulse, and for the sake of simplicity it can be regarded as the same in that the jumper is seeking to increase the value of work. Hence, the server in tennis will use a very long arm, and hyperextend the back so as to increase the range of the movement, while the golfer will transfer weight on to the back leg during the back-lift, and on to the front leg during the forward swing to produce an increased range of movement.

Newton's laws have many implications for movement patterns with which the student of skill analysis must become familiar. Accurate film/video/photographic analysis can reveal the contact time and the work distance, while dynamometers, strain gauges, tensiometers and force platforms can give us the value of the force, thus introducing us to some of the tools of the trade.

Movement is effected by the bones of the body which comprise a structure of levers. A lever has a pivot, located either at one end or at some point between the ends, hence the bones can form a lever system comparable to the action of a pair of scissors with a pivot at one end or a pair of sugar tongs with the pivot at the opposite end. Physicists define these for us as first, second, and third class levers respectively. Many of the levers used in sport are like the sugar tongs, for example the tennis serve. The racket (the resistance) is in the hand, the pivot is the shoulder joint, and the muscle force is applied at points between the shoulder and the hand. The true classification of a lever, however, must be their efficiency in creating a force to produce the movement. In this second classification, a long lever is force effective and a short lever is termed speed effective.

For example, in the running movement the leg pushing against the surface needs to be force effective, so it is made long with complete extension of the hip, knee and ankle joints. Failure to produce this effect will reduce the level of the force created against the surface. Once the leg has fully extended it needs to return to a position from which to work again quickly, hence the knee is bent, shortening the lever and making it quicker for the leg to recover. In this instance the coach needs to observe the extension and flexion qualities of the levers.

Many movements created by the body involve rotation. Indeed, it is safe to say that most sports involve the creation and control of rotation. While the act of running in a straight line might appear to be a linear movement, the legs and the arms both rotate about their pivots, in particular the hips and shoulders. To promote rotation we need to apply a force which is not directed through the centre of gravity. For example, the high-jumper at take-off needs to produce a force which will subsequently rotate the body into efficient positions to effect bar clearance. This is done by taking off from the inside of the foot, with the arms and free leg aiding rotation by moving across the body.

Rotation is effected by controlling the length of the appropriate levers. For example, the gymnast who wishes to perform the complicated movement of a triple back somersault will 'pike' about the hips, shortening the length of the body lever. This will increase the speed of rotation. In terms of physics, the action decreases the moments of inertia, so increasing angular momentum (speed of the body). These are all terms which the study of Newton's laws will familiarise us with. When the gymnast is trying to execute the aesthetic movement of the 'hollow back' somersault, during which the rotation must be slow for control, the body lever needs to be kept long, in effect increasing the body's moments of inertia, and decreasing angular momentum.

In studying angular motion the student must become familiar with the various planes and axes of movement relating to the body. For example, in diving and trampolining movements such as the somersault the body might rotate about the 'short axis' of the body, and at the same time about the 'long axis' of the body in twisting movements. By way of a more complicated illustration, the pirouette movement calls for the performer to rotate about the long axis in the transverse plain. A full explanation of these terms is beyond the scope of this text.

Earlier, I stated that many movements in sport involve the control of rotation. This introduces the study of stability. For example, the gymnast alighting from a piece of apparatus must control their landing. This is achieved by contracting the muscles and straightening a joint, so as to reduce the effect of speed. This is known as creating a 'counter couple'. The rugby players forming a scrum will place their bodies as low as possible, and place their feet as wide apart as the circumstances allow. This illustrates that to increase stability the centre of gravity of the body must be low, and the base for support extensive. Stability also involves the control of friction, a resistive force, and the athlete or footballer might place spikes or studs of varying length in their boots or shoes in order to increase this force. The skier might use a special wax on the ski to decrease the effect of friction.

Associated with rotation is what is termed a 'hinge moment'. The application of this relates to the slowing or the stopping of one end of a lever, causing the opposite end of the lever to speed up. The classic example is when one alights from a moving vehicle. When the feet hit the floor the lower extremity of the body stops while the upper extremity speeds up. This process of acceleration can take place about any axis and in any plane; stop the left side and the right side speeds up, stop the bottom of the lever and the top speeds up. All throwing and striking actions illustrate the hinge moment effect. When the right-handed golfer hits a ball, the left side braces, speeding up the right side which carries the club. In the fast bowling action of cricket, the front leg braces, halting the lower sections of the body and speeding up the top section carrying the ball.

Certain sports call for the body to be projected through the air, as in any jumping activity. Throwing activities call for the body to launch a missile. In aquatic sports, either the body or a boat is forced to move through water. This introduces the complicated study of aerodynamics and hydrodynamics. Anyone participating in aquatic sports such as swimming and rowing, and in activities involving flight, such as throwing and kicking, will need to make this study in order to produce efficiency. In very simple terms, this means examining the forces which can aid locomotion through the particular medium, and also the forces which impede movement. These forces are termed 'lift' or 'buoyancy', for those aiding the movement, and 'drag' for the frictional forces. For lift or buoyancy to exist, the forces aiding motion must be greater than those resisting the movement. The swimmer achieves propulsion (thrust/lift) from the action of the arms, legs, and in some cases, the trunk. The streamlining of the body through the water, using an efficient technique such as removing excess hair, can reduce drag. The manufacturers of disci and javelin certainly have the aim of reducing drag when they produce aerodynamic javelins and high spin discus. These forces are different to the forces mentioned previously since they do not act through the centre of gravity. Instead they act through a point known as the centre of buoyancy or the centre of pressure. Unlike the centre of gravity (the point of balance) these are not obvious and have to be calculated. The difference between the centre of gravity and the centre of buoyancy or pressure is known as the 'pitching moment'. When this moment 'arm' is long, the faster the body will rotate about the theoretical point. To redress this imbalance the swimmer might have to work harder with the legs to keep a streamlined position through the water, while the thrower will have to spin the missile more at release.

As far as flight activities are concerned, one needs to have an understanding of trajectories and the mechanics affecting flight range. In simple terms a missile loses speed by a set factor known as the gravitational moment, until it reaches its maximum height. From the high point it then gains speed, at the same rate, until it returns to the ground. Normally, the flight path is an extended parabola, where the time taken for the missile to reach the high point is the same as the time taken for it to return from the high point to the ground. Aspects such as the angle of projection and the angle of attack are of significant importance, and must form part of the study for anyone who wishes to perfect skill in this very specialised area.

This area of study also introduces us to such terms as 'swerve' and 'spin', skills required by the cricket bowler or tennis player who wish to get the ball to turn off the pitch or swing/swerve in the air. Again this requires an understanding of flight forces and the factors which can affect flight. It requires an understanding of air pressures and pressures created by the skill of the performer, and how movement is affected by pressure changes. Anyone wishing to succeed in throwing events, particularly bowling in cricket, and in certain racket sports, must have this level of understanding to reach the highest ranking.

Games which involve 'striking' such as tennis, hockey, cricket or baseball, and those which involve 'rebounding', introduce a further study. The material of the striking surface such as wood or racket strings, the texture of the rebounding surface such as a cricket pitch or the walls of a squash court, and the density of the material of the ball can all change the nature of a skill. To fully understand sport, such a study is essential.

I trust that this brief introduction will have encouraged the reader to make a positive study of this important science. By using all of the aids which technology has produced for us, accurate skill analysis, linked to perfection, is possible. However, there remains one aspect of skill analysis which is of equal importance to perfecting a movement. There is no doubt that an inefficient movement can produce injury, and with it a forced rest or even premature retirement from the sport. For example, the thrower/server whose action is inefficient may develop javelin or tennis 'elbow'. The player who cannot jump or land correctly will damage the ligaments and tendons of the ankle. Hence, the study is not only about attaining perfection, but extending the career of a player as well.

The average player or coach is unlikely to have this level of understanding. However there are now specialists in this field, in particular at universities where the study of sport is offered as a degree option, who can make the necessary contribution to a team. The contribution made by sports scientists is fast gathering momentum, so much so that the employment of such people will be the norm in less than a decade.

Evaluation techniques

The compilation of evaluation profiles for elite sportsmen and women is fast becoming the norm, not only for individual sports, but also for team games, where they provide the manager and trainer with important data on the fitness of the playing squad.

The idea of fitness profiling came into vogue in Europe in the early 1950s, when Physical Education degrees from the USA started to have an impact. The subject 'Tests and Measurements' became part of the syllabus at colleges training Physical Education teachers. Fitness profiling developed steadily until reaching the level of sophistication it currently enjoys, since the revolution in electronics has made the collection, interpretation and recording of data far more widespread. Indeed, many local authority owned sports centres now offer quite elaborate fitness profiling to their fee-paying members.

Benefits of assessment

Much of the book so far has been related to the training of the 'S' factors (speed, strength, stamina, suppleness and skill). All of these can be evaluated by simple tests, as can all of the associated cross-components, such as power, speed endurance and strength endurance. There would, in fact, be little point in entering a specific phase of training unless the athlete were to emerge from the programme with an improvement in the relevant quality, so assessment gives essential feedback to both the coach and the athlete.

In sports such as track and field athletics or swimming, the yard-stick could be one's personal best time or distance. However, there are a number of errors possible in assessing 'one-off' performances. Wind assistance and the facilities available affect performance, and errors can be made in timing or measurement. Hence a much broader assessment of fitness and achievement is required.

Evaluation tests and measurements not only enable the coach to measure improvement, or possible regression, but to diagnose specific weaknesses and problems. The early identification of problems will allow greater time for correction and cut down on the chances of reducing the final performance.

It is also possible to use some tests as a prediction for future performance, and in the long-term this can lead to talent identification. This procedure has been undertaken in some Eastern Bloc countries in track and field athletics and gymnastics. The evaluation profiles, used predominantly with younger performers, include details of the height of the parents, the child's postural analysis, mobility, medical and dental examinations, a sprint to determine speed potential, a run to determine aerobic fitness, a sargent jump and a grip strength analysis. The performers may also be subjected to basic technical skill tests in several disciplines. As they develop, the subjects might undergo laboratory tests, and are sometimes subjected to psychological tests.

If more widely applied, such talent identification might lead to a reduction in the number of hours wasted by coaches on performers who do not possess the necessary physiological make-up to enable them to become world-class. However, whether the procedures for talent identification are ethical is debatable. There is no consideration, either, of the 'late developer', nor is there any thought as to the effectiveness, or otherwise, of always placing the better, more experienced coaches with the performers of proven ability.

Tests and measurements can also be an excellent source of motivation. For example, a key player in a soccer team can be motivated to work on flexibility if he is shown a 'sit and reach' test result which has indicated a poor range of movement. Further motivation can be provided when a colleague records a superior result.

The tests can be used as a valuable coaching aid when administered within a large group. Performers of similar ability in the different 'S' factors can be put to work together, giving a better training regime. In this way performers will not be asked to work in a group which is too advanced, or in a group which does not work at a high enough level.

Achievement can be monitored through a series of sophisticated laboratory tests by a research physiologist. For example, the VO_2 max. test measures precise work loads together with the amount of oxygen used and the amount of carbon dioxide produced. However, these tests require very expensive equipment and anyone who wishes to undergo this form of evaluation should refer to chapter 12 for information on sports physiologists. Hence, the principle aim here will be to introduce the reader to what is known as field testing, which requires only simple equipment such as a stopwatch, tape measure or grids. A step-by-step account of all methods of evaluation and relevant norms is not feasible here; readers requiring these should refer to specialist publications.

Points to consider in compiling a test

When constructing a test, or battery of tests, a number of points must be considered. They are as follows.

1) *Validation*   How valid is the test in measuring what you hope it will measure? For example, the broadjump differential test is excellent and reliable for measuring leg power, and any sportsman or woman who requires leg power as an integral part of their sport will always score highly on this test. By comparison, the Harvard Step Test is a poor predictor of the ability to run a fast 800 metres.

2) *Reliability*   How reliable is the test in a retest situation? The reliability of a test frequently rests in the hands of those administering it, in particular how the tester standardises a particular test in both the original and retest situations. Most of the tests outlined in this chapter have a good degree of reliability.

3) *Scoring*   It is possible to record raw scores, such as a broadjump differential of 70cm (28in). However, the raw scores can be converted to 'T' scores by applying statistical techniques and producing a table of norms. Many texts devoted to this area will include norms for most of the valid tests outlined here.

4) *Grouping of individual tests*   A number of tests can be grouped together to produce an approximation of a fitness index. A common grouping is the JCR test, that being the vertical jump, chinning and a 10 x 10m shuttle run.

As well as recording the main elements of fitness, a good evaluation profile also includes some basic anthropometric measurements and other details relevant to health and fitness. These might be listed as on page 116.

Name

Age

Height

Weight

Height of Father: ❑❑❑❑   Mother: ❑❑❑❑ (for the young performer)

Body measurements: Length of inside leg ❑❑❑❑   Arm span ❑❑❑❑

Measurements: Waist

                     Hips

                     Chest

Physiological tests should cover:

1) lung capacity measurements as attained from the recording of
    forced exhalation into a peak-flow meter
2) pulse count
3) average breathing rate
4) body fat percentages.

Body fat percentages

Measuring body fat percentage is an easy method of discovering
correct bodyweight and composition. Beneath the skin is a layer of
subcutaneous fat, and the percentage of total body fat can be
measured by taking the 'skinfold' at selected points on the body. The
only equipment needed is an inexpensive pair of callipers, as shown
in fig. 60.
    The method is quite simple:

1) ensure that all of the skinfold measurements are located on the
    right side of the body and that the measurements are taken in
    millimetres
2) pick up the skinfold between the thumb and the index finger so
    as to include two thicknesses of skin and subcutaneous fat
3) apply the callipers about one centimetre from the fingers and at
    a depth about equal to the thickness of the fold
4) repeat the procedure three times as the measurement may vary,
    and take an average

5) in order to standardise, measurements should be taken by the same person and at the same time of day, preferably in the morning.

The following sites may be used for determining percentage body fat:

1) triceps – the skinfold should be taken midway between the top of the shoulder and the tip of the elbow. The arm must stay alongside the body
2) biceps – at a point midway between the elbow and the arm pit
3) subscapular – just below the tip of the shoulder blade
4) suprailiac – just above the crest of the hip.

Fig. 60 Measuring body fat with callipers

For individuals aged 17 years and above, the total percentage of body fat can be found by totalling the sum of the four skinfolds and, referring to the chart below, locating the correct age and sex columns and reading across. (A different method is used for younger people, an explanation of which is beyond the scope of this book.)

As a guideline, the average man is 15–17 per cent body fat, while the average woman is between 18 and 22 per cent. It is common to find male distance runners with fat percentages of less than 10 per cent and women with less than 12 per cent.

To support the body fat percentage it is often helpful to obtain information regarding the measurement of the width of limbs – for example, around the thighs, arms and chest. This information becomes especially useful during periods of strength training, or muscle hypertrophy, which occur in bodybuilding or weightlifting; or, alternatively, at times where weight loss is required for peak efficiency.

From these introductory tests the evaluator must then consider the 'S' factor components of fitness.

Skinfold measurement conversion tables

Column one represents the total calliper measurements in mm. The other columns give percentage of body fat relative to age and gender.

Skinfolds (mm)	Males (age in years)				Females (age in years)			
	17-29	30-39	40-49	50+	16-29	30-39	40-49	50+
15	4.8	——	——	——	10.5	——	——	——
20	8.1	12.2	12.2	12.6	14.1	17.0	19.8	21.4
25	10.5	14.2	15.0	15.6	16.8	19.4	22.2	24.0
30	12.9	16.2	17.7	18.6	19.5	21.8	24.5	26.6
35	14.7	17.7	19.6	20.8	21.5	23.7	26.4	28.5
40	16.4	19.2	21.4	22.9	23.4	25.5	28.2	30.3
45	17.7	20.4	23.0	24.7	25.0	26.9	29.6	31.9
50	19.0	21.5	24.6	26.5	26.5	28.2	31.0	33.4
55	20.1	22.5	25.9	27.9	27.8	29.4	32.1	34.6
60	21.2	23.5	27.1	29.2	29.1	30.6	33.2	35.7
65	22.2	24.3	28.2	30.4	30.2	31.6	34.1	36.7
70	23.1	25.1	29.3	31.6	31.2	32.5	35.0	37.7
75	24.0	25.9	30.3	32.7	32.2	33.4	35.9	38.7
80	24.8	26.6	31.2	33.8	33.1	34.3	36.7	39.6
85	25.5	27.2	32.1	34.8	34.0	35.1	37.5	40.4
90	26.2	27.8	33.0	35.8	34.8	35.8	38.3	41.2
95	26.9	28.4	33.7	36.6	35.6	36.5	39.0	41.9
100	27.6	29.0	34.4	37.4	36.4	37.2	39.7	42.6
105	28.2	29.6	35.1	38.2	37.1	37.9	40.4	43.3
110	28.8	30.1	35.8	39.0	37.8	38.6	41.0	43.9
115	29.4	30.6	36.4	39.7	38.4	39.1	41.5	44.5
120	30.0	31.1	37.0	40.4	39.0	39.6	42.0	45.1
125	30.5	31.5	37.6	41.1	39.6	40.1	42.5	45.7
130	31.0	31.9	38.2	41.8	40.2	40.6	43.0	46.2
135	31.5	32.3	38.7	42.4	40.8	41.1	43.5	46.7
140	32.0	32.7	39.2	43.0	41.3	41.6	44.0	47.2
145	32.5	33.1	39.7	43.6	41.8	42.1	44.5	47.7
150	32.9	33.5	40.2	44.1	42.3	42.6	45.0	48.2
155	33.3	33.9	40.7	44.6	42.8	43.1	45.4	48.7
160	33.7	34.3	41.2	45.1	43.3	43.6	45.8	49.2
165	34.1	34.6	41.6	45.6	43.7	44.0	46.2	49.6
170	34.5	34.8	42.0	46.1	44.1	44.4	46.6	50.0
175	34.9	——	——	——	——	44.8	47.0	50.4
180	35.3	——	——	——	——	45.2	47.4	50.8
185	35.6	——	——	——	——	45.6	47.8	51.2
190	35.9	——	——	——	——	45.9	48.2	51.6
195	——	——	——	——	——	46.2	48.5	52.0
200	——	——	——	——	——	46.5	48.8	52.4
205	——	——	——	——	——		49.1	52.7
210	——	——	——	——	——		49.4	53.0

Speed

The most accurate field test to evaluate true speed is the 30-metre sprint. The performer toes a starting line with the evaluator at another line 30 metres away. The running surface must be level grass or some other prepared surface. The performer starts to sprint towards the evaluator. When the leg of the performer commences the run, the stopwatch is started, and when the torso reaches the line the watch is stopped. Alternatively, photo-electric devices can time even more accurately.

Strength

Strength levels can be evaluated using inexpensive dynamometers, or spring scales. They can measure leg, back or grip strength and also pushing strength, and are used in the following ways.

Grip strength

The right hand is tested first. The dynamometer is placed on the hand so that its edge lies between the first and second joints of the fingers, with the dial towards the palm. The subject may use any movements to obtain maximum grip, but the arm must not touch the body or any other object. The subject must place the dynamometer above the head and squeeze it with maximum force, bringing the arm down as the force is applied. The arm should remain straight throughout. The coach reads the dynamometer, returns the pointer to zero, and records the score. The procedure is repeated with the left hand.

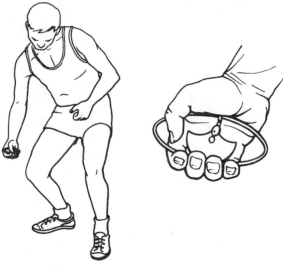

Fig. 61 Measuring grip strength

Back and leg strength

Several back and leg strength dynamometers are available, but those relying on compression are not required to test for back and leg strength, as only lifting power is necessary. For this reason, a chain of at least 50cm (20in) in length, with a handle attached, should be available. In the back lift the legs must remain straight as the performer exerts force on the chain. In the leg lift the back must remain straight with the knees bent. Force is exerted as the subject attempts to straighten the legs. This lift may be done with a belt around the waist and attached to the handle/chain. The techniques are demonstrated in figs 62 and 63.

If you cannot get dynamometers, use established isolated weight training exercises, in particular those requiring low skill levels, or where the skill involved has been totally mastered. Such 'lifts' include bench press, squat, seated press, isolated arm curls, the snatch and the clean and jerk. Here one measures a person's best maximum performance for a single repetition, as might be done when positioning people in an Olympic lifting competition.

Fig. 62 Measuring back strength

Fig. 63 Measuring leg strength

Stamina

Three distinct areas of stamina were identified in chapter 5: aerobic efficiency, local muscular endurance and anaerobic efficiency. Each has to be measured using distinct methods.

Aerobic efficiency

Aerobic efficiency can be measured by a run such as the 'Cooper twelve-minute run', or an established road circuit close to the training ground. You can also use the Harvard Step Test Index (HSTI).

The Cooper twelve-minute run is performed on a standard, internationally recognised athletics track. The performers start running round and round the track from the start line, and after twelve minutes a signal is given to stop and the total distance run is measured. Good male rugby backs, hockey players and footballers should cover around 3,000m in the time.

The Harvard Step Test relies largely on pulse recovery after exercise. Originally constructed for college men, the test has been modified and now exists in a short and long form.

The performer steps up and down, at a rate of 30 steps per minute, on to a bench that will vary in height between 50cm (20in) and 35cm (12in), depending upon the age and the sex of the performer. The rhythm of the step test is important, and prior to the start of the test the evaluator should demonstrate the cadence while calling the step number aloud.

The subject mounts the bench, using either foot, and stands erect on top of the bench, with both feet together. The leading foot then steps down first, followed by the other foot, to the original position. This is one complete cycle. The cadence can be checked either by the use of a metronome or a stopwatch, and two beats per cycle are allowed. After five minutes of stepping, the evaluator will call for the subjects to stop and sit down.

Each subject should have a partner who will have rested for the duration of the stepping. After one minute the partner counts the subject's pulse for 30 seconds and records the result; this figure is referred to in the equation below as P1. Two further pulse counts are made, each over a period of 30 seconds, the first between 2 minutes and 2 minutes 30 seconds (P2), and the next between 3 minutes and 3 minutes 30 seconds (P3).

Two formulae are available to calculate the HSTI, one for the five-minute step test (the long test), and another for the shorter test where the subject may not have been able to sustain the rhythm, or has been unable to complete the test. Long-form calculations can be made using the formula:

$$HSTI = \frac{15,000}{P1 + P2 + P3}$$

In the short form of the test, the time at which the subject stops should be recorded, and the pulse recorded as described. The results are calculated by the formula:

$$HSTI = \frac{\text{Duration of stepping in seconds}}{5.5 \times P1 + P2 + P3}$$

In the long form of the test, an excellent score, expected of most international sports performers, would be 100 or above, a poor score would be below 50. In the short form of the test a good score would be 80 or above, and a poor score would again be below 50.

While both the Cooper twelve-minute run and the Harvard Step Test have a place in any evaluation programme, recent advances in the appreciation of aerobic fitness have given us what is commonly known as the 'bleep' test or 'multi-stage' fitness test. In basic terms this consists of a shuttle run over 20m, at a pace determined by a pre-recorded cassette tape. The bleeps on the tape indicate the turning point of the shuttle, and also the end of a particular stage, and as the tape runs the time span between the bleeps becomes progressively shorter, so demanding a faster run. Initially the space between the bleeps is fairly long, hence the tempo of the run is slow. Once the participant can no longer keep pace with the bleeps, the test is concluded for that individual, and the appropriate stage of the test recorded. Stage one is very easy; stage eight will prove difficult for many participants in games which do not require a high level of aerobic fitness; while stage 14 will cause very fit athletes some distress.

The advantage of the test is that it is easy to administer, and fairly large groups can be accommodated at a single session. The incentive to do well, and score highly, is brought about by the competitive nature of the test. There is the indirect competition against the speed of the recorder, and direct competition against other members of the group. Hence, it is ideal for highly motivated people. The disadvantage is that the turning at the end of each short run can cause some discomfort. With major games players it is best done on their normal playing surface and in their normal playing footwear. However, it can very readily be adapted for use in any indoor area which will permit a run of 20 metres.

The tape, together with the necessary evaluation charts and directions, can be obtained from almost any National Coaching Foundation Centres. The test represents an excellent means of assessing maximal oxygen uptake, hence it is a very valuable tool in the field of evaluation.

Local muscular endurance

Local muscular endurance can be evaluated by established circuit training exercises. The evaluator must count the number of repetitions that can be performed in one minute. Examples of these exercises are outlined in figs 64–9 and include bar jumps, sit-ups, press-ups, chins, dips and squat thrusts. Standardisation of the tests is a problem due to the variety in individual style and technique, so it is important to establish a set method for performing each exercise, and the subject should not deviate from this model. Any exercises performed with an incorrect technique should be omitted from the final score.

The exercises shown are only guidelines and there are a host of similar exercises which could be included in an evaluation profile, providing they can be standardised.

Fig. 64 Sit-ups 1. The performer lies back while the partner holds his feet to keep the legs flat on the floor. At a signal the performer sits up to cross right elbow towards left knee and returns instantly to the floor. Then he repeats with left elbow towards right knee. The partner counts the number of successful sit-ups

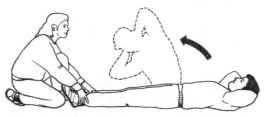

Fig. 65 Sit-ups 2. The performer lies back with feet close to hips, held down by partner, and tries to sit up as in fig. 64

Fig. 66 Press-ups. In extended front support position and with back straight, the arms are bent to allow the chin to touch the floor, keeping head in natural alignment. Straighten arms to starting position. The partner counts out loud, and any movement where the arms do not reach the right angle position with the chin touching the floor are discounted

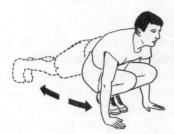

Fig. 67 Squat thrusts. In long front support position, draw knees with both legs together up to touch elbows and return to long front support position. The partner marks the tucked and extended leg position on floor with chalk, counting out loud each movement and discounting any short ones

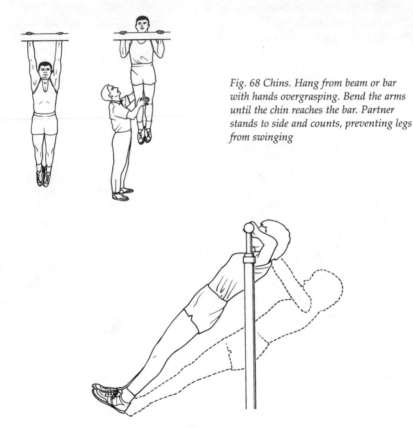

Fig. 68 Chins. Hang from beam or bar with hands overgrasping. Bend the arms until the chin reaches the bar. Partner stands to side and counts, preventing legs from swinging

Fig. 69 Modified chins for women. Take the long sitting position with beam or bar at stretch height from the sit, and push feet forwards to extend the trunk. Then bend the arms to pull the body towards the beam

Anaerobic efficiency

Several methods exist to measure anaerobic efficiency. For the elite performer, a 1,000-metre run, performed at full effort, gives an accurate estimate of anaerobic capacity. Good-class male discus throwers, weighing over 100kg (224lb) for example, have recorded times of 2 minutes 40 seconds for this standardised run when performed on a good quality athletics track.

Another accurate test of anaerobic efficiency is the 400-metre 'drop-off' test. Here the subject is timed running at full speed over 100 metres. After a five-minute recovery period, he or she runs 400 metres at full speed, and the time is again recorded. In order to convert the 400-metre time to a 100-metre 'split-time', it is divided by four. The 100-metre sprint time is then subtracted from the split-time, giving the drop-off time. An example of this technique is shown in the result of a top-class female hockey player:

100m time = 13.0 seconds
400m time = 60.0 seconds   60 ÷ 4 = 15 seconds
15 – 13 = a 'drop-off' time of 2 seconds.

When this is compared to the result of a top-class female 400-metre athlete the difference in anaerobic efficiency is remarkable:

100m time = 11.8 seconds
400m time = 50.0 seconds   50 ÷ 4 = 12.5 seconds
12.5 – 11.8 = a 'drop-off' time of 0.7 seconds.

The aim is always to reduce the drop-off time by increasing anaerobic efficiency.

Suppleness

When assessing flexibility in a laboratory a physiologist might use goniometers or flexiometers to obtain information, but equally reliable results can be obtained from field tests using simple tape measures and grids. Such tests include the 'sit and reach' test, designed to measure hamstring flexibility, the 'back hyperextension' test, to measure mobility in the lower regions of the spine, and 'lateral flexion' tests, to evaluate the movement about the spine in the lateral plane.

The 'sit and reach' test

The subject adopts the long-seated position on the floor, with the toes in line with the edge of a bench and the knees pressed firmly to the ground. A grid, or tape, is positioned on the bench with the zero on a scratch line placed at the subject's feet, so that the area in front of the line shows a negative reading and the area behind it a positive reading. The subject should sit up out of the hips and reach forwards towards the grid, pushing the fingertips as far as possible along the tape. The knees must remain on the ground and he or she should attempt to relax. The furthest distance that the subject is able to reach along the tape is recorded. When he or she has recovered, the procedure is repeated.

Many top-class soccer players have been known to record negative scores, that is, they are unable to touch their toes. Good-level high jumpers and gymnasts can reach over 40cm (16in) along the scale. Anyone recording less than 10cm (4in) would be well-advised to increase flexibility training, with particular emphasis on the hip and hamstring region. *See* fig. 70.

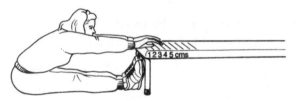

Fig. 70 'Sit and reach' test

Back hyperextension tests

The subject lies flat on the bench, face downwards, with the hips level with the end of the bench. A partner holds the subject's feet down on the bench, and fastens a tape measure to their neck with an elastic collar. The subject hyperextends the back, while the tape measure records the vertical displacement. A simple, automatic measuring device can be made as detailed in fig. 71.

While some footballers and middle distance runners might record scores of less than 30cm (12in) for this test, many fast bowlers in cricket, swimmers, gymnasts, hurdlers and high jumpers could score over 80cm (28in). Most high-class sportsmen and women should be hoping to score at least 50cm (20in).

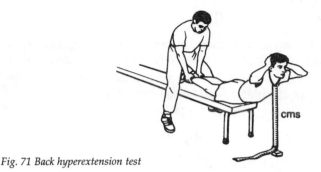

Fig. 71 Back hyperextension test

Lateral flexion tests

Lateral flexion may be evaluated by marking a 1m (3ft) horizontal measuring scale on a wall. The scale should be at shoulder height to the performer and should be drawn deep enough to cater for the difference in height of all the subjects. A line is drawn on the floor, at right angles to the wall and opposite the 33cm (13in) mark on the wall scale. The right-handed subject stands with feet together and at right angles to the floor line, approximately one arm's length away from the wall. Without moving the feet, the right arm is raised sideways, to shoulder level, with the fingers extended. From this position the subject twists, in a clockwise direction, as far as possible to touch the wall scale with the right hand. The farthest point reached on the scale and held for two seconds is then recorded. For left-handed performers the scale is reversed, reading from right to left. *See* fig. 72.

The flexibility tests should be performed in a controlled manner and in all cases there should be two attempts with the best score recorded.

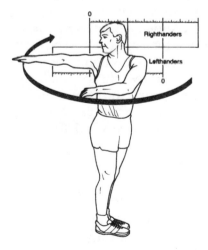

Fig. 72 Lateral flexion test

Skill

Most individual sportsmen and women, or sporting bodies, have their own methods of evaluating skill relevant to their sport. However, tests which are vaguely termed 'gross muscle co-ordination tests' could also be of use. For details, *see* chapter 17.

Related and cross-component areas

Probably one of the most important areas for evaluation, certainly in soccer, rugby, hockey, and track and field athletics, is power. There are a number of standardised tests which are very reliable, including the vertical jump, the standing broadjump differential, and series of jumps such as the triple jump. Probably the most reliable is the standing broadjump differential.

A scratch line is marked on the floor and a second line marked at the height of the performer, along the floor away from the scratch line. With both feet placed behind the first line, the performer attempts to jump beyond the body height line. One metre beyond this mark indicates excellent power potential for men, as does a distance of 60cm (24in) for women.

An alternative is the sargent jump. A chalkboard or a piece of card or paper is marked with horizontal lines at 1cm (0.5in) intervals, covering 1m 50cm (5ft). For clarity a different coloured line can be drawn every 5cm. The board is hung so that its lower edge is 1m 50cm from the floor.

The subject faces the wall, under the board with their feet on the floor, and stretches one hand as high as possible up the board. This mark is noted. He or she then stands sideways beside the board and leaps vertically to touch as high up the board as possible. The difference between this and the first recorded height, is measured.

An excellent sargent jump for a man would be over one metre, with some women recording at least 60cm (24in). Top-class women long-jumpers might score one metre, while top-class males in the same event would score above this mark, indicating massive leg power.

The throws and jumps decathlon, originally designed to motivate athletes during training, can also be used for evaluation of cross-component effects.

The training diary

For evaluation profiles to have any significant meaning, the data collected must be recorded and stored for future reference. For the coach a card index system is advisable, while the individual should include all of their own results in a personal training diary.

A training diary is an integral part of the planned approach to training for peak performance. While it can be used to detail the results of tests as outlined earlier, or to record competition results, there is a massive amount of data that needs to be recorded to help both the evaluation and the planning process. Although a training diary will vary according to the individual performer and the individual sport, there are certain common items that might be included in any diary of this nature:

1) date and venue of training
2) proposed training routine, actual training routine
3) training conditions, weather, etc.
4) the intensity of training – total poundage of weights lifted, total mileage run, etc.
5) personal analysis of training session
6) personal details – weight, resting pulse rate, exercise pulse rate, breathing rate
7) diet
8) sleep
9) cyclical changes for women athletes.

Quite a number of governing bodies have their own training diaries available for participants. An example of a page from one commonly used in athletics, and produced by *Arena* publications, is shown on page 130.

The importance of regularity

Regular, well-constructed tests can indicate the efficacy of a training programme, and have been known to predict the onset of illness, motivate a player to train harder, or improve a specific quality of fitness, and so enhance the overall level of performance.

A number of top-class rugby and soccer teams include evaluation profiling as a monthly record of a player's achievements. Should a player become injured, the coach might insist on a return to pre-injury test results before permitting that player to return to the squad.

On page 131 is an example of a fitness profile which I have used successfully for a number of years with groups of elite sportsmen and women from a variety of sports. It has also been used with groups of students in their final year at school. Very little specialist equipment is needed other than a tape measure and a stopwatch. Tests 2, 6 and 7 can be excluded from the profile when the necessary equipment is not available.

MORNING					GENERAL COMMENTS (How I felt/session quality etc)	TRAINING COMPANIONS	WEATHER CONDITIONS		
Sleeping hours	Breath count	Pulse count	Body weight					Mileage	Total weights

MONTH:			TRAINING SESSION*	
Day	Date	VENUE		ABBREVIATIONS USED:

The battery of tests is compiled to permit easy organisation with fairly large groups of people. Test 1 can be done first, last or at a different time, as it needs an outdoor track or a larger indoor facility; tests 2–8 can be performed in a circuit using the facility of a standard gymnasium; tests 9–11 are for local endurance and can be done as a group; test 12, the aerobic fitness test, must be done last since it is fatiguing. A short rest period between each section should be allowed in order to produce more realistic results.

Fitness Profile

Name.. Age......... Ht........... Wt...............

Group	Test	Date								
		Score	Pts	Score	Pts	Score	Pts	Score	Pts
A	1. 30m sprint								
	2. Skinfolds								
	3. Broad jump								
B	4. Sit reach								
	5. Back hypers								
	6. Grip								
	7. Peak flow								
	8. Criss cross								
	9. Sit ups/min								
C	10. Squat jumps/min								
	11. Bar jumps/min								
D	12. Multi-stage run								
	13.								
	14.								

Comments ....
Date ....

Players from sports such as rugby, soccer, hockey, and many other team games, can be evaluated using a slightly different technique, incorporating tests which call for more specific skills. The following battery of tests (*see* pages 132–5) is one which I have used successfully in the sport of rugby. Tests 7 and 8 are specific to rugby, however I have used the same tests in both soccer and rugby, asking the soccer players to 'dribble' the ball rather than carry and pick the ball up. Using these modified skills, the norms are still fairly accurate.

Test 1 is used to assess aerobic efficiency; test 2 – pure speed; tests 3, 4 and 5 – local muscular endurance; test 6 – power and power endurance; tests 7 and 8 – specific endurance skills; test 9 – speed endurance.

The Wilf Paish rugby football tests

Test 1   The Cooper twelve-minute run or multi-stage fitness test.

Test 2   30-metre sprint time, best of three attempts (*see* page 119).

Test 3   Squat thrusts per minute (*see* page 124).

Test 4   Sit-ups per minute (*see* page 123).

Test 5   Press-ups per minute (*see* page 123).

Test 6   Stamina bound over 22 metres, shuttle system, immediate turn-abouts, in following sequence: 1) hop right leg; 2) giant strides; 3) hop left leg; 4) giant strides; 5) double foot bounds; 6) sprint. Total time taken for the shuttle sequence. Speed turning is very important.

Test 7   Zig-zag run (*see* fig. A). The time taken to run from A to B, pick up a ball and run to C, zig-zag between cones to D, and then zig-zag back to C. Sprint to E, put the ball down and sprint to F.

Test 8   Star run (*see* fig. B). Balls are placed at A and E. The player starts at A with the ball and runs to E, changes the balls over, sprints around the cone at B and back to E to change the balls over. He then runs round cones C and D in turn, changing the ball over at E each time before returning to A. Total time taken to complete the agility run.

Test 9   Diagonal pitch run (*see* fig. C). Time taken to sprint from A to B, to C to D, and finish back at A.

See pages 133–5 for scoring system.

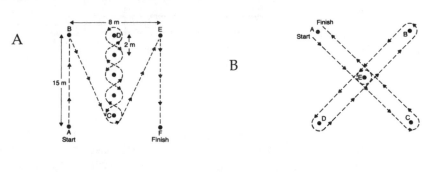

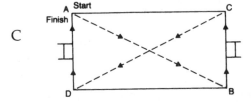

Rugby football evaluation norm tables

The norms were constructed over a period of four years from extensive tests with Keighley Rugby League Football Club, Halifax Rugby League Football Club and members of the Great Britain squad.

Forward/back differential

In certain situations a coach might need to compare the test results of a heavy forward with a much lighter back. When making such a comparison, a total of 50 points should be added to those achieved by the forward, when the total for all nine of the tests have been added together.

Total points score ratings based on international and national status players:

800 points	Excellent
700 points	Very good
600 points	Good
500 points	Average
Below 500 points	Below average and in need of remedial treatment

Injury/return situation

In rugby football, a coach is frequently faced with a situation of deciding when a key player is ready to return to squad training and playing. The tests have been used to very good effect with several clubs. The injured player must score the same total from the tests as was scored when injury-free.

	1 12 min run	2 30m sprint	3 squat thrust/ min	4 sit ups/ min	5 press ups/ min	6 stamina bound (secs)	7 zig zag (secs)	8 star run (secs)	9 diag pitch (secs)
100	4000M	3.5	90	65	100	30	16.0	10.0	60
99	4000	3.5	90	65	99	30	16.0	10.0	60
98	3990	3.5	90	65	98	30	16.1	10.0	60
97	3980	3.5	89	64	97	31	16.2	10.1	61
96	3970	3.6	89	64	96	31	16.3	10.1	61
95	3960	3.6	88	63	95	32	16.4	10.2	62
94	3950	3.6	88	63	94	32	16.5	10.2	62
93	3940	3.7	87	62	93	33	16.6	10.3	63
92	3930	3.7	87	62	92	33	16.7	10.3	63
91	3920	3.7	86	61	91	34	16.8	10.4	64
90	3910	3.8	86	61	90	34	16.9	10.4	64
89	3900	3.8	85	60	89	35	17.0	10.5	65
88	3890	3.8	85	60	88	35	17.1	10.5	65
87	3880	3.9	84	59	87	36	17.2	10.6	66
86	3870	3.9	84	59	86	36	17.3	10.6	66
85	3860	3.9	83	58	85	37	17.4	10.7	67
84	3850	4.0	83	58	84	37	17.5	10.7	67
83	3840	4.0	82	57	83	38	17.6	10.8	68
82	3830	4.0	82	57	82	38	17.7	10.8	68
81	3820	4.1	81	56	81	39	17.8	10.9	69
80	3810	4.1	81	56	80	39	17.9	10.9	69
79	3800	4.1	80	54	79	40	18.0	11.0	70
78	3790	4.2	80	54	78	40	18.1	11.0	70
77	3780	4.2	79	53	77	41	18.2	11.1	71
76	3770	4.2	79	53	76	41	18.3	11.1	71
75	3760	4.3	78	52	75	42	18.4	11.2	72
74	3750	4.3	78	52	74	42	18.5	11.2	72
73	3740	4.3	77	51	73	43	18.6	11.3	73
72	3730	4.4	77	51	72	43	18.7	11.3	73
71	3720	4.4	76	50	71	44	18.8	11.4	74
70	3710	4.4	76	50	70	44	18.9	11.4	74
69	3700	4.5	75	49	69	45	19.0	11.5	75
68	3690	4.5	75	49	68	45	19.1	11.5	75
67	3680	4.5	74	48	67	46	19.2	11.6	76
66	3670	4.6	74	48	66	46	19.3	11.6	77
65	3660	4.6	73	47	65	47	19.4	11.7	77
64	3650	4.6	73	47	64	47	19.5	11.7	78
63	3640	4.7	72	46	63	48	19.6	11.8	78
62	3630	4.7	72	46	62	48	19.7	11.8	79
61	3620	4.7	71	45	61	49	19.8	11.9	79
60	3610	4.8	71	45	60	49	19.9	11.9	80
59	3600	4.8	70	44	59	50	20.0	12.0	80
58	3590	4.8	70	44	58	50	20.1	12.0	81
57	3580	4.9	69	43	57	51	20.2	12.1	81
56	3570	4.9	69	43	56	51	20.3	12.1	82
55	3560	4.9	68	42	55	52	20.4	12.2	82
54	3550	5.0	68	42	54	52	20.5	12.2	83
53	3540	5.0	67	41	53	53	20.6	12.3	83
52	3530	5.0	67	41	52	53	20.7	12.3	84
51	3520	5.1	66	40	51	54	20.8	12.4	84
50	3510	5.1	66	40	50	54	20.9	12.4	84
49	3500	5.1	65	39	49	55	21.0	12.5	85
48	3480	5.2	65	39	49	55	21.1	12.5	85
47	3460	5.2	64	38	48	56	21.2	12.6	85
46	3440	5.2	64	38	48	56	21.3	12.6	86
45	3420	5.3	63	37	47	57	21.4	12.7	86
44	3400	5.3	63	37	47	57	21.5	12.7	86
43	3380	5.3	62	36	46	58	21.6	12.8	87
42	3360	5.4	62	36	46	58	21.7	12.8	87
41	3340	5.4	61	35	45	59	21.8	12.9	87
40	3320	5.4	61	35	45	59	21.9	12.9	88
39	3300	5.5	60	34	44	60	22.0	13.0	88

	1 12 min run	2 30m sprint	3 squat thrust/ min	4 sit ups/ min	5 press ups/ min	6 stamina bound (secs)	7 zig zag (secs)	8 star run (secs)	9 diag pitch (secs)
38	3280	5.5	60	34	44	60	22.1	13.1	88
37	3260	5.5	59	33	43	61	22.2	13.2	89
36	3240	5.6	59	33	43	61	22.3	13.3	89
35	3220	5.6	58	32	42	62	22.4	13.4	89
34	3200	5.6	58	32	42	62	22.5	13.5	90
33	3180	5.7	57	31	41	63	22.6	13.6	90
32	3160	5.7	56	31	41	63	22.7	13.7	90
31	3140	5.7	55	30	40	64	22.8	13.8	91
30	3120	5.8	54	30	40	64	22.9	13.9	91
29	3100	5.8	53	29	39	65	23.0	14.0	91
28	3080	5.8	52	29	39	65	23.1	14.1	92
27	3060	5.9	51	28	38	66	23.2	14.2	92
26	3040	5.9	50	28	38	66	23.3	14.3	92
25	3020	5.9	49	27	37	67	23.4	14.4	93
24	3000	6.0	48	27	37	67	23.5	14.5	93
23	2980	6.0	47	26	36	68	23.6	14.6	93
22	2960	6.0	46	26	36	68	23.7	14.7	94
21	2940	6.1	45	25	35	69	23.8	14.8	94
20	2920	6.1	44	25	35	69	23.9	14.9	94
19	2900	6.1	43	24	34	70	24.0	15.0	95
18	2880	6.2	42	24	34	70	24.1	15.1	95
17	2860	6.2	41	23	33	71	24.2	15.2	95
16	2840	6.2	40	23	33	71	24.3	15.3	96
15	2820	6.3	39	22	32	72	24.4	15.4	96
14	2810	6.3	38	22	32	72	24.5	15.5	96
13	2800	6.3	37	21	31	73	24.6	15.6	97
12	2780	6.4	36	21	31	73	24.7	15.7	97
11	2760	6.4	35	20	30	74	24.8	15.8	97
10	2740	6.4	34	20	30	74	24.9	15.9	98
9	2720	6.5	33	19	29	75	25.0	16.0	98
8	2700	6.5	32	19	29	75	25.1	16.1	98
7	2680	6.5	31	18	28	76	25.2	16.2	99
6	2660	6.6	30	18	28	76	25.3	16.3	99
5	2640	6.6	29	17	27	77	25.4	16.4	99
4	2620	6.6	28	17	27	77	25.5	16.5	100
3	2600	6.7	27	16	26	78	25.6	16.6	100
2	2580	6.7	26	16	26	78	25.7	16.7	100
1	2560	6.7	25	15	25	78	25.8	16.8	100

Year plan

As indicated earlier in the chapter, evaluation should be part of an on-going programme, fitted into a normal year plan. An example of how this can be achieved is shown on page 137.

This year plan is one used by a world-class javelin thrower, but is applicable to any thrower. The idea can be used for all sports. The year is broken down into the various phases of training. Each of the major training components is listed in vertical columns and represents the number of sessions the person would do in that week, for example 1 x 3 miles, sprint 2 sessions 6 x 50m and 4 x 150m full recovery. The last column indicates the tests which are performed at the start, the middle and the end of a training phase.

The abbreviations used are:

Spr = sprint; *B.J. Diff.* = Broadjump differential; *Sit R.* = Sit and reach test; *Back Hyp.* = Back hyper-extension; *Lat. M* = Lateral mobility; *1,000m* = 1,000 metres run timed; *12 min run* = Cooper's 12-minute run round track; *Sit/min* = Sit-ups per minute; *Chins* = Pull-ups on bar per minute; *Dips* = Dips on parallel bars per minute; *Sq. Thrusts* = Squat thrusts per minute; *Sq. Jumps* = Squat jumps per minute; *Power Cl* = Power clean with weights 1 repetition max.; *Power Sn* = Power snatch with weights 1 repetition max.; *F. Squat* = Front squat with weights 1 repetition max.; *Seat Press* = Seated press with weights 1 repetition max.; *Bench Press* = Bench press with weights 1 repetition max.; *Grip Str.* = Grip strength using dynamometer; *Pent* = throws/jumps pentathlon, *see* pages 40–1: first five events of each or selected five events.

Name .... Training Sequence ....

Session per week

Period	Emph	Run	Spr	Weights	Bound	Med Ball	Circuit	Tech	Other	TESTS
Oct.		1								
Nov.	Endurance		2	2	1	1	1	1		30m spr., B.J.Diff., Sit.R., Back Hyp., Lat.M., 1,000m, 12min run, end bound. Sit/min, Chins, Dips, Sq.Thrusts, Sq.Jumps.
Dec.										
Jan.	Gross Strength									30m spr., B.J.Diff., Sit.R., Back Hyp., Lat.M., Power Cl., Power Sn., F.Squat, Seat Press, Bench Press, Grip Str.
Feb.										
Mar.	Specific Strength Power									30m spr., B.J.Diff., Sit.R., Back Hyp., Lat.M., Power Cl., Power Sn., F.Squat, Seat Press, Bench Press, Jump Pent., Throws Pent. 20m hop right/left/timed and difference between right and left leg recorded.
Apr.										
May	Skill Speed									30m spr., B.J.Diff., Sit.R., Back Hyp., Lat.M., Mean of six technique drills. Javelin: Drill 1 standing throw, Drill 2 throw from 3 strides, Drill 3 throw from 5 strides, Drill 4 throw from 9 strides, Drill 5 overhead shot throw forwards, Drill 6 overhead shot throw backwards.
June										
Sept.										

Support agencies

In the modern world of top-level sport it is no longer possible to survive with just endowed physical characteristics and a trainer; top clubs now enlist the help of a coach, fitness adviser, sprint trainer, nutritionist or psychological adviser. World-class tennis players have been advised on their fitness training by leading coaches from track and field athletics; golfers have had their swings analysed by bio-mechanics specialists using high-speed photography coupled with computer analysis techniques; racing car drivers have been fitted with biotelemetric devices to record how their hearts react under conditions of extreme stress, and the results have been analysed by sports physiologists. There is now a world of sports scientists who can influence the performance of athletes at the very highest level.

However, the function of the support agents must incorporate far more than the scientist and the paramedical groups. Many world-class performers now also rely heavily on managers and agents. Therefore, in defining 'support agencies' one is not looking at the administrative structures of sport – the bodies responsible for fix-tures, playing conduct, circle of rules, discipline committees, etc. – but people who work directly to enhance the performance of the individual – managers and agents, coaching/training staff, paramedics and sports scientists.

The manager and agent

Managers and agents are relatively new to sport. I am not referring to the team manager, but rather the manager or agent who works for, and is paid by, the individual sportsman or woman, a role necessary primarily because of the impact of television on sport.

Sporting heroes and heroines are now asked to endorse products or work as public relations people for industry – indeed they now undertake much of the work which used to be reserved for stars of the entertainment industry. With a massive potential income they need managers and agents who can do all of the necessary mundane administration, permitting the sportsmen and women to get on with their training and competitions. Indeed, many sports stars share agents and managers with pop stars. They offer their clients a complete package, looking after all of their business interests, tax claims, investments, etc.

The boxing manager has been a part of the professional sport almost since its inception. They arrange the matches and agree the terms of the contracts. Quite a number of other sports, principally athletics, have recently adopted a similar arrangement. Promoters of events the world over obviously find it easier to work with an agent who might represent a number of sportspeople, rather than trying to negotiate with the individual performer. In this situation, the agent is able to provide the promoter with a clutch of stars who can enhance the potential of his programme. Hence there exists, in what is theoretically an amateur field, a group of people who negotiate racing or playing contracts in return for a percentage of appearance money. This can, and frequently does, produce a situation where top performers are encouraged to compete too frequently.

The coach or trainer

The argument: 'To what extent is coaching an art, or a science?' is ongoing. When one considers the role of the coach and the enormous scope of this role, one might assume that it is that of an artist guided by scientific underpinning.

One of the most important tasks in being an efficient coach is that of dealing with people, being able to work with both the old and the young and acquire a state of understanding and trust. In this way the job is an art. But it is also a science, linking the principles of biomechanics, physiology and psychology to an activity.

Do all sportsmen and women need coaches? Certainly beginners must be taught the fundamentals of their sport, and teaching leads into coaching. But once the basics are mastered most players go on to play the game for pleasure rather than advance to elite performance. Those who do wish to progress must seek further guidance from a coach.

Coaches play a variety of roles, from the dominant force making all of the decisions, to the athlete's servant, offering advice and criticism only when asked to do so. However, in order to survive – survival and status being measured by success – the coach needs to fill a further three roles, as 'the guide, the mentor and the whip'.

In order to guide, a coach needs technical competence, knowledge of the sport and its conditioning requirements, and a grasp of strategy in competition. Much of this is a scientific understanding, though it can be derived through natural development and association with a particular sport.

As a mentor, the coach must be adept in working with people and be prepared to give up a great deal of his or her time. Sensitivity and realism in the setting of goals are essential. The targets of the coach should be compatible with those of the athlete. Co-operation is also important; the coach must be able to co-operate with those in the immediate environment, for example other coaches, other athletes, club members and officials and those in the hierarchy of the sport.

As the whip, the coach should be one of the major driving forces behind the team or the individual athlete, and leadership qualities are therefore essential. The athlete looks upon the coach to assess the situation, evaluate performance, and adapt, either by change or progression.

Taking all things into consideration, many athletes would acknowledge that as well as fulfilling all of the above roles, the coach also becomes a friend, and it does help if this happens!

The medics and paramedics

Doctors

Most sportsmen and women will recognise the essential service the medical profession has to offer. Top-level sport places a tremendous stress upon the anatomical and physiological structure of the body. Should the stress become too great, the body starts to break down. This will manifest itself in a deterioration in performance and restrictions in training, even a total loss of income.

While the injury to the sportsman or woman might be obvious in a contact game, especially if it involves broken bones, other stress-related injuries are less obvious and need expert diagnosis. There are many injuries that incapacitate athletes which even the best doctors fail to diagnose. The resulting pain can restrict training, lower confidence levels and ultimately produce a frustration that can encourage premature retirement from the sport. This is particularly so with lower-back injuries, which, by their very nature, are difficult to diagnose and tend to take months or even years to respond to treatment.

Pain is an indication to the body that all is not well. Athletes often try to 'run off' an injury, but this must be discouraged, as must the disguising of pain by the over use of freeze-sprays, or even pain-killing tablets and local anaesthetic injections. Minor injuries can turn into debilitating ones if subjected to further stress. At the first sign of injury, the performer should stop exercising, take some precautionary first aid measures, and then, if the painful symptoms do not subside, consult a doctor.

Doctors should not only be consulted for diagnosis of injuries. There is a whole host of things that can go wrong with the physiological structure of the body, which regular, or emergency, visits to the doctor can correct. For example, low red cell counts, which drastically reduce efficiency especially amongst those involved in endurance events, can be detected by analysing a blood sample. Similar methods can be used to detect changes in the immune system of the body, which, if allowed to go uncorrected, will reduce performance.

An athlete should visit the doctor over anything untoward, particularly symptoms of lethargy, regular sore throats or irregular defaecation, as they could be an indication that too great a stress is being placed upon the body and a warning that breakdown is possible.

Physiotherapists

Most professional clubs employ their own physiotherapist. A true physiotherapist should not be confused with the old-fashioned 'liniament man', the 'rubber' or the 'pounder' who was seldom qualified and frequently did more harm than good. These people are disappearing from the modern sporting scene, and their place is being taken by people who have had to undergo rigorous training as part of a medically recognised course.

The role of the physiotherapist should not be a diagnostic one; that should always remain the function of the doctor. However, once an injury has been diagnosed physiotherapists play an important role in the rehabilitation process. A good physio will have at his or her disposal a whole range of electronic aids, including ultrasound and lasers, which can help considerably towards shortening a rehabilitation period.

The team physiotherapist also has a very important role to play in the immediate pre-competition period. When players are on edge, 'psyching' themselves up for the big occasion, the tender massage of the physiotherapist can calm the nerves and allow energy to be directed towards beating the opposition.

Chiropractors

While in some countries chiropractors are accepted as part of national medicine, their services are still not officially recognised in other parts of the world. Yet many people, in particular those suffering from lower-back problems, find that a chiropractor provides their only means of remaining in sport. They can frequently sort out problems for which the normal doctor/physiotherapist link fails to find a successful remedy.

Chiropodists

Infected toes, frequently caused by tight-fitting footwear, are common in sport. The feet act as the transmission area for the energy promoted by the body, similar to the function of the tyres on a motor car. A bruised toe or ingrowing toenail can make foot contact painful, and painful feet cannot be ignored.

Dentists

The top athlete must develop the habit of regular dental check-ups. Teeth and gums can become infected and cause pain which will have a detrimental effect upon performance.

Sports scientists

Many universities now offer degrees in sports science. It is a difficult degree to organise because it involves the study of a number of very specialised disciplines which are not always well related to each other, for example physiology, biomechanics and psychology. These in turn each produce specialists.

Physiologists

Sports physiologists will have spent most of their study time examining work physiology – how the body reacts to various training regimes, how the adaptation process takes place, factors that can limit adaptation and so on. Those working in a laboratory will have at their disposal an array of sophisticated evaluation equipment, capable of providing the individual sportsman or woman with a very elaborate evaluation profile. Most of them will also have an assortment of ergometers (treadmill, bicycle, etc.) on which energy consumption can be analysed under very stressful working conditions. At present, only a few people in sport appreciate terms such as 'V0$_2$ max.' (a measurement of one's maximum work potential), but as the drive to improve standards continues, so will such terms become a regular feature of elite sport.

Biomechanics experts

The title 'biomechanics expert' is also new to sport. In basic terms this is a person who applies the laws of physics to the motion of the human body. These skills have been considerably enhanced by the revolution that has taken place in the electronics industry; the basic tools of the biomechanics expert's trade are the high-speed sequence camera and the force platform.

A player who believes that his or her performance is hindered by an inadequacy in an aspect of technique can have it placed under fine scrutiny by the biomechanics expert. The technique can be analysed, time and again, and electronic models, based on computer findings, used to make comparisons and find any shortcomings. Immediate fault correction is possible from looking at instant video replay during practice, although high-speed cine film analysis is currently the best method for the specialist who wants to provide a player with feedback because of its superior quality.

In certain sports, in particular those in which jumping is a feature, not only can techniques be analysed, but computer read-outs can give details of the precise nature of the force applied. The biomechanics specialist has accordingly come to play an invaluable role in technical fault correction.

Like the sports physiologist, the specialist in biomechanics is likely to be found in a university department of Physical Education, and most of them are only too prepared to share their knowledge with the practical performer.

Sports psychologists

Most people involved in sport will recognise that the ultimate level of performance, the razor's edge between defeat or victory, is more likely to be influenced by the psychological rather than the physiological. Several world-class teams, individuals and their coaches, have sought the help of a sports psychologist. When used correctly, their contribution towards success can be invaluable.

In many respects, coaches make excellent self-taught psychologists. By mixing with competitors during training and competition, they learn to recognise how different individuals adapt to stress and to prescribe effective remedies. However, if true specialist help is required, then sports psychologists can be consulted at university Physical Education departments. Sports psychology deals with several distinct subjects: learning and teaching, athlete–coach interaction, aspiration levels and goal-setting, pre-event preparation and post-event analysis.

Learning and teaching
Learning and teaching involve the various theories of how people learn physical skill and how they are taught. It is concerned with motivation, who and what provides the desire to learn and perfect a skill. Complex skills can be learned and taught by a combination of whole and part learning (*see* chapter 7). The player and coach must use all of these learning situations to facilitate skill perfection.

Athlete–coach interaction

A good teaching relationship is determined by the interaction of personality. An extremely extrovert coach and introverted player are unlikely to get on, or even understand each other. Many psychologists examine coaches from their position as leaders, seeing them as 'dictator' or 'father figure' according to their personality. However, while psychologists can identify personality types, their power to change these is highly limited. They can, however, identify potential areas of conflict.

Aspiration levels and goal-setting

From time to time athletes will ask: 'How good do I want to be? Do I wish to be world-class? Should I just be a "fun" player?' There is little point in setting goals unless they are realistic, and unless the player is prepared to make the necessary commitment to achieve them. The top-level player will have to make many sacrifices, in particular of personal time and a professional career. In the long term it is a matter of priorities and the choice must be that of the individual. The elite performer may find that frequently compiling a checklist of the sacrifices made in order to achieve the necessary goals serves as a reminder to stick to the planned course. 'Without dedication nothing great is ever achieved' (G.H.G. Dyson).

Pre-event preparation

Preparation can be divided into short-term and long-term procedures. The short term may take the form of a pre-event pep talk, a final psyching session; it will vary considerably from individual to individual, both performer and coach. To pitch it correctly the coach may need to consult a good psychologist on what might be said, or better still what should not be said. Individuals experience various levels of arousal, and one has to find the right one in order to achieve the best performance; a pre-match talk that overexcites a competitor may not, in fact, be of help.

When the pep talk is directed at the players in a team, it should serve only as a focal point for the task in hand. For the individual-based sports, however, much of the pre-event focussing is similar to hypnotism. It demands tremendous concentration to produce what people in sport frequently term 'tunnel vision', a state of mind where nothing can distract the focus of attention away from winning. During this essential pre-match 'psyching' phase, it is easy to let officials, fellow competitors or spectators interrupt; only those with total commitment to its value succeed in achieving the 'tunnel vision' state.

There are a number of long-term psychological training methods available to the coach. One of the best is termed 'autogenic training'. Again, a variety of systems are used, but, in one form or another, it is essential for those wishing to reach the top. One method involves the performer(s) viewing a film or video of the opposition immediately prior to a training session. The coach comments on inadequacies in their performance. This is followed by a psyching session designed to introduce an even higher state of arousal than would normally be possible. As a result, the athlete's stress level is high at the start of the session and, with the elite, this always enhances training performance.

There are a number of autogenic training techniques, all of which will bring about a beneficial response from the individual concerned. Players and coaches should consult a recognised sports psychologist for the best one to use.

Post-event analysis

For most coaches the pre-match 'pep' talk is relatively easy, as most players will be in a responsive, aroused state. However, the same cannot be said for the post-match contribution. When players are successful, any post-event debriefing, or analysis, is quite easy. It becomes a problem when the result is unfavourable. No one loses deliberately, whereas one always wins deliberately. Therefore the situation can only be resolved by careful planning and preparation. Perhaps when the feelings of defeat are still within the dressing rooms, it is not the time to analyse the result and illustrate weaknesses in tactics or patterns of play. However, if left too long after defeat, the true value of any analysis and recrimination might be lost. The good coach becomes a self-taught psychologist through experience, and a sense of 'when the time is right' becomes instinctive. Players must be told the truth, but the skill is waiting for the right moment. Again the sports psychologist could provide expert advice.

Pharmacology

The place of the pharmacologist in a book of this nature is controversial. Of course, pharmacology has made a massive contribution through the correct agencies of the medical profession. However, without condoning the situation, it would be unrealistic for the author not to recognise the contribution that the illegal use of certain drugs has made to top-level sport. Sports such as weightlifting, bodybuilding and the heavy throwing events can never be the same again following the introduction of anabolic steroids. Perhaps the same can be said of blood doping in the endurance events, and, more recently, the appearance on the market of a pill that can have an identical effect to blood doping.

The truth is that the use of drugs to enhance performance is not allowed, so those who resort to them break a rule and ignore the most accepted ethic of the sport, that of 'fair play'. However, since the rewards in sport remain so high, there will always be those who are prepared to take the risk and cheat.

While the governing bodies of sport undertake testing at most major fixtures, and some implement a 'spot' check system any time throughout the year, most of the cheats avoid detection, and that continues to encourage the risk-takers.

The technologist

The contribution of the technologist over recent decades might not be so obvious, but has, in fact, been enormous. Playing surfaces, clothing, equipment and physiotherapy aids have changed enormously, and they are only the tip of the iceberg.

Organisations

In many countries there are 'Institutions of Sport', 'Departments of Sport', 'Coaching Resource Centres', and so on, some of which actually train coaches for sport, while others provide information packages and support material that can make the coach's job easier. In any advanced country in the world, a coach with a problem should be able to find a coaching resource centre and receive help; an excellent example in the United Kingdom is the National Coaching Foundation. Details concerning any of the support agencies discussed in this chapter can be found by contacting the national or local sports council.

Women in sport

We now live in a society in which many gender barriers have been removed. However, sport may be one area where the appearance of equality is more cosmetic than reality. Certain clubs in the UK, particularly cricket and golf, restrict their membership to men only, while some countries do not permit women to participate in sport at all, much to the concern of movements such as the International Olympic Committee. While the western world has progressed in the area of equality, in most third world countries, especially the Moslem states, it remains a long way off.

Recently, the International Amateur Athletics Association carried out a survey in the sport of track and field athletics, the results of which are almost certainly reflected in other sports throughout the world. Very few countries make real attempts to offer post-school girls the opportunity to participate in sport at any level approaching that which is offered to men, indeed the majority participating in the survey did not offer any comprehensive recruitment plan for women. Almost 90 per cent of the countries surveyed did not have any women coaches appointed at a professional level, and very few of the nations had any women serving the sport at executive level. So while progress has been rapid, there still remains a great deal of 'catching up' to do.

During the latter part of this century women's participation in sport has increased dramatically, not only in traditional 'women's' sports, but also in sports which were previously considered exclusive to men, such as soccer and rugby. Participation has increased both at grass roots level and at the highest competitive level. In some sports, such as track and field and distance swimming, women are fast closing the gap on men in terms of speed, and there is speculation that their performances might surpass those of men in certain areas, especially when skill, flexibility and endurance are major components.

Many women have improved through following training regimes

initially designed for men, but concern is now being expressed as to whether training loads developed and proven for men are correct for producing elite female performers, or whether they place women's health and fitness at risk. If this is the case, how should the treatment of female athletes differ from that of their male counterparts?

Any differences between the training of male and female sports-people appear to be determined by three basic factors: physiological differences, anthropometrical differences and socio-psychological pressures. Some coaches believe that a male athlete's level of work and intensity of training will not harm a woman athlete if under-taken within her own capacity, and indeed, may encourage her to do better. However, it might also be impossible for a woman training at this level, and under this kind of stress, to ever reach her own true potential, as injuries, health disorders and psychological demoralisa-tion could prevent it. These three factors have to be addressed before deciding on whether a woman's training should be the same as a man's and if not, how it should differ.

Physiological differences

There are some differences in anatomical and physiological structure between the sexes in childhood, but the onset of female puberty between the ages of approximately 11 and 14 highlights and exacer-bates them. During puberty the body prepares itself for the demands of adulthood, quite often in a haphazard way, with layers of fatty tis-sue being deposited in certain regions, while the hormones strive to maintain a balance. Fatty tissue becomes more apparent as the teens progress. Unfortunately, most of this fatty tissue is deposited around the hips and bust, and a thoughtless comment from a casual observer can make a promising athlete self conscious or, worse still, drive her out of the sport. This is seen regularly in gymnastics and athletics, and it is a great loss when all that would be required to restore a proper balance is a sensible diet and a well-structured training pro-gramme, designed to produce a more athletic shape.

Similarly, problems can also occur when a flippant remark, from a coach or relative, leads to a young girl over-reacting and developing either of the chronic eating disorders, anorexia nervosa and bulimia nervosa. Girls who participate in sports for which a low amount of body fat is desirable, such as gymnastics, dancing, horse riding, middle- and ultra-distance running, are especially likely to suffer from these illnesses. It is considered fashionable to be thin anyway, and being thin is a quality approved of by those people that matter in the young sportswoman's life: the coach, rivals and the media. Many young women have difficulty in conforming to this ideal, how-ever, especially when it is not within their genetic make-up.

With the onset of menarche, the young athlete will experience special difficulties and problems, even when a regular cycle has developed. Women involved in high-level endurance training may experience irregularity or even absence of periods for much of their sporting career. This is known as amenorrhoea. Others are likely to find that the common complaint of pre-menstrual tension prior to a period, or pain when it arrives, affects performance.

Most coaches and performers will recognise the symptoms associated with hormonal changes, but if they are perceived simply as moodiness, or lack of motivation, they may lead the coach to develop a negative attitude towards the athlete involved. It requires a good relationship, or reasonable self-awareness in the athlete, to recognise the symptoms and adapt accordingly.

Hormones

An insight into the role of oestrogen and progesterone, the female sex hormones, can be of help in understanding variations in mood, irregularities in performance, both in training and in competition, and weight fluctuations within the monthly cycle.

During the first 14 days of the cycle, oestrogen is dominant, causing a cheerful mood and easy-going attitude, with an anabolic effect on the metabolism. After ovulation, progesterone comes to the forefront, and for some women it can cause depression, aggressiveness, exhaustion, irritability, fluid retention and headaches. This state may even last until three days into the next cycle and usually gets progressively worse as the period approaches. Bleeding occurs for three, and up to a maximum of seven days, with a small blood loss.

Fluid retention at this time can increase bodyweight by 0.5–2kg (1–4.5lb), while in some cases 4kg (9lb) has been recorded. This can make targets set in competition or training more difficult to attain.

Although the onset of the period may bring relief from fluid retention it can also mean that the functional capacity of the sportswoman is reduced due to stomach cramps, back pain and headaches. In some cases anaemia can result, with a devastating effect upon most sports, in particular those where endurance is a high priority. Other changes include an increase in lung capacity, an increase in pulse rate, an increased risk of infection and a proneness to accident and injury. Likewise there is a relative decrease in muscle strength capacity, the ability to control bodyweight, the internal pressure of the eye, the steadiness of the arm and hands, and the levels of concentration and of motor capacity and co-ordination.

The coach wishing to train the woman towards peak performance must recognise these cyclic changes and incorporate them into the training schedule. For example:

- skill training that requires steadiness of the arm and hand, and co-ordination of the eye, should not be emphasised during the pre-menstrual phase
- the training of endurance events should respect changes in lung capacity, pulse rate and water retention
- allowances must be made for changes of muscle state in training for events calling for high levels of speed and strength.

Fig. 73 indicates how training loads can change throughout the menstrual cycle, although it should be borne in mind that there will be some variation within this basic framework for each individual.

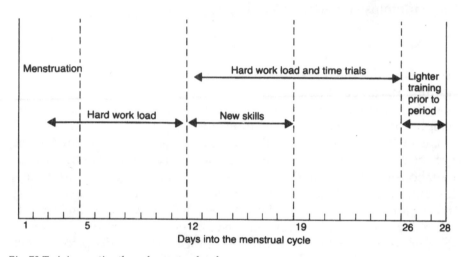

Fig. 73 Training routine through menstrual cycle

Anthropometrical differences

Women have several anthropometrical limitations that reduce their chances of ever equalling the sporting performances of men. The mammary glands are a major handicap until a woman matures as an athlete, probably in her late teens. At this point any fatty tissue may be redistributed or disappear completely, under the influence of a sensible diet or higher training loads. Genetically, women have a different chromosomal make-up that has an effect upon the structure and chemical composition of the body tissues.

On average, a woman is between 10 and 12 centimetres (4.5in) shorter than a man, and can also be in the region of 10kg (22lb) lighter, although women participating in sport often cross these barriers, as can be seen in the extreme somatotypes. In general, women have a relatively longer torso with a shorter leg length.

The main difference in the skeleton structure is in the pubic region where the female structure is broader, shallower and at a more obtuse angle, to allow for child bearing. The femur bone can often incline inwards giving a knock-kneed look. Differences can also be found in several other joints.

With musculature, the woman has far less muscle mass than her male counterpart, and three quarters as much fat again as a man, spread evenly around the body. Heavier training loads and constant calorie counting can reduce the fat, but men do have an immediate advantage. Body fat contributes approximately 20–25 per cent of bodyweight in the average woman, compared to only 10–15 per cent in men. Due to the extra muscle mass of a male, the muscular strength of a female performing the same activity is likely to be only 55–85 per cent of a man's.

Socio-psychological pressures

Along with improved female performance in sport, public opinion on the appearance, and the role, of women athletes has undergone a considerable change. Aggression, which was associated with competitive sport, also used to be associated with masculinity. Young women used to be allowed to enjoy competitive sport until social pressures, such as the influence of peer groups or the institution of marriage took over, and women continuing to participate in sports were considered as freaks. Fortunately, recent trends have brought sporting prowess for women more into vogue. The craze for healthier lifestyles and fitter bodies has made sporting activities such as jogging, swimming and cycling far more popular. Often the participants have found that they do possess a certain amount of ability, and have gone on to enjoy the stimulus of competition.

At times some women may feel that they have a double battle to fight. While they can be respected for their sporting prowess, there is also pressure on them to appear feminine. With ever-increasing financial rewards coming to those who are successful, women certainly find it helpful to look the part – athletic maybe, but also pretty, feminine and appealing. One only needs to look at the fashion worn by our female athletes to realise how important this is to the athlete, the manufacturer and the media.

Should a woman perform badly, critical observers suggest that it is due to her female figure or her womanly attitude. Should she perform well, the criticism then is that she is 'butch' or 'plays like a man'. It seems that a sportswoman is expected to play two roles, that of being a good athlete, and that of being a good woman. Failure to succeed in either of these roles may ultimately be construed as being the fault of trying to do well in the other.

Perhaps the sportswoman might also feel that pressure arises because of the media and associated advertisements. How often do we see sportswomen appearing on advertisements for cosmetics, fashion, etc? While we occasionally see articles in women's magazines featuring sportswomen, they are seldom, if ever, related to femininity. Some women find the role of parenthood conflicts with sport; taking time off to have a baby represents a great interruption in a sporting career.

The fact remains that should a woman improve her performance levels significantly, the critics never examine the training regimes that might have produced the improvement, rather they intimate that it is related to the implantation of a foreign hormone. It is known that many of the world track and field records were established by eastern bloc countries and, more recently, China. While there is evidence of a certain level of drug abuse, the women are seldom given credit for the many hours they dedicated to their training. While ergogenic aids can help, they are certainly not a substitute for hard work, especially for women.

There is no doubt that in taking any testosterone-related compound the benefits are considerably greater for women than for men. Because of the relatively low levels of natural testosterone in the female body, very small doses can have a dramatic effect. Indeed, the levels necessary can be so low as to hardly change the testosterone–epitestosterone ratio, the guide for the dope testers. This may mean that women athletes will soon be required to offer blood samples for analysis rather than the urine sample accepted for men. Fortunately, in many sports, the gender test is almost a thing of the past. To an informed observer, it becomes increasingly uncertain as to why women should suffer the indignity of having their gender doubted. In this modern era of sport I have no evidence at all of any man who has tried to masquerade as a woman. Since the chromatin test is unreliable in as many as 20 per cent of cases, this is reason enough for disbanding gender verification.

The influence of training

Training can improve a woman's performance to such an extent that she may perform better at a sport than the 'average' male – this is especially so in events requiring a high degree of skill. In some activities, such as long distance running and swimming, and more recently in the power events, women are closing the gap on men, even at the elite level of performance.

Women's increased strength and power could be the result of a gradual genetic change (probably brought about by nutrition), increased training loads, or hormonal influences, some of which might be transplanted artificially. The truth is that the factors that influence levels of performance are all trainable, these being speed, strength, stamina, skill and flexibility, and the performances of women will continue to improve while these can be improved. However, the evolutionary pattern of performances for women is likely to follow that of their male counterparts, which would indicate that they will at some point start to 'level out' unless the standards are artificially enhanced. Nevertheless, training provides considerable scope for improvement, within certain limits.

Strength

For many years strength activities using resistance techniques were shunned for women, the thought being that it would cause 'masculinisation'. Without doubt, there is a degree of muscle hypertrophy when women do weight training, however the level of hypertrophy is small when compared with men, due mainly to the low circulating levels of testosterone. Indeed, the levels are less than 10 per cent of that of the adult male.

It is generally recognised that the main factor influencing muscle growth is the male sex hormone. This puts the woman at a distinct disadvantage. It is also recognised that both insulin and the growth hormone have a significant effect (*see* page 37). In view of this, perhaps one should attempt to stimulate naturally the production of insulin and the growth hormone in women. Both of these hormone-related compounds respond to exercise, and it has been found that activity of a more aerobic nature can further increase the levels of both insulin growth factor (IGF) and the growth hormone. The same researchers found that levels of both IGF and the growth hormone are lower when the intensity of training is higher. Research also indicates that the effects are greater during the second half of the menstrual cycle.

This would indicate that there is a need to tailor strength training programmes for women using a system of extensive rather than intensive training. In other words, keep the resistance lower and the sets/reps combination higher. There might also be some merit in increasing the frequency of weight training during the second half of the menstrual cycle with the hopes of facilitating a greater growth hormone response.

Power

The improved standards exhibited by many sportswomen can be attributed to a better understanding of the development of power. It has been seen that power is influenced by speed, strength and flexibility. Because of their innately lower levels, there is a danger that sportswomen will concentrate solely on developing strength, but this can produce a decrease in both speed and flexibility as they are not necessarily compatible with strength. In view of this, the female performer should be encouraged to undertake plyometric training, where a series of rapid, muscular contractions are completed in succession (*see* chapter 4).

Since power is associated with force development (strength), it is unlikely that the female can ever become as powerful as the man. The gap can be made smaller by training, however the development of power in women has so far been delayed because of the belief that such training can damage a woman's body, causing conditions like prolapse of the womb and difficult pregnancies. There is little evidence to support these findings.

A woman should also look towards the development of specific strength by using a system designed to tailor strength requirements to an individual and her sport, such as resistance pulleys and elastics. While at times it might be necessary to modify equipment such as weighted jackets, and to lower resistance levels with both elastics and pulleys, the system does offer a very good form of training for women. In particular, there is an instantly perceivable relationship between these specific exercises for sports such as tennis, golf and athletics, as opposed to formal weight training.

Speed

Training for women to improve speed does not differ from that for men, neither do its benefits. *See* chapter 2.

Endurance

The physiologist determines the level of endurance by measuring what is known as the VO_2 max. This represents the ability of the cardio-vascular system to transport oxygen to the active tissues. A woman's VO_2 max. is lower than that of a man by as much as 25 per cent because women have, on average, a smaller heart and lungs. However, it can be improved by systematic training, to the extent that a woman can raise her level to something in the region of 25 per cent greater than the average man's.

Research indicates that women depend more upon the aerobic production of energy and fat combustion than men, and they certainly do appear to get more benefit from endurance-based sports than power-based ones. Also, women appear to have a greater ability to utilise lipids, thus explaining their bias towards low-intensity, long-duration events.

The strength–weight ratio of a person has a profound effect upon sports, especially those biased towards endurance. Hence, the person who has an excess of body fat, which is dead weight, is likely to perform less well. It should be the aim of most women in sport to reduce their body fat levels to less than 15 per cent, and even as low as 10 per cent for those involved in endurance sports. One woman who has achieved an excellent physique with good muscle definition, in a sport where many performers might be criticised for being too heavy, is Martina Navratilova.

Skill

While women would find difficulty challenging men in terms of strength, speed and endurance, there is no evidence to suggest that they have decreased skill thresholds, and there is a considerable body of research to suggest that, as long as the skills are not related to a strength component, the performance of the female can equal that of the male. These tests have mainly been performed by psychologists and skill analysts looking at eye and muscle co-ordination.

In fact, in hurdling and high jumping, women's skill levels can be higher than men's. This is due to the flexibility afforded to the pelvic region by the greater tilt of the innominate bone of the woman, so placing the lower limbs in a more efficient alignment.

Suppleness

From evaluation profiles compiled with the basic flexibility field tests outlined in chapter 6, women were found to have a greater range of movement than men in the trunk, the arm and shoulder region, elbow hyperextension and the hip.

Almost certainly attributable to the anatomical structure of the woman, these can be of great significance in events such as track and field athletics, gymnastics, swimming and racket sports. There are, however, exceptions to the rule, in that a man who has worked progressively on his flexibility can attain levels equal to those of a trained woman.

Gynaecological considerations

The various effects of the menstrual cycle upon performance were examined earlier. An additional effect is that women can miss seven per cent of their training time, as much as four days every cycle. When the margin between success and failure is measured in a fraction of one per cent, women who wish to train for peak performance cannot afford to miss this amount of valuable training.

Fortunately, pharmacologists have given women hope. While mild pain killers and diuretics can reduce some of the minor symptoms of menstruation, as can diet, the birth control pill has revolutionised the situation. Nowadays it is quite common for the team doctor to pre-scribe the oral contraceptive pill to regulate the cycle in order to reduce the negative symptoms of menstruation, and avoid the period of high fluid retention coinciding with major competitions.

Unfortunately, the pill is not without its side effects. Long-term use is not recommended because of its links with cardio-circulatory illnesses, infections of the urinary tract and the risk of blood clotting. Many athletes have reported more extreme changes in mood and greater fluid retention and swollen breasts than normal, even when taking low dosage oestrogen and progestogen pills, although for most sportswomen these effects are less on the pill than off it.

The oral contraceptive pill reduces the levels of vitamin C in the body, and if this is allowed to go uncorrected then it would con-tribute towards anaemia and a reduced immunity to infection. Hence a woman on the birth control pill is well-advised to supplement her dietary intake of vitamin C by at least 500mg per day. They also suffer reduced levels of magnesium and zinc and should therefore supplement these minerals too.

Amenorrhea

The absence of periods, or amenorrhea, is more common in sportswomen than in the population at large. It is especially notice-able in women undertaking very high training loads. Women with regular menses prior to starting training usually continue with them during intensive training, but women with irregular periods usually continue to suffer irregularity or become amenorrheic. Therefore the best method of predicting the regularity of a menstrual cycle is to establish what the pattern was prior to training. In general, athletic girls tend to experience menarche later than the average woman.

Diet and nutrition

There is no doubt that diet has a profound effect upon the menstrual cycle. Nutrition is discussed in detail in chapter 14, but in some respects sportswomen require special consideration. Not only do their demands differ from those of the average woman, but they also differ from those of the sportsman.

Women require nutritional therapy in certain areas, especially to counteract the negative aspects of menstruation.

Iron

Two-thirds of the iron present in the body is in the form of haemoglobin, the red oxygen-carrying pigment of the blood. The rest is present in myoglobin in the liver, spleen, bone marrow and muscles. On average there are 3.5–4.5g ($^1/_8$–$^1/_7$oz) iron present in the body and these stores are dependent upon iron absorbed from the diet. Iron can be in the form of organic 'haem', found in meat, and this can be absorbed without any outside help; non-haem iron requires the presence of vitamin C for efficient absorption.

The best sources of iron are seafoods such as cockles and winkles, dried brewers yeast, wheatbran, cooked liver and kidney and wholemeal bread. Certain vegetables, especially watercress and spinach, are also rich in iron.

Iron deficiency produces tiredness, a lack of stamina, changes in palor and giddiness. However, the ultimate test of deficiency is a blood haemoglobin count taken by a doctor. If anaemia exists, the doctor can recommend several iron supplements. The daily recommended intake of iron for women is 15–18mg. Often a multi-mineral and vitamin tablet will suffice, though during high-intensity training the potency has to be increased.

Vitamin C

In addition to aiding the absorption of iron, vitamin C is important in providing resistance to infection, working as an anti-oxidant, controlling blood cholesterol levels, and maintaining healthy bones, teeth, blood and sexual organs. Unfortunately, much of this water-soluble vitamin is lost in the processing of food, but it can be found in good quantities in certain fruit juices, rose hip syrup, and blackcurrants. The most effective way of taking the vitamin is in the form of ascorbic acid tablets, available from a pharmacist.

Vitamin B$_6$

Vitamin B$_6$ is a water-soluble vitamin, commonly used in the treatment of pre-menstrual tension, and depression induced by the oral contraceptive pill. The vitamin has a co-enzymic effect on the conversion of fatty acids, and it is especially beneficial when taken in conjunction with Evening Primrose Oil. Most sportswomen are advised to consume at least 25mg of B$_6$ per day, and as much as 150mg if they are on the pill.

Other dietary requirements

In addition, a woman who wishes to train for peak performance should follow the guidelines below as a help in dealing with weight and for general health.

1) Reduce the level of caffeine in the diet. Many people drink far too much coffee, and coffee affects the body's metabolism. Substituting fruit or herbal teas might help.
2) Reduce or remove completely all chocolate from the diet.
3) Reduce the quantities of sugar, salt and dairy produce.
4) Reduce carbonated drinks, particularly Colas.
5) Avoid smoking totally and reduce the levels of alcohol.

There is evidence to suggest that 3g of Evening Primrose Oil taken prior to menstruation can have a beneficial effect upon performance. The following list of supplements, together with their daily requirements should help those in doubt:

Vitamin C: 3g per day
Vitamin B₆: 150mg per day
Total 'B' complex
Vitamin E: 3 days prior to menstruation, 300mg daily
Iron: on prescription
Zinc: 10mg daily
Magnesium: 10mg daily.

Medical implications

In recent years the incidence of medical disorders such as amenorrhea and osteoporosis in relatively young people who undergo intensive training is alarming the medical profession worldwide. As mentioned earlier, women are subjected to role models to a greater degree than men, and western society seems to suggest that the lean body is associated with fitness. Magazines which imply that many of the role models almost completely eliminate fats from their diet only serve to exacerbate the problem. The medical profession is aware that menstruation is affected by body fat and that low body fat levels will induce amenorrhea. They are also aware that should the percentage body fat level drop below 10 per cent, the level is too low to transport the steroid hormones and fat-soluble vitamins. The medical profession are certain that the incidence of premature osteoporosis is related to low body fat levels, probably due to the relationship of the fat-soluble vitamin D and the calcium available for building bone. Accompanying this deterioration in the bone structure is the associated risk of all types of fractures, especially those related to frequent impact.

The avoidance of fats brings with it eating fads and the associated eating disorders such as anorexia nervosa and bulimia. People so affected will eat very little, induce vomiting soon after eating, and resort to laxatives, diuretics and appetite suppressants. Many young athletes are kept alive merely by eating large quantities of chocolate. While these problems are also common within society in general, they are highlighted in sport because the training demands that enough energy is made available to fuel the activity.

The fact that so few coaches in sport are women, and that male coaches may not be aware of the tell-tale symptoms, means that the situation can remain undetected until it is almost too late.

Nutrition

All too frequently, the difference between success and failure is as little as a fraction of one per cent. When players of international status have similar endowed abilities, and train along similar lines, the final result can be determined in favour of those who eat correctly. And it is true to say 'We are what we eat', since it is our food intake that ultimately determines our physiological functioning.

The sports competitor has to consider nutrition in respect of its dominant role in the following:

- strength–weight ratio
- muscle protein rebuilding
- muscle glycogen content
- water and electrolyte balance
- aerobic capacity
- injury healing rate
- resistance to infections
- intestinal hurry (*see* chapter 15).

Strength–weight ratio

When a person eats more food than is required for the energy expended, the superfluous energy from the food is converted to fat. The fat is deposited about the body, thus increasing bodyweight and almost certainly reducing efficiency. Every individual has an optimum weight, relative to strength; should weight increase, without an added increase in strength, then efficiency is reduced. It is relatively easy to calculate the amount of energy one expends, with the following equation:

$$\text{energy output} = \text{basal rate} + \text{chores} + \text{sport energy}$$

The first element on the right of the equation, the basal rate, is determined by weight, height, age and gender. It represents the energy required to fuel 24 hours of bed rest, as follows:

Men		Women	
Weight	Calories	Weight	Calories
64kg (140lb)	1,500	45kg (100lb)	1,225
73kg (160lb)	1,640	54kg (120lb)	1,320
82kg (180lb)	1,730	64kg (140lb)	1,400
91kg (200lb)	1,815	73kg (160lb)	1,485
100kg (220lb)	1,900	82kg (180lb)	1,575

The above table is based on a height norm of 178cm (5ft 10in) for men and 168cm (5ft 6in) for women. In each case add or subtract 30KCal per 2.5cm (1in), as the taller the person, the greater the energy expenditure. The age norm is 25 years, with a reduction of four per cent for each decade above that age, and a reduction of four per cent for each decade below it, as energy requirements decline with age.

Chores are what we have to perform to live: standing, walking, washing, eating, dressing, undressing and, of course, working for one's living. As an indication of the energy used by chores, it requires 1.5 calories per kilogram of weight to stand for one hour, this being the energy necessary to keep the postural muscles in a state of contraction.

Nutritional researchers have arrived at some reasonably accurate computation for the extra energy above the basal level expended by chores, as shown in the table below.

Activity	Above Basal
Quiet sitting	30%
Light activity (office work)	50%
Moderate activity (housework)	70%
Heavy occupational work	100%

For example, the first part of the equation for a 25-year-old woman typist who is 168cm (5ft 6in) tall, weighing 64kg (140lb) becomes: 1,400 calories (basal rate) + 700 calories (chores allowance 50%) = 2,100 calories per day.

To this total must be added the amount an individual expends in energy in practising sport. It takes 51 calories per minute to fuel a full effort sprint, and 10 calories per minute (for a performer of standard weight, age and height) to play a game of squash.

The above equation for a 35-year-old male squash player who is 188cm (6ft 2in) tall, weighing 91kg (200lb) and whose occupation is an architect/valuer becomes: 1,800 calories (basal rate) + 1,260 calories (chores and occupation) + 540 (sport energy) = 3,600 calories per day.

He would therefore need to eat the equivalent of 3,600 calories a day to maintain the energy balance. It is possible to calculate the energy expended in any sport, but this is too broad a topic to be included here.

Muscle protein rebuilding

The act of stressing a muscle, as in training, causes the protein in the muscle to break down, and once this happens the natural repair process in the body overcompensates and makes the muscle stronger. Muscle protein is rebuilt via the intricate action of the growth hormone and the protein taken in as part of a person's diet. The body must have protein, since it cannot manufacture it from other basic nutrients.

Muscle glycogen content

Glycogen is the basic food which all muscles require for contraction. The final fuel for muscular energy is a substance known as adenosine-tri phosphate, but it has to be liberated by metabolising carbohydrate glycogen. The food we eat is eventually converted to glycogen, so that the energy cycle can continue, however less stress is placed on the body when the fuel for muscular contraction is taken in in the form of carbohydrates.

Water and electrolyte balance

'Man cannot live by bread alone'; fluid (water) is essential. All the cells of our body are bathed in a fluid, the chemical composition of which must be kept constant. The maintenance of this stable environment is known as homeostasis and it is totally controlled by what we eat and drink. Unless the body gets the correct balance of minerals and trace elements it cannot function correctly and, as a result, physical performance will be reduced.

Aerobic capacity

Aerobic capacity is the ability of the body to cope with activities of a sustained nature such as a marathon run, long-distance swimming or cross-country skiing. It refers to energy obtained from our food and fully metabolised in the presence of oxygen. While in certain situations we can derive energy from both fats and protein, the body works most efficiently when it derives its energy from carbohydrates. Unfortunately, the body only has a reserve of about 2,500 calories, hence the other nutrients have to be used as a source of energy.

Fats can yield twice as much energy as carbohydrates, but they are very inefficient in the way they use oxygen to produce their energy. Proteins yield about the same amount of energy as carbohydrates, but in their metabolism produce more toxic by-products. This again emphasises the need for the active performer to include sufficient carbohydrate in his or her diet.

Oxygen is transported around the body by haemoglobin contained in the blood, and the haemoglobin level is influenced by the iron content in the diet. Anaemia commonly affects people in sport, particularly women, and has to be treated quickly with supplements of iron and vitamin C, otherwise aerobic capacity will suffer. However, by eating certain offal meats, and certain green vegetables, the natural level of iron can be kept fairly constant. Should an athlete feel lethargic for no reason at all, it could indicate that a blood test is necessary to see whether or not there is an iron deficiency.

Injury healing rate

Injuries heal faster on a well-balanced diet, vitamin E being particularly important.

Resistance to infection

As is well known, vitamin C is a virus fighter. Unless the body gets the correct balance of basic nutrients, vitamins and minerals, the immune system of the body is impaired, thus lowering its resistance to infection.

Basic food needs for sport

To appreciate fully how nutritional science can help the sportsman and woman, it is necessary to understand what the basic foodstuffs are and the effect they have upon the body.

An effective diet must contain protein, fats, carbohydrates, vitamins, minerals, liquids and roughage. Sport disturbs the chemical balance of the body so it must return back to normal as quickly as possible. Nutrition plays an important role in keeping this delicate chemical balance, so that the various cells work in an efficient environment.

Proteins

Proteins are the cell builders. They are a chemical combination of carbon, oxygen, hydrogen and nitrogen. Of the three basic nutrients, protein is the only one completely essential to the body. The cells of the body are composed of protein and they are constantly undergoing change and being broken down in the general wear and tear of life. Protein rebuilds the cells, particularly those of the muscles. Training and competing breaks down the protein in the muscles, but in rebuilding, nature makes them stronger through the intricate action of protein and certain hormones available in the body.

Protein also contributes to the enzyme pool, so making the chemical process of life more efficient. They have a marked effect upon the production and action of certain hormones, which again makes this process of life the remarkable function it is.

Another very important aspect of the role played by proteins is in maintaining the delicate nitrogen balance, for protein is the body's only source of this essential element. Research indicates that the nitrogen balance is best maintained when the protein ingested is of animal, rather than vegetable, derivation. There is also some evidence to show that proteins have a stimulatory effect upon the nervous system, keeping the body alert, aware and capable of making split-second decisions, all very important aspects of peak performance in sport. Hence, a diet low in protein is certain to reduce efficiency.

Protein is available to the body in the form of amino acids. There are over 20 known amino acids, some of which are termed essential. As long as the body has a supply of these essential amino acids, then it is capable of manufacturing the others.

In 1956 the United Nations Committee for Food and Agriculture ranked the most common sources of protein. Eggs were found to contain the best balance of essential amino acids (though not complete) and were given a 100 per cent rating. This does not mean that an egg is composed entirely of protein, it is just the percentage given to enable one to place the other foods in rank order. The chart is as follows:

eggs	100%
fish/meat	70%
soya beans	69%
milk	60%
rice	56%
corn	41%

By mixing proteins the biological value can be increased. For example:

eggs + potato	137%
eggs + milk	122%
eggs + wheat	118%.

Most nutritionists believe that the average person will get sufficient protein from the normal diet, which for an adult is 1g per kilogramme of bodyweight ($^1/_{10}$ oz per each 6lb), and for a child, 2g per kilogramme of bodyweight. The person involved in high-level sport also requires 2g of protein per kilogramme bodyweight. It is unlikely that any person who follows a good, balanced diet is going to be short of protein, however we like to take out an added 'insurance' with elite players through supplementation in the form of tablets containing a very carefully balanced supply of amino acids. The supporting theory relating to amino acid therapy is beyond the scope of this text, but suffice it to say that at the time of writing amino acids are the vogue supplement for top class sportspeople.

Carbohydrates

Carbohydrates are combinations of carbon, hydrogen and oxygen. They are not essential, as the body has the capacity to manufacture them from the other basic nutrients, however, they represent a very convenient source of energy because of their efficient combustion when converted to energy. The body is able to store about 2,500 calories of carbohydrates, however, this is not enough to fuel the energy requirements of most participants, so some energy must be derived from the combustion of fats and proteins.

The athlete should derive about 60 per cent of his or her energy requirements from carbohydrates. Two sources are available: sugars and starches. Those involved in sports should consider a ratio of 60 per cent starches to 40 per cent sugars, which places minimal strain upon the digestive system.

One should guard against a sudden ingestion of sugars, as could come from taking excess glucose tablets or drinks in the belief that they will boost energy by increasing blood sugar levels. In fact, it could produce the opposite effect, creating an insulin reaction, which the body might take as a precautionary measure through its natural feed-back mechanism.

The following table shows foods rich in carbohydrates.

Food	g carbohydrates per 100g food
rice	86.8
cornflakes	85.4
honey	76.4
jam	69.2
bread (white)	54.3
bread (brown)	48.4
chips	37.3
potatoes (boiled)	19.7
bananas	19.2
apples	12.0

Fats

If sportsmen and women listened to advice given to the general public by a large body of nutritionists, their efficiency would be considerably impaired. For those involved in very high outputs of energy, the deposition of fatty tissue about the body should not be a problem. Fats represent a massive potential store of energy, their yield, per unit weight, being about 2.5 times greater than that of carbohydrates. The disadvantage is that they require significantly more oxygen when combusted. Therefore, since respiratory capacity is often limited, over-reliance on fats for energy is a disadvantage for high-intensity exercise. They are, however, essential for all sportsmen and women who should get at least 20 per cent of their energy from fats. They also fuel a large proportion of the overdraft of 2,500 calories. Fats are also essential in that they bind the fat-soluble vitamins A, D, E and K.

Fats can be derived from both animal and vegetable sources. Vegetable fats are thought to have less harmful effects upon the body when taken in excess. The efficient athlete will probably need to make use of both sources.

Food	g fat per 100g food
margarine	81.5
butter	81.0
nuts	53.5
bacon	40.5
cheese	34.5
lamb	30.2
pork	29.6
eggs	10.9

It is most unlikely that any player will fall short of the essential basic levels of the three main nutrients; in fact, they will almost certainly take in more than is sufficient to meet the energy requirements.

Vitamins

In contrast to fats, it is by no means certain that the athlete will get enough vitamins from a normal diet. Although the study of vitamins has been with us now for over a century, few people know what they are or what they do. A fairly safe and simple idea is to regard them as the catalyst of nutritional chemistry. That is, they speed up, or make more efficient, the chemical processes involved in getting the nutrients from the food we eat.

Vitamins are divided into two basic classifications: those which are fat-soluble, namely A, D, E and K, and the water-soluble vitamins of the B and C groups.

Vitamin A
Vitamin A can be taken directly into the body through one of the fish liver oils or via the carotine in fruit and vegetables. It is important as it keeps the skin, teeth, gums and other soft tissues in a good state of health. The table on page 170 gives an indication of the foods containing vitamin A. Supplementation should not be necessary.

Vitamin B group
The vitamin B group is a complex of vitamins, all related to one another. Some of them carry out similar functions to each other, but the higher group has a special effect upon the body. As B vitamins are water-soluble their life is limited, hence a daily intake is necessary.

Vitamin B_1, thiamine, is needed to keep the cells of the body well nourished. It converts carbohydrates to usable glucose, and has a 'toning' effect upon the heart muscles. It is found in wheatgerm oil and is almost totally destroyed by cooking and storage.

Without the enzymic effect of vitamin B_2, riboflavin, the body could not produce energy efficiently. It also has a profound effect upon the body's ability to produce energy from fats, and is derived from the same source as vitamin B_1.

The action of vitamin B_3, niacin, is similar to that of B_2, and it is essential in carbohydrate metabolism, as well as in aiding the correct functioning of B_1 and B_2. It is found in yeast products, nuts, fish and meat.

Vitamin B_5, pantothenic acid, converts all of the three main nutrients to energy. It has a 'calming' effect upon the body during stress, and helps fight infections in the blood stream. Vitamin B_5 is obtained from wheat, meat, fish, poultry and vegetables.

Vitamin B$_6$, pyrodoxine, aids the metabolism of proteins, controls the sodium and potassium blood levels, and plays a vital role in the production of red blood cells. This vitamin is found in whole grains, nuts, eggs and beans.

Vitamin B$_{12}$ has a profound effect upon the correct functioning of many of our cells, our blood, our liver and our nervous system. However, its most recognised role is that of aiding the production of red blood cells. It is found in most dairy products.

Folic acid is essential for both physical and mental well-being. It works in close association with other B vitamins, especially B$_6$ and B$_{12}$, and vitamin C. Its main work is associated with the brain and nervous system. It is found in root vegetables, green leaves and lean meat.

The vogue vitamin in sport is vitamin B$_{15}$. Research indicates that it helps in producing energy when under great stress. While the indiscriminate use of vitamin supplementation is not recommended, an additional intake of this one is worthwhile, although if one eats well, including green vegetables, meat, beans and eggs in the diet, even this might not be necessary. However, just to add that little extra 'insurance', brewer's yeast and wheatgerm extract are a cheap dietary addition.

Vitamin C (ascorbic acid)

Vitamin C is the best-known of the vitamins to the population at large, because of the high-pressure sale associated with certain drinks and fruit. Vitamin C has an effect upon most connective tissue; it helps in the healing of wounds and tissue injury; it helps the body fight infections; and it is essential in the absorption of iron. Even from this very brief review its importance to the athlete can be readily recognised. Vitamin C is available in most fruits and vegetables.

Vitamin D

Vitamin D is known as the sunlight vitamin, as sunlight entering through the skin combines with ergesterol (an oily substance found under the skin) to produce it. This vitamin helps our body to use calcium and phosphorus to provide us with healthy bones and teeth. Hence those players in contact sports, where broken bones are a common hazard, should get plenty of it. Vitamin D also has a profound effect upon the liver and kidneys, two vital organs that are highly stressed in training for peak performance.

Many athletes go to warm sunny climates for special adaptive training. It has been found that sunlight can increase testosterone levels, and have a beneficial effect upon the circulatory system. Perhaps those who wish for peak performance should look into the use of full spectrum lighting, which is now available in many health and fitness centres throughout the world.

Vitamin E
Vitamin E captured public interest a decade or so ago, because of its purported effect upon libido. Whatever the truth of that, there is strong evidence to suggest that vitamin E helps the fatigued muscle to recover quickly. It also helps in the healing of soft-tissue injuries. For these reasons it might be worth supplementing after every game. Vitamin E is available in most nuts, seeds and oils.

There are of course other vitamins, but those listed here are the most important ones to the active sportsman or woman.

Vitamin intake
The following table gives an indication of the daily requirements of vitamins for the healthy, active athlete.

Vitamin A	5000I.U. (International Units)
Vitamin B_1	1.4mg
Vitamin B_2	1.6mg
Vitamin B_3	30mg
Vitamin B_5	10mg
Vitamin B_6	2mg
Vitamin B_{12}	2mg
Vitamin C	100mg
Vitamin D	400I.U.
Vitamin E	30I.U.

Minerals

Most people believe that minerals and vitamins are the same, and that their action on the body is similar. This couldn't be further from the truth. Basically, there are two groups of minerals that have an effect upon the health and stability of the body. The first is the 'salt' group which aids the delicate fluid-electrolyte balance, ensuring that the cells function in a stable environment. These include sodium, potassium and chlorine. The second group are those responsible for the well-being of bones, teeth and tissues, and include calcium, phosphorus, magnesium, cobalt, zinc and iron.

For most of the year, there will be no need to supplement minerals. However, for important matches in hot conditions, electrolyte-balanced drinks can restore lost minerals during and after a game.

Going shopping

With this basic nutritional outline complete, there remains the vital question of what to eat, in terms of the food we can buy from the shops, as opposed to the scientific constituents.

The following table represents the basic nutrients, vitamins and certain minerals, together with the foods from which they are best obtained. The table is compiled in order of cost effectiveness.

Protein	bread, milk, cheese, chicken, eggs, cereal, liver, fish
Carbohydrates	sugar, bread, potatoes, cereal
Calcium	milk, cheese, carrots
Iron	liver, baked beans, potatoes, bread, peas
Phosphor	meat, fish, cheese, nuts
Vitamin A	carrots, liver, margarine, milk
Vitamin B$_1$	cereals, bread, peas, milk, pork
Vitamin B$_2$	liver, cereal, milk, eggs, cheese
Vitamin B$_3$	cereal, potatoes, liver, bread
Vitamin C	fruit juice, fresh vegetables, fruit
Vitamin D	margarine, butter, eggs, fish
Vitamin E	meat, fish, cheese, nuts.

While fats are not included, if one eats wisely from this list each day, then little will be left to chance. It is better to concentrate on these foods than to give a long list of what should be avoided. There are, of course, foods such as those deep fried in fat, which, when taken in excess, can place an extra stress on a body. Fat has a long transit time in the gut, and moderation is the key word of the day.

Mealtimes

The question of when to eat is critical but is difficult to standardise, and must include special considerations for eating during the training period and before matches, as well as normal eating.

The body clock is best kept to time by eating at regular intervals. This is usually determined by the nature of one's employment, setting a pattern to which the body gradually adapts. For most athletes this means the normal three conveniently spaced meals each day. Anything other than a very light snack between these must be avoided. Cooked meals are no more nutritious than cold ones.

It is important to avoid eating late at night as digestion is impaired, and evening meals should be complete by 8 p.m., though this will be a problem on conventional training nights. One must avoid overeating; just sufficient to quench the appetite is all that is required. Remember to monitor bodyweight!

Prior to training

Most sportsmen and women train during the evenings from about 7 p.m. and should therefore try to take a light meal at 4 p.m. The nature of his or her employment might well make this difficult, but he or she must avoid the 'empty tank' syndrome, produced by an excessively long break between eating and training. If the athlete has to travel directly to training from work, the situation is even harder, and he or she can only hope to 'top-up' the system by eating a quick energy chocolate bar. Training on a full stomach is equally to be avoided as the food will not be digested.

It is theoretically possible to 'carbohydrate load' on the last meal prior to training, by eating foods rich in starch such as pasta. This situation will also apply to a match played after a normal working day.

The pre-match meal

A number of factors influence the meal before a competition, the most important one being the starting time of the match. Most take place in the early afternoon and this is probably the easiest situation to cater for. The athlete should prepare with a brunch at about 10 a.m. consisting of cereals, fruit juice, toast, preserves and a beverage. This will provide the energy required in an easy form.

However, the starting time of the match might not be so convenient, and it is only possible to give general guidelines to cover all situations. First, a pre-match meal should be finished three hours before the scheduled start of the match. In this situation almost any food from the list in the previous section can be taken. Fatty foods such as chips, fried fish and steaks are to be avoided as they have a long transit time in the gut and will produce discomfort during the game, thereby reducing efficiency. A small glass of fortified wine before such a meal aids digestion, but larger quantities and other alcohols must be avoided.

Secondly, if the athlete cannot eat three hours before the match but has to leave a shorter interval, he or she should concentrate on quickly digested foods from the starch group, such as pasta or sandwiches. Salad materials are to be avoided as they are frequently hard to digest. When the interval is very short, then only foods containing glucose, fructose and simple sugars, such as confectionary bars, should be taken. One should avoid eating anything at all less than an hour before, as the pre-match 'psyching' will affect blood supply to the gut and hence digestion.

Special diets

Training harder will certainly force a change in eating habits, as extra training increases the energy requirements. Monitor bodyweight daily.

While some players might be naturally large there is always a need to improve one's strength–weight ratio. This can only be done by increasing the muscle content and decreasing the fat content of the body. This implies a systematised strength-training programme together with an attempt to 'burn off' excess fat by regular bouts of sustained running, and can only be done in the 'closed' season. Eat well from the foods on the recommended list, and supplement them with amino acids to aid strength development and muscle bulk.

Although losing weight is the usual aim, in some situations a player might need to increase it. This isn't easy, as in most cases it requires a stimulation of the growth hormone. Evidence suggests that this can be done by standardised strength-training techniques and food supplements such as skimmed milk and protein powder foods.

Vegetarians

Some sportsmen and women are vegetarians, yet can still have an adequate sports diet. They particularly need to eat cheese and eggs, in much the same way as non-vegetarians eat meat. However, the vegetarian diet may lack iron, which is not readily available to the body in its vegetable sources, so supplementation might be necessary.

Sportsmen and women on vegan diets need to look very carefully at what they eat with a well-qualified nutritionist, to make sure that they get the correct balance of amino acids, minerals and vitamins.

Ergogenic aids

We live in a so-called 'health food' age and are constantly reminded by advertisers of the need to eat healthily. It is hard to understand what is meant by the term 'healthy eating'. When a person eats a well-constructed diet, with the right balance of basic nutrients, then that person will be eating healthily. In most cases advertisers are trying to market a 'wonder' product that can add a different dimension to a person's life through taking a 'supplement'. All supplements are precisely that – potions to supplement a normal healthy diet, and as such they should not be necessary. Most go towards making very expensive, and at times colourful, urine!

With the advent of improved dope testing procedures, and thus the added risk of detection, athletes will be searching for any substance that might just tip the balance in their favour. The health food market has been quick to take advantage of the situation and offer the miracle potion which can turn the 'average' into the 'world-beater'. Perhaps it is coincidental that the appearance of 'vogue' supplements seems to follow an identical four-year cycle to the Olympic Games? It is possible to justify any of the supplements by pseudo-scientific reasoning, however it is very difficult to find valid research to support the claims. If the world-record holder takes it then it must be good . . .

The athlete is faced with a very difficult problem. Should they believe what the advertisers say and invest in a product that might possibly help them to realise their life's ambition, without any firm evidence supporting its efficacy? In most cases the product does not come cheaply, and one is therefore considering committing a large proportion of available income. In such a situation the athlete is very gullible and there is no reliable source of information for them to take as reference. To receive a totally unbiased reference is difficult. Often the only literature available is a glossy advertisement leaflet, complete with an endorsement from a champion, an endorsement which is only of real value to the champion! I am certain that the information is available in research departments throughout the world, however the athlete may not wish to hear the truth: there is no substitute for hard work.

The supplement currently in 'vogue' is creatine, in one of its various forms. Several well-established sources have provided evidence that it works on race horses, and from my own work, albeit not in a very controlled situation, there is evidence that it can help people working at an intense rate for a period of between 15 seconds and one minute.

Making reference to the energy systems described in chapter 5, we can note that adenosine tri-phosphate can be recreated by the use of creatine phosphate. Hence, raw creatine must be converted to creatine phosphate. This conversion probably takes place in the liver and is enzyme-aided. It appears also that the enzyme activity is improved by the availability of ubiquinone, vitamin Q, which the market provides in the from of Co-enzyme Q 10.

Creatine is abundantly available in red meat, so does this place the vegetarian at a disadvantage? The body can also make creatine from amino acids, in particular arginine and glycine. Might selective amino acid supplementation therefore be a better source? At mitochondria and cytoplasmic level the prescence of inosine (yet another supplement) can speed up the resynthesis of adenosine tri-phosphate.

The situation is a confusing one and will be made clearer when the precise source of creatine is known – how it is produced, from what it is produced, and how pure the substance is. The bi-product of creatine metabolism is a substance known as creatinine, which is known to be toxic. Since athletes are mainly of the 'more is better' school, it becomes uncertain as to the level of creatinine the body can tolerate before it becomes dangerous. Finally, what percentage of supplemented creatine actually finds its way into becoming creatine phosphate? Perhaps there is some merit in eating quantities of red meat?

Another 'vogue' supplement is carnitine L. Carnitine is found in the muscles and in the liver, probably as a store for future use. Carnitine is related to the 'B' group of vitamins and it can be synthesised in the body utilising vitamin C. It is suggested that carnitine is involved in the transportation of fatty acids to the mitochondria. Fatty acids represent an enormous and valuable source of energy, particularly when it is needed for a sustained period of time, as in marathon running and other ultra-endurance events. The availability of fatty acids will have a 'sparing' effect upon energy produced from carbohydrates. It does this by placing a restriction on the activity of Co-enzyme A, saving the energy produced this way so that it can be used in a more efficient form during the 'emergency' stages of a lengthy event.

Earlier I mentioned vitamin Q, which appears to play a significant role in the production of various forms of energy. It is available in foods such as oily fish, beef, chicken, nuts and soya oil, so making sure that these foods are available in the normal diet might prove cheaper and more efficient than taking any form of supplement. However, this approach does create a problem with the athlete who says 'I don't like fish; I don't like green vegetables'. My answer is always 'Perhaps you will not like winning!'

Researchers have also made the sporting world aware of the need for hydration. Athletes have always been aware of the natural desire to drink after exercise, particularly when the exercise takes place in a hot, humid environment. The physical exercise has created a system whereby the heat generated by the work needs to be stabilised so that the core body temperature does not escalate. This is hormonally controlled and is influenced by the electrolyte balance in the body fluids. Years ago the automatic reaction to dehydration was to take salt tablets, a limited approach to correcting the levels of sodium. The body is very quick to adapt to prolonged periods of sweating, but not to instant changes as is the case with violent exercise. There is therefore a definite need to take precautionary measures.

There is evidence that once the body becomes dehydrated, even at a level as low as two per cent, then performance levels are adversely affected. The precautionary measure is to rehydrate before, during and after any form of exercise which can cause this type of stress. The water bottle with secure mouthpiece is now a common sight in sport. (Again, advertisers have been very quick to recognise this fact and produce logo-emblazoned bottles.) The problem is what to put in them? Manufacturers produce a wide variety of drinks for these circumstances. Some produce a well-balanced electrolyte-enriched fluid, while others manufacture a drink containing energy replacements, utilising glucose polymers or similar non-sugar substances. There is no doubt that energy taken in this form, during prolonged exercise, will enhance performance, but the drinks can also be used very effectively in post-exercise energy replacement. It is recognised that energy is best replaced very soon after exercise. If the process is delayed by an hour or more, then the replacement is slowed considerably, and it can take several days to re-establish the norm. Exercise has an inhibiting effect upon the appetite; most foods are not palatable soon after vigorous exercise, hence the energy replacement drink offers the option of 'killing two birds with one stone'.

This whole area of nutrition is one which athletes and coaches must now study, and even seek professional advice on, when striving for success at the highest level.

To summarise, I would recommend that an athlete should make sure they eat the following each day:

- adequate protein in the form of meat, eggs, cheese or a vegetarian substitute
- at least two root vegetables – one white (e.g potato), one coloured, (e.g. carrot)
- at least two green vegetables – one legume and one leafy
- at least two types of fruit – one citrus and one fleshy
- enough liquid to keep the urine 'sweet' (lacking odour) and clear.

Familiarisation

Most international performers will be required to compete in a variety of different countries, in different climates, environments and under different conditions for competition, all of which create additional stresses prior to competition. For example, competitors who took part in the 1968 Olympic Games in Mexico City had to familiarise themselves with the rarefied atmosphere of 2,250m (7,500ft) above sea level, a hot, humid climate, and, for many of them, an initial jet-lag. Those who wish to aspire to international level must give very careful thought to these varying conditions when preparing for distant international tours.

Temperature

A player from a temperate climate will experience discomfort when forced to compete in a tropical or even sub-tropical environment, as will people from equatorial regions when competing in a much cooler environment. English cricketers find themselves having to play in the heat of Australia, the Indian sub-continent and the West Indies, where the energy-sapping heat can have a dramatic effect upon performance, unless certain precautionary measures are taken. West Indian cricketers, playing in almost Arctic conditions in April in the north of England, cannot expect to give their best without some acclimatisation.

For sports like rugby, cricket and hockey, the weather also affects pitches. Rugby players who are only familiar with playing on the lush grass of Australian pitches experience difficulties when faced with the variety an English winter can offer – the very hard pitches of the early and late season, frost-bound pitches, or the soft, slippery surfaces frequently encountered in mid-winter. The first things they need to consider are their footwear and protective clothing.

Having to compete in very hot, humid conditions is the most common problem for international competitors. The only true way to acclimatise is to go to the country well in advance of the competition, and gradually get used to working in the different conditions. The emphasis must be on 'gradual', taking all of the necessary clothing precautions, e.g. hats, and other items designed for exercise in a hot climate. Certain types of skin will also require the protection of barrier creams.

In such conditions, dehydration is a real problem, hence the fluid intake must be increased. Without doubt, bottled water is the most suitable drink. Large quantities of fruit juice and carbonated drinks must be avoided as they are likely to produce an upset stomach. If a drink is too cold, it passes through the system too quickly. Increasing one's dietary salt certainly isn't necessary as the body very quickly adapts to the changes in its mineral balance, although in the short term the specially formulated, slow-release salt tablets might prove helpful. Specially prepared electrolyte drinks will help in a similar way, but they must be taken in moderation, as a rapid ingestion of any mineral will trigger off a homeostatic reaction in the body. They are useful during a playing interval in games such as soccer, rugby and hockey. The safest method is to experiment with various preparations as part of the training programme for such eventualities. The surest way to reduce the possible effects of dehydration is to drink water before, during and after exercise, but it is important to remember that the water must not be too cold.

Performers suffering from dehydration sometimes have to produce a urine sample for dope testers. This can be very stressful, with the athlete still unable to produce a sample several hours, and several pints of fluid, after the event. Patience and yet more fluid will eventually bring the desired response.

Altitude

At high altitudes the active muscles are partially starved of oxygen. The oxygen in the atmosphere lacks the pressure to allow the most efficient gaseous exchange in the lungs. However, by staying at altitude for a period of time, the body gradually starts to compensate by encouraging the red-blood-cell-producing mechanisms to produce more cells to carry oxygen, so increasing the level of oxygen available for activity. Despite this, the gas transfer in the lungs will still not be as efficient as at sea level; no amount of acclimatisation will permit the visitor to match the native because a heredity factor has given those people living at high altitudes a slightly different lung membrane, which allows a more efficient transfer of gas. This factor is gradually making its presence felt at international level in middle- and long-distance running events, where the Kenyans and Ethiopians are currently taking all the honours. Eventually, other high-altitude nations such as Peru and Chile are likely to excel in these events, once they have established strict training regimes.

The increase in red blood cells remains for several days after returning to sea level, and a number of athletes take advantage of this by training at altitude before major competitions. However, judging precisely when to return to sea level is difficult since the duration of the extra cells varies from athlete to athlete. A further problem with altitude training is that taking athletes away from their normal domestic environment can create emotional or psychological problems that far outweigh any physiological advantages. As far as the individual is concerned, one can only recommend 'try it and see'. It works for some people.

Time shift

Time changes, particularly when coupled with jet-lag, present a major problem, and one that many people involved in sport fail to recognise. The body has a 'body clock' mechanism, according to which it expects to do certain things at certain intervals. If there is a forced time change, such as flying to another continent to compete, then the body is unlikely to perform at its best. For example, in an Olympic Games held in North America, qualification rounds are frequently held at 9 a.m. Because of the routine of the Games, this will mean arising at 5 a.m. which, for the European, could be the equivalent of midnight as far as a personal body clock is concerned. Hence, to familiarise oneself the situation must be created in advance in training at home. The athlete would need to get up at midnight and go through the preliminaries, leading up to a training performance at 4 a.m. This might sound drastic, but it could produce that little extra that leads to a winning performance.

Jet-lag and flying

Some people cope with flying across time-zones with little change from their normal routine, while in others it can produce upsets as severe as feverish conditions with raised body temperatures. Some people are also terrified of flying, and have to be transported to major sporting functions by boat. Sea sickness is probably the lesser of the two evils!

Opinion is divided as to the best method of accommodating jet-lag. There are those who favour the quick flight out to compete almost the same day, and this is probably suitable for a one-off race, or a single match. The underlying philosophy behind this is that the effects of jet-lag are seldom immediate, and are most commonly experienced on the two days following the flight, when the body clock has had time to make its adjustments. The other body of opinion favours a long stay prior to the competition to allow the body clock adequate time to adjust itself.

Jet-lag is compounded by the conditions of air travel. On a long-haul flight, for example across the Atlantic, the body is forced into a confined space, with air conditioning, for several hours, and it is difficult for most people to sleep well in this atmosphere. In addition, there is the problem of dehydration, with associated dry and sore throats. While there are no-smoking areas, the fact that people do smoke in other areas of the aeroplane produces some overall pollution, which most sportsmen and women find irritating. The simple answer is to drink water frequently, limiting the amount of carbonated and fruit drinks to those provided with a meal. Alcohol should be limited or preferably avoided altogether, as it helps to promote dehydration.

Sitting in a confined space frequently causes fluid to pool about the ankles. The best solution is to remove tight-fitting shoes and give the ankles some exercise, with the occasional walkabout. Indeed, some airlines provide slippers/socks to help reduce the effects of this problem.

Boredom is another problem, but the airlines recognise this, and counter it with frequent bar/meal services and films. In this situation however, there is the obvious danger of overeating, or even eating unfamiliar foods, which is likely to cause stomach upset and which could adversely affect performance at a later date.

Unfamiliar cuisine

The type of food eaten in foreign countries, and at times the standard of hygiene in its preparation, can cause considerable discomfort to those who are not cautious in what they eat. The simple answer here is to stick to familiar food, drink only bottled water, wash all fruit in bottled water and restrict the amount of carbonated water and drinks such as fresh orange juice.

The problem does not arise in major events such as the Olympic Games, since international food is always served and is prepared under the most stringent hygiene conditions. It happens during small team trips, and slightly longer European fixtures, indeed some national teams now take their own food and chefs with them. Again, the obvious answer is to be cautious, to stick to familiar food and to seek treatment the instant there are signs of a stomach upset. It is possible to take a preventitive drug, but these are not without their side-effects. Seafoods are obviously to be avoided as the reaction to contaminated shellfish is very debilitating. As in all aspects of training for sport, prepare in advance, even in respect of food.

Know yourself

There may be other aspects of travel that could impinge upon an individual's performance in sport, and athletes should try to become aware of any idiosyncrasies. Training for peak performance requires careful thought and long-term planning to assure that the fewest possible factors are left to chance.

Training for major ball games

Elite performers in team ball games encounter problems that performers in individual sports do not. An athlete or boxer can peak for a one-off situation such as the Olympic Games; the elite performer in team ball games might have to produce a number of peak performances over a half year, or even over as much as nine months. The individual sportsman or woman is in total control of his or her own destiny; the major games player has to rely upon co-operation from other team members, knowing only too well that the chain is as strong as its weakest link. The individual athlete can undertake a period of relatively light work, lasting up to one week or more, prior to, or following, a major competition. If the major games player who had matches each weekend were to do this, it would mean a week without training.

By the very nature of the beast, the major games players only remain satisfied when working on the skill aspect of the sport, i.e. kicking, striking and passing, and left to themselves are likely to neglect flexibility, strength, power and endurance. The performer, or coach, should refer to the year plan listed on pages 136–7, and not give way to the temptation to drop elements of it.

To drive the point home, remember that there must be a two-week period of total recovery at the end of the season, where relaxation to re-charge the system is high on the list of priorities, and that the period of rest should be followed by a period during which the emphasis in training is upon endurance. This period should then be followed by one emphasising strength and bridging the components of strength endurance. Following this, in sequence, there should be periods of training that highlight specific strength, power, speed, and finally sport preparation, prior to the next competitive period.

The amount of time devoted to each of the components will be determined by the duration of the non-competitive period. For example, in the United Kingdom, soccer players only enjoy a 'closed' period of about 14 weeks, and rugby and hockey players slightly more, while cricketers usually get a break of over 25 weeks.

However, there is a problem with many elite performers, in particular in rugby league and cricket, whereby players can also get a contract in the southern hemisphere, which means that they are in a period of competition for the whole year. This is to be discouraged, certainly for an extended period of several years. It does not allow time for relaxation and recovery from the stress of one competitive season before the next is contemplated. Also, the closed period is one in which fitness levels are improved, new skills learned, and others modified. An extended period of all-year-round competition will only detract from the ultimate performance level.

Once the period of component emphasis is identified, there is a need to allocate the time spent on training each component. This will be determined by the total amount of time available each week.

To make sure that each component of fitness receives an adequate proportion of time, the unit plan is recommended.

The unit plan

A total of 10 units is allocated to the training programme. The time duration for each unit is determined by the total amount of time available for training. For example, if a performer has 10 hours each week to devote to training, each unit time is one hour. Should the total time be only five hours, then each unit time is 30 minutes.

For example, a soccer player in the month of April might have the following training distribution.

	No. units	Unit time	Total time
Speed	2	45 mins	90 mins
Strength	2	"	90 mins
Stamina	1	"	45 mins
Skill	4	"	180 mins
Suppleness	1	"	45 mins
	10		7½ hours

Using the above example, the player on the endurance (stamina) component might do the following, on different days of the week:

3-mile sustained run	20 minutes
5 x 300m with a 4-minute recovery	25 minutes
Total Time	45 minutes

Similarly, flexibility training might be split into three sessions, each of 15 minutes, prior to some of the skill sessions.

With the unit plan the opportunity exists to highlight a particular strength or weakness. For example, if a performer believes that strength levels might be low, then extra time can be devoted to it. However, it is important when using this system that the total number of units still add up to 10. This will mean reducing the unit value of another component to allow for the extra strength promotion.

Again, using the example above, the strength component could be increased by one unit, making a total of three, the skill component reduced by one unit, making that a total of three, while the total remains at 10 units.

Speed

The speed examined will be that of running, since all of the sports included in this section need to develop this ability to a very high degree.

For speed, one needs to sprint for a short distance, and allow an adequate time for the energy system to be replenished, as described in chapter 2. For ball-game players, 5 x 50m sprints using a handicap penalty is effective. It relies heavily upon the competitive nature of the individuals attracted to these sports to maintain their interest.

Ideally, the training area should be an athletics track with a synthetic surface, an all-weather playing surface, or a good-quality grass surface.

The training session is divided into a number of heats with a minimum of five and a maximum of eight players in each heat. Each group then runs a normal sprint race over a distance of 50m. The winner, and each subsequent winner, receives a penalty of one metre, which is never restored, in the block of five sprints. In the perfect world it should produce a different winner each time. The competitive nature of the activity encourages full effort, and stopwatch time can be used as an added incentive, with records kept of personal best times.

The exercise can be made more interesting and specific by adopting a number of different starting poses. For example, the rugby player can start in the full prone position and the hockey player in a standing start as for a penalty corner.

The emphasis must be on speed, and winning. Ideally the squad should be divided into groups of relatively equal sprinting ability using a promotion and relegation system to ensure a good level of competition.

Speed endurance

This is the aspect of training which few major games players enjoy. It is a hard, painful experience when done correctly, and will involve the player running fast, just sub-maximally, for an extended period (*see* chapter 5). The appropriate distance for the ball game team is between 150m and 300m, or 20–50 seconds. The number of repetitions and the recovery period will vary according to the group.

The following samples should serve as helpful guidelines:

5 x 300m @ 40–50 secs	5 mins recovery
8 x 150m @ 20 secs	2 mins recovery
120m, 140m, 160m, 180m, 200m,	
180m, 160m, 140m, 120m	walk back recovery

A useful variation is to have the players sprint along the sides and diagonals of their pitch (*see* page 132). In most sports this will be at least 300m.

Strength

There is only one way to increase strength and that is to exercise muscles against a resistance. Ideally, this should be in the form of weight training, using the modern 'stack' systems. The major games player is looking for all-round strength, and almost certainly the best method is to use the 'simple' system (*see* page 28) or the 'combination' system. Since the games player only needs to become strong enough to perform better in their chosen sport, heavy weight training is not advocated, but rather an eight-item routine is recommended, selecting three exercises for the upper body, three for the lower body and two for the trunk, keeping in mind that there will be a need for both extending and flexing movements. The player should work at levels between 60–90 per cent of maximum. This will dictate the number of sets and repetitions.

The player must also realise that weight training can be used to strengthen a particular part of the body in order to remedy a specific weakness, or as part of remedial work following an injury.

Strength endurance

This area could also be termed local muscular endurance (LME). It reflects the ability of the body to cope with a relatively high level of work placed upon a specific group of muscles, such as is experienced during a maximum period of an exercise, e.g. sit-ups.

For major games players, a twelve-item circuit, exercising the main muscle groups of the body in rotation, is recommended (*see* pages 67–8).

In team training a timed approach should be used, rather than performing a set number of repetitions at each station. The following offers a number of time variables, each exercise being performed at the station for a period of time, followed by a period of recovery before moving on to the next station.

Exercise time	*Recovery time*
30 secs	1 min.
30 secs	30 secs
40 secs	20 secs

Three or four circuits should be completed, depending upon the total amount of time allocated. Some coaches favour doing the complete routine at one station before moving to the next, while others favour the more conventional circuit approach, performing just one set of repetitions at each station to complete a single circuit, the total circuit then being repeated two or three times to achieve the stipulated dose.

Specific strength

To achieve specific strength, the player needs to perform exercises similar in nature to those used in the specific sport, only against a resistance. Elastic, rope, and pulleys, etc. can be secured to a bat, stick or boot so as to provide the resistance. For example, fig 74 (no. 2) shows a batsman performing a cricket stroke against the resistance of a rope that is controlled over a horizontal bar. The partner can vary the degree of tension on the rope to bring about the specific strengthening effect.

A number of these specific strength exercises can be placed in a skill/strength circuit and applied in an identical way to the circuit used to promote local muscular endurance.

For example, a typical skill/strength circuit for a cricketer could be:

1) bowling action against elastic resistance
2) straight-bat shot against rope tension
3) bowling action against high pulley and weight
4) back hyperextension against high pulley and weight
5) arm/shoulder overhead throw medicine ball
6) leg isolation – drills with weighted ball
7) accuracy throw
8) leg kick medicine ball
9) back hyperextension medicine ball
10) cross-bat shot against rope tension.

Fig. 74 Skill circuit for cricket

Elastic

1 Bowling action elastic

2 Straight bat shot

3 Bowling action pulley

4 Back strength high pulley

5 Bowling action – back leg isolation

6 Accuracy throw

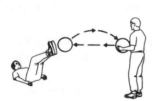

7 Leg extension – medicine ball

8 Leg flexion – medicine ball

9 Back hyperextension – medicine ball

10 Raise leg throw – medicine ball

11 Overhead throw – medicine ball

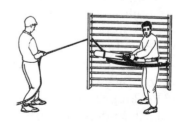

12 Cross-bat shot

Similar circuits can be devised for all of the major games using pulleys, elastic, medicine balls and weighted balls. For example, old rugby/soccer balls can be filled with sand or lead shot to provide a resistance exercise that only uses the skill of the specific sport.

By applying a resistance of any form, the actual skill pattern of that movement is slightly changed. However, strength developed this way is more likely to have a positive transfer of training to the skill itself than, for example, isolated weight training exercises.

Stamina/aerobic endurance

Aerobic endurance forms the foundation on which all other aspects of fitness are moulded. It determines the efficiency of the heart and lungs to continually pump oxygenated blood to the active muscle tissues. A period of aerobic fitness should immediately follow the post-season rest period.

To perform aerobic fitness training one should exercise at a fairly low intensity level, for a period of about 30 minutes, increasing to at least double that as the aerobic conditioning phase progresses. Once a reasonable level of aerobic fitness has been developed, one or two 30-minute sessions per week should be sufficient to keep the level primed. The most efficient way to do this is to run for a sustained period; the running can be on the road, provided good footwear is worn, or on grass or sand. Running can be sustained or more intermittent in the case of fartlek running (*see* page 59).

It will be very difficult for all players to develop aerobic fitness at the same level and rate of progression, mainly because of the differences in physique. Hence, for sustained runs of between 5 and 8 kilometres (3–5 miles), a handicap system should be considered so as to provide motivation for those with a physique unsuited to this type of work. While there should be very little difference between the endurance capacities of defenders and strikers in soccer, the goalkeeper being the exception, in both codes of rugby, the heavier forward will find sustained running considerably harder than the smaller back. In almost all cases, aerobic efficiency will be strongly influenced by bodyweight. Indeed, many players use their bodyweight as an excuse for not doing this type of work, but they must not be allowed to get away with it. There is also a strong tendency for major games players to neglect this mundane work, in the mistaken belief that it can be developed through a game-type situation. This cannot be the case, as the intermittent nature of the game restricts the pressure which is placed on the system by the sustained nature of continuous work.

As aerobic sessions must not deteriorate into very low intensity work, a time or a competitive incentive should be used to keep the level up. Good, fit, male hockey, soccer, American Football and rugby backs should be capable of sustaining 5–6-minute miles. Heavier players should be capable of averaging 6–8 minutes. Fit young women games players must be capable of sustaining a 6–8-minute-per-mile pace for a period of three miles.

Aerobic fitness is not developed overnight, but must be worked at over a period of years, but one thing is certain, the time spent on it will pay handsome dividends.

Skill training (team fitness)

It is not the intention in this text to discuss this aspect in detail, as the many books on individual sports cover it in depth. However, its position in a training programme is very important, although unfortunately too many major games players devote a disproportionate amount of time to this aspect of training and neglect the other important aspects of fitness.

Skill endurance

Skill levels are frequently influenced by endurance. When fatigue becomes evident, levels of co-ordination and speed co-ordination start to deteriorate. The body must be trained to cope with this situation by adopting a system of 'overload' training. This type of training is frequently termed 'pressure training' and calls for a skill to be repeated many times in a short period.

Pressure training must be specific, and will almost certainly require training partners and a good supply of balls, or an efficient system of returning the balls to the skill executor. Classic examples of this type of work could be corner kicking and receiving in soccer/hockey, and line out or scrummaging work in rugby. A specific skill is isolated and then put under pressure in a game-type situation, without permitting the full game pattern to flow (*see* chapter 7).

Certain skills can be included in a skill circuit, as explained in the specific strength aspect of this chapter – the skill tests listed on page 132 are ideal for this type of work. However, in this situation, the emphasis must be placed upon endurance.

A number of the skills are also ideal for using in repetitive shuttle relay-type practices. A good example of this type of work is in picking up, passing/throwing and catching skills in rugby or cricket.

5	4	3	2	1	0	A	B	C	D	E
					$\mid$					
x	x	x	x	x	0^1	x	x	x	x	x

The training groups should be divided into teams. Player 1 starts with a ball in his hand and runs to put it down on line 0–0¹, continues running to touch player A, and then stands behind player E. Player A runs, picks up the ball, passes it to player 2, and joins the team behind player 5. Each player then continues the movements in sequence. The shuttle run can continue for a certain period of time or for a set number of repetitions. There are many variations of this type of work, involving hitting, kicking or dribbling movements as in hockey and soccer.

The well-informed coach should have a good repertoire of shuttle-type relays and out-and-back relays.

Suppleness

Suppleness is one of the most neglected areas among major games players. In many cases, a well-planned flexibility training programme can restrict the incidence of common muscle injuries, such as those experienced with a torn hamstring. Many players pay lip service to suppleness by performing a few callisthenic or stretching exercises as part of a warm-up routine, but elite players should do at least one specific flexibility session each week, in addition to those done as part of a warm-up routine. The best techniques to use are those employing joint isolation with active and passive partners, also using a PNF system (*see* chapter 6).

The training day

An increasingly professional approach to sport, with more full-time players relying on their sport to provide their income, means that players have time to apply a scientific approach to their training. Those players who have to earn their living from some additional form of occupation can still copy the basic format outlined here. For most clubs there is a danger of copying what appears to be the norm in soccer; spending 90 per cent of their training time devoted to rehearsing skills. Using this approach it is doubtful that skill levels improve proportionately to the time devoted to them. One thing is certain, the player is unlikely to get faster, stronger and more powerful, as skill rehearsal will not improve these qualities significantly. I am also of the opinion that too much skill work is psychologically damaging, particularly when skill levels are very high.

With more time available for training, there is a danger of not allowing the body enough time to fully recover from the effects of high-activity training. I cannot emphasise enough that rest must form part of any training plan. Devoting too much time to physical exercise can cause the body to place itself in a catabolic situation, where stress leads to a breakdown rather than an adaptation. In such a state the immune system starts to break down, increasing the risk of infections, and the collagen system deteriorates, making a player more prone to injury as well as increasing the time taken for healing and recovery.

In most playing situations the match day will dictate when the players rest. Many professional clubs have a training session up to two hours before the match itself. For many it forms part of a skill rehearsal, however there is little evidence of it having any beneficial effect upon the game itself. It would be far better for the players to relax, reserve their stores of energy, and at an appropriate time start to focus their minds on the preparation necessary for elite performance. Similarly, most clubs rest the day after a match. While the advantages of this might seem obvious, there is more merit in calling the players in for a recovery session, taking the form of mild exercising and stretching, to stimulate the venous return system. This allows an opportunity to recognise any muscle soreness or centres of pain that could indicate a potential injury. The early treatment of a mild injury will assure a speedier rehabilitation.

Tournaments place an even greater strain on the players, as they have to play several games 'back to back', with very short recovery intervals spacing the games. Here there is an advantage in having a large, very fit squad, that has been prepared specifically for this type of stress. In this situation all of the recovery aids, for example physiotherapy, relaxation aids, energy and rehydration replacement supplements, etc. should be exploited to the full.

Total time available

Most good-class clubs, other than the full-time professional soccer clubs, only train for a maximum of three sessions per week, each of about two hours. This will mean that most players have to do almost as much again on their own, and it leaves the coach/trainer/player to make a decision as to which components should be left to the player's own devices. Most will find that the pure strength and aerobic endurance components are suited to individual development, whereas the components such as speed, which needs competition, and skill, which needs other team members present, are best developed in the squad situation.

Facilities

While some clubs only have the use of a grass pitch with limited floodlighting, most ambitious clubs take advantage of at least one weekly session in a gymnasium or sports centre. Such facilities are essential.

Hard, uneven or slippery surfaces in the depth of winter, where the main concern is to keep warm rather than attempt to develop a specific component of fitness, are not conducive to purposeful training. Some far-sighted clubs and individuals even take advantage of a weekly session at a local synthetic-surfaced athletics track. However, when the weather is good, the pitch is one of the best training areas, and full use should be made of it. Stands and terracing also offer the imaginative coach facilities that can add variety to any training session.

What to do

This, in part, will be determined by the amount of time available, and what the coach decides should form part of one's own personal training programme, as opposed to the squad training programme.

To make sure that all of the various components of fitness are covered, a monthly plan should be adopted. A typical plan for a rugby side based on three sessions per week might be as follows:

	30 mins	*30 mins*	*30 mins*
Week 1			
Day 1	Aerobic endurance: run drills, etc. (PNF)	Skill endurance: skill circuit	Speed: 6 x 50m sprint
Day 2	Speed: 40m, 60m 80m x 2	Speed endurance: 4 x 300m, 5 min. recovery	Skill: tactics team plays
Day 3	Speed: 120m, 140m, 160m, 180m, 200m	Speed endurance: local muscular endurance circuit	Skill: team plays
Week 2			
Day 1	Aerobic endurance: running drills and PNF	Speed: bounding	Skill: team plays
Day 2	Speed: 2 sets of 5 x 50m as handicap sprints	Speed endurance: 4 diagonal pitch runs	Skill endurance: skill relays
Day 3	Aerobic drills and PNF and local muscular endurance	Speed: 8 x diagonal sprints	Skill: team plays

Week 3

Day 1	Speed: 10 x 50m	Speed endurance: 6 x 300m, 5 min. recovery	Skill endurance: skill relays
Day 2	Aerobic running drills, PNF and local muscular endurance circuit	Speed: 6 x 120m, walk back recovery	Skill: team plays
Day 3	Speed: 40m, 60m, 80m x 3	Speed endurance: 6 diagonal pitch runs	Skill: team plays

Week 4

Day 1	Speed: team relays, shuttles out	Speed endurance: 120m, 140m, 160m, 180m, 200m	Skill endurance: skill circuit
Day 2	Aerobic running drills, bounding	Speed: bounding	Skill: team plays
Day 3	Speed: 10 x 50m	Speed endurance: 3 x 600m, 8 min. recovery	Skill: team plays

A plan of this nature gives sufficient variation to prevent boredom, but is repetitive enough to be purposeful. The coach must make full use of skill relays, and skill circuits, to include all of the skill factors in a game. For example, the rugby coach must include passing, catching, tackling, being tackled etc. in the circuits. There is no real limit to the variety of skills which the innovative coach can include.

Using a training programme such as this requires a degree of pre-training organisation. By attempting to train three specific components in one evening, time will be at a premium, hence there has to be a slick changeover. The components should be done in the order listed, otherwise maximum benefit will not be achieved from a component such as sprinting. Team discipline is essential, as vital minutes can be lost if players arrive late, leave early or chat.

What to avoid

Many professional clubs, particularly those involved in seasonal sports such as soccer, rugby and cricket, only do any form of fitness training in an intensive period just before the season starts. This is almost certainly determined by tradition rather than any systematic approach to training. In many instances, the total time allotted to pre-season training is in the region of a month. This is nearly always preceded by a period of the same duration of almost total inactivity. Hence there is seldom a period during which there is a build up of the intensity of training. The result is that many players approach the season enthusiastically but often fatigued.

This approach will also not permit any significant development in the qualities of speed, strength, speed endurance and strength endurance. The evidence is overwhelming to support the fact that if these specific personal qualities are not stimulated, at least weekly, they will regress to a pre-trained state. Hence time must be permitted during the playing season to stimulate the systems responsible for speed, strength and the related qualities. Indeed, it is sufficient to say that, of the 'S' factors, skill is the factor which regresses the slowest. Once a person has learned to swim, the skill remains until the muscles deteriorate to the extent that they can no longer provide the propulsive power. With as little as three days confined to ones bed, it is possible to see how quickly strength regresses!

The solution is to refer again to chapter 8, examine the schedules detailed in this chapter, and then devise a scheme of work to suit the specific needs of the team.

CHAPTER 17

Training for combat sports

Combat sports consist of a wide variety of skills which, on the face of it, have only one common component in that they are individual- and not team-based. The boxer, for example, will need a slightly different mix of the various components of fitness than will the fencer, wrestler or judo performer. However, in terms of physiological demands, the sports are all quite similar in that the body is involved in a high level of physical activity for a short duration, seldom exceeding three minutes. Bouts of activity are spaced with periods of recovery, hence the intermittent nature of the work is predetermined.

Boxing is quite unique as a sport, in that it is the only sport whereby the primary aim is to make your opponent incapable of continuing in the contest, by forcing a temporary loss of consciousness. In conditioning, the boxer has to rehearse a situation whereby energy is expended in delivering a blow and must also prepare for the energy-sapping mechanisms of receiving a blow.

Training components

The following qualities rate amongst the top five essential training components for the combat sportsman or woman, though they are not listed in rank order:

1) local muscular endurance of the arms and legs
2) gross strength
3) speed of arm and leg movements
4) cardio-vascular efficiency
5) skill.

194

The fact that a component such as flexibility is not listed does not mean that it should be excluded from a training regime.

Combat sports, other than during an Olympic Games, do not have the clearly defined seasons of the major team games and participants are not usually required to compete for an extended season of several months. Participants can almost select their competitions and then peak towards those occasions. Hence, for this group of sports it becomes *what* to do rather than *when* to do it.

Local muscular endurance

To develop local muscular endurance the player must perform work tasks of a high extent and a fairly low intensity. The ideal methods available are circuit training and high-repetition weight or resistance training.

A ten- or twelve-item circuit should be selected, similar to the one listed on pages 67–8. Either the repetition system, or the timed system, is appropriate. Ideally the full circuit should be completed two or three times each week, changing the system to permit a degree of variety. In addition to this, the performer is advised to do 100 repetitions of three different exercises every morning, soon after awakening – press-ups, sit ups and squat jumps are appropriate. The time taken to perform such a routine is minimal, in total less than 10 minutes, but the small sacrifice will repay the performer with considerably enhanced local muscular endurance.

High repetition weight training, working at a level of 50 per cent of the one rep maximum and keeping the extent of training high, will help to improve this quality. The timed approach is ideal for combat sports, initially starting with an exercise time of one minute, followed by a recovery period of one minute. An eight-item schedule should prove efficient, using the main muscle groups of the body (arms, trunk and legs) in rotation. Once the athlete is familiar with this type of approach, the extent of training can be improved and made more specific by miming more closely what happens in a contest, e.g. 3 x 3 mins with a one-minute recovery. This is certainly not a schedule for the faint-hearted.

The combat sports take place within the confines of a fairly small, restricted area. The basic leg movements are of a skipping, side-stepping nature rather than the striding action of a runner, hence skipping and side-stepping movements must form part of any systematic training routine. Skipping with a rope is an ideal movement, since it conditions both the arms and the legs. The tempo and the duration can be varied to bring about an adaptive response.

Bar jumps, side-stepping and criss-cross movements are also ideal for both training and evaluation techniques (*see* pages 196–7).

Bar jumps

While a bar placed between two gymnasium benches is ideal, a single reversed bench with the balance side upwards, provides an ideal piece of training apparatus. The performer starts with both feet to one side of the bench and jumps across the bench to take up an identical double-foot landing position. This sideways jump is repeated in quick succession at a rate of one per second (*see* fig. 75).

Side stepping movements

Two chalk lines are marked out one metre either side of a central line on a firm, reliable surface. The performer starts with the feet straddling the central line. With a side-stepping movement the bodyweight is shifted quickly to place the right foot over the right side line, then, with a similar side stepping movement, cross the centre line to place the left foot over the left side line. The movement is performed for one minute, a score being made each time the centre line is crossed (*see* fig. 76).

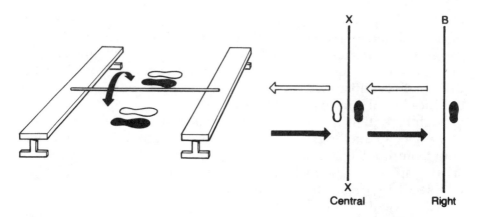

Fig. 75 Bar jumps

Fig. 76 Side stepping

Criss-cross movements

Another useful exercise is the criss-cross movement. A square of 1m x 1m is constructed on the floor and divided into four equal parts, numbered 1–4. The performer starts with both feet in square 1 and jumps with both feet together to land wholly in square 2, then to squares 3 and 4 in rotation. The number of complete sequences 1–4, minus the number of mistakes, in one minute is recorded.

The above movements can all be performed for five sets of one minute each, spaced with a one-minute recovery.

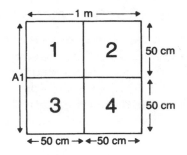

Fig. 77 Criss-cross movements

Gross strength

While gross strength might not appear to be a prerequisite for a fencer, it is instantly recognised as a most important quality for the boxer, wrestler, or martial art practitioner. However, a scientific approach must be taken to the development of strength with a careful eye kept on strength–weight ratio. With high-intensity, or even high-extent weight training, there is likely to be an increase in muscle bulk, with an associated weight increase, that could push the competitor into a higher weight category. This might not be a desirable effect.

The performer should adopt a variety of strength training techniques. The elite performer might be a novice to weight training, hence advice must be sought as to developing an efficient lifting technique. Once this has been developed the information in chapter 3 should be used. The combat sportsman or woman should firstly consider the simple approach, then progress towards the combination or tri-set system. The boxer or wrestler, who will almost certainly require greater strength levels, must consider one of the more advanced systems using very heavy weights, in the region of 90 per cent of the one repetition maximum.

When specific peaking is required, the performer should firstly develop a level of strength endurance using a more extensive system of training, before progressing on to the intensive method for maximum strength gain.

In contests such as wrestling, it will certainly mean sustaining an almost isometric contraction for a period of time, until submission is gained, or a skill advantage position is secured. This situation must be mirrored in strength training for these sports.

Speed of limb movements

This quality, like sprinting, is an endowed one. A person is born with muscle fibres, nerve supply and blood supply, all of which help to facilitate fast movements. As an endowed quality there exists a maximum speed potential, and it is towards achieving this potential that all speed training must be directed. As speed can be affected by other components of fitness, such as strength, flexibility and skill, it must not be considered in isolation. It follows, therefore, that some of the movements described for speed endurance, such as skipping and side stepping, could also have a transfer of training effect upon the quality of speed.

In training, the combat sportsman or woman can use punch bags, shadow boxing/fencing movements, and other traditional techniques that enhance speed of movement. Probably the most rewarding avenue to explore is to work with speed balls, or over-inflated basketballs or soccer balls.

The speed ball should be familiar to all boxers. Its basic principle can be experienced by pushing a hard basketball or soccer ball against a wall. The performer should stand just slightly further away from the wall than the length of the arms, and then perform a rebound pushing movement at maximum speed. Indeed, once the performer has mastered the technique, the ball moves so quickly that it appears to be static against the wall. The level of the arms, relative to the shoulders, can be varied to bring about a desired effect.

Plyometrics should be used to develop the speed of leg movement. The bounding activities, depth jumping and medicine ball work described on pages 39–48, are ideal.

Cardio-vascular efficiency

As always, sustained running is the activity most likely to bring about the best adaptive response. The exercise period should last at least 30 minutes and those who wish to aspire to high levels of fitness should do a minimum of three sessions each week. While an early morning session is common within this group of sports, and ideal for those who wish to shed weight, it can be done effectively at any time of the day. The pace of the sustained run will vary considerably from person to person. However, good, fit, young men should aim for a sustained speed of 6–7 minutes per mile while women will, in most cases, be about one minute per mile slower.

Skill training

Skill training must be specific and related to the individual sport. Time must be spent in the organisation of the practice to make sure that it is purposeful, and sessions should be devoted to skill endurance, skill speed/power and tactics. A coach should always be present to make sure that the objectives of the practice are achieved. Full use should be made of coaching aids such as videos, instant analysis and the correction of faults. (*See* chapter 7.)

Training diary

The individual combat performer should be encouraged to keep a training diary, which should include both a forecast of work and the actual work performed. By documentation it is possible, at the end of a training cycle, to analyse and correct any mistakes.

Training for racket sports

While it is possible to group the racket sports under one heading for convenience sake, the fact is that at the elite level there is now a massive difference between the fitness components of tennis, squash, badminton, etc. However, while specific requirements do indeed differ from sport to sport, there are many components they hold in common.

It has been reported that champion tennis players practise for up to three hours prior to major matches. If this is true, then they are enduring up to five hours or more of high-level physical activity. It should not be assumed that the fitness levels required by the badminton or squash player are in any way inferior to those of the tennis player.

The key areas of fitness that the racket sports player must develop are: specific strength/power, specific speed about the court, local muscular endurance, cardio-vascular efficiency, and skill. This does not mean that other components of fitness, such as flexibility, are to be ignored, but that they can be integrated into a programme of training, while the specific areas identified receive special emphasis.

Specific strength

Like all of the specific components of fitness, strength has to be developed out of already strong and powerful muscles. Hence a foundation of strength, and strength endurance, has to be developed. This must be done by systematic weight training, using any of the systems described in chapter 3. Initially, the foundation has to be based on strength endurance using an 'extensive' method, such as the simple or combination system. Once the body is familiar with exercising against this form of resistance, an 'intensive' method, designed to promote gross strength, should be followed.

It must be remembered that the promotion of strength is not an instant recipe for success. While strength gains can be fairly rapid, strength training is a long-term investment, which will pay dividends over years rather than months.

Although there does not appear to be a firmly defined season for those at the very highest international level, especially for those who compete in the Antipodes, racket sports are nevertheless seasonal. This allows the performer to peak for a specific competition period, which may extend over a period of months (*see* chapter 1 for a full explanation of 'peaking').

The basic requirement for strength promotion is that one should spend several weeks on each of the areas of strength endurance and gross strength as part of a complete fitness programme. Moreover, these components must not be ignored once the tournament season has started. They regress fairly quickly, but it only requires a weekly session to maintain levels. During the season the player should follow a strength retention schedule whereby eight exercises are selected and performed at the 3 x 8 of 75 per cent maximum.

Specific strength training should take the form of four different methods: weight training, pulley and rope work, medicine ball activities and muscle group isolation skills.

Weight training

The weight training exercises are of a kind where the movement pattern in shifting the weight is similar to that which might be performed in executing a particular stroke, such as the straight arm pull-over for the tennis service.

Pulley and rope work

Rope and elastic are secured to a convenient part of the racket and the action of a shot is performed against the resistance of an attached weight. Alternatively, this can be done against the controlled resistance of a partner, in which case a horizontal bar or beam is required for strokes such as the service, while a vertical bar is required for cross-body shots, such as the forehand and backhand drives (*see* fig. 74).

Medicine ball

A weighted ball is thrown to a partner, or against a wall, and then caught on the rebound for subsequent repetitions, using an arm movement similar to that performed in the execution of the strokes (*see* figs 28, 29 and 30 for overhead shots and fig. 26 for cross-body shots).

Muscle group isolation drills

Muscle group isolation drills are strength-promoting activities, during which a muscle group, such as the right leg (*see* fig. 78), is isolated so that more pressure is placed upon the left shoulder and lower back. Similarly, the left leg can be raised to make the right side work harder to push the body over the fulcrum (*see* fig. 79).

Speed and power

The speed component of movements must not be ignored while the player is performing exercises on a specific strength. Throughout all of the activities the player must work against the resistance at maximum speed. It is only by exerting a large force, over a short period of time, that power can be trained.

Fig. 78 Skill isolation, rear leg isolated

Fig. 79 Skill isolation, front leg raised on platform

Specific speed about the court

The key to success in racket sports is to get the body into the right position on the court, to play the stroke, and to try to dictate play by forcing your opponent about the court, so making them tired or forcing them to hurry a stroke.

It is unlikely that the dominant player in a rally will have to run more than four or five strides, but speed off the mark is of paramount importance. Moving about the court involves a combination of forwards running, backwards running, side stepping, turning, stopping and changing direction, all done with accuracy to position the body to play an effective stroke. This calls for tremendous speed, power and agility in the lower limbs.

Initially, in the preparatory period of training, the player should practise sprinting over a short distance, say about 30 metres, preferably on a synthetic surface and using the correct footwear. To get maximum benefit, it is best done competitively by racing against other players. As the season approaches, this should be superseded by sprinting of a more specific nature, changing the distance, direction and starting position so as to approach what is likely to be experienced on the court of play. Sprinting about a court, however, as part of a game will not be enough. It must be done in isolation, where the focus of attention is speed of leg movement and not getting into position to play a shot.

Sprinting speed is also considerably influenced by gross strength and flexibility, and these should be trained as outlined in chapters 4 and 6.

Plyometric training is, without doubt, the best method for developing the agility to move about the court at peak, controlled speed. The movements involve very powerful contractions of the leg muscles to force changes in speed and direction. The basic activities include bounding, in all of its many forms, depth jumping and kicking medicine balls (*see* chapter 4).

When performing plyometric activities, the performer must be conscious of the speed of the movement. He or she must always attempt to produce maximum power from the muscles. Advanced plyometric training should only be done by mature players who have first developed the necessary strength and co-ordination through more formal strength training techniques and sprinting.

Ideally, the racket player would do at least one plyometric session each week of the year, with probably two sessions at the peak of the out-of-season conditioning phase.

Local muscular endurance

One has only to observe top tournament players to appreciate exactly how long some rallies can last, the sheer power of each stroke, the dynamic movements necessary to gain a positional advantage, and to realise the precise contribution that local muscular endurance can make. Indeed, during a long rally this will probably be the deciding factor, because as fatigue develops, both power and skill deteriorate.

Local muscular endurance is best developed by 'extensive' weight training and circuit training (*see* chapter 5). Sportsmen and women can learn a lot from each other, so chapters 16 and 17 which examine the major games player and the combat sports player will offer the racket player some useful advice. Indeed, the movements about a court could be described as a cross between those of a boxer and a soccer player.

As the onset of the season approaches, the circuit should become more specific, introducing a number of the activities described in chapter 5.

Cardio-vascular efficiency

Few racket sport players enjoy this aspect of training, but it is the foundation upon which all other aspects of fitness are based. While some of the activities listed under local muscular endurance will contribute a certain amount to this aspect of fitness, the best way to improve it is to run, at a sustained pace, for at least 30 minutes. Initially, many good-class players will find this hard, and will frequently offer boredom as an excuse for not doing it. However, once the early discomfort associated with this type of work is no more than a memory, improvements are rapid and many players even get to enjoy the sustained running session.

During the early stages of training for endurance the player is advised to run for a period of time, rather than for a set distance. Like most aspects of fitness, it has to be developed gradually, and most players will have to build up to the 30-minute target in stages. Those who are unfamiliar with this type of work are advised to mix jogging and walking for a period of 30 minutes and gradually, as the weeks progress, to reduce the walking and increase the running content, until a 30-minute run is comfortable. This takes weeks rather than months. Soon after the target of 30 minutes slow, sustained running has been achieved, the player should be encouraged to increase the tempo.

The player should consider doing this type of work for two sessions each week during the peak of the out-of-season endurance phase, and for one session each week during the playing season.

Skill training

Individual players have to work with their coaches to develop the skill of their specific game, a practice which is beyond the scope of this book. But one thing is certain – skill training must be an all-year-round activity. Once a systematic approach to training has been adopted, there will be significant improvements in strength, power, speed and flexibility, all of which will have an influence upon technique. Unless skills are kept in harmony with these improvements they could need almost total re-education at a future date.

During skill training sessions, the player must be put under pressure to practice a specific stroke. The skill is isolated so that specific weaknesses can be rectified, and is then, at a later stage, returned to the game situation.

Schedule

It now only remains to fit all of the components of fitness into a care-fully-planned schedule. Training at least twice a day on different components of fitness, especially during the out-of-season condition-ing phase, will certainly be necessary. A weekly schedule, during the conditioning phase of the year, might read as follows.

	Session 1	*Session 2*
Day 1	30-minute sustained endurance run.	Flexibility PNF, strength training with weights.
Day 2	Flexibility with active partner, skill training (matchplay).	Speed training, 6 x 50m full effort sprints, full recovery.
Day 3	30-minute sustained endurance run.	Plyometrics, bounding, medicine ball work.
Day 4	Flexibility PNF, strength training with weights.	Circuit training for local muscular endurance.
Day 5	Plyometrics, bounding, medicine ball work.	Skill circuit – isolation drills, ropes, pulleys, elastics.
Day 6	---------------------------- R E S T ----------------------------	
Day 7	Skill training (pressure).	Speed training – specific; sprinting using sideways and backwards running from a variety of starting positions.

Training diary

A training diary should be kept to record the progress of training and to document it for future analysis.

Training for individual sports

As far as training is concerned, sports centred on individual performance such as athletics, gymnastics, golf and swimming, are not as complicated to plan as team sports. Apart from international events – the Olympic Games, Commonwealth Games, and World and European championships – the individual is relatively free to select when and how often to compete. This makes the phasing of training and the associated peaking much easier to plan and put into practice.

However, the individual sportsman and woman live in fear of being injured, with the attendant frustration of not being able to train and having to observe the success of others. Although team game players experience similar frustrations, their teams continue to play week-in and week-out, and the injured player can recover and regain his or her place in the team. For individual sport performers, competitions missed are gone for ever. On the other hand, individuals are unlikely to receive contact injuries, and can minimise the chance of stress-related injuries through training strength, power, and flexibility.

While on the surface it might appear difficult to treat such diverse sports as golf and swimming together, there are common components in their training, and it is these features that will be highlighted in this chapter.

The individual performer will need to train appropriately for all of the 'S' factors, allowing, at times, for the specificity of each. For example, the thrower from field events, the golfer, the swimmer and the gymnast will all need arm strength; the middle-distance runner and the swimmer will need local muscular endurance; the jumper and the gymnast both have to produce 'flight'. It will be up to the individual athlete to appreciate the common components of each, and then select from the total training structure the appropriate aspects for their own individual needs.

Remember that a performer is only as strong as the weakest link, and that any weaknesses must be removed by extra training.

Speed

While both strength and flexibility have a cross-component effect upon speed, the only way to train true speed is to make the respective limbs and levers function quickly (*see* chapter 2).

The sprinter and the gymnast might perform short sprints on a fast surface over a distance of 30–60 metres. The swimmer could also do short sprints as part of 'land' training (the swimmer has the problem that his or her sport is performed in a resistant medium, but speed movements have to be practised out of water).

Arm speed, as required by the sprinter, thrower, golfer, swimmer and gymnast, can be trained with the speed ball and basketball rebound drills.

Speed of arm movement could be a focal point during skill isolation drills. Drills of this nature require tremendous concentration and commitment to the end result from the performer. All speed movements require the fast muscle fibres to work quickly, are energy-demanding and require a long recovery time before subsequent movements can be performed.

Power-promoting activities such as plyometrics, medicine ball work on both arms and legs, and specific weight training, can also have a profound effect upon both arm and leg speed (*see* chapter 4).

Speed endurance

Activities such as sprinting, middle-distance running and most swimming events call for a high level of speed endurance. When the muscles are required to work very quickly for an extended period of time, the performer has to become familiar with the high-activity bi-products which build up in the muscles. Within a short period of time, about 40 seconds, the muscles are forced to stop contracting or reduce the level of activity. Hence, those involved in activities requiring speed endurance must work at a very intense level for about 40 seconds, and then allow the muscles time to recover before subsequent bouts of activity. The recovery period needs to be about ten times as long as the activity and the number of repetitions limited to about four or five, otherwise the recovery process cannot function correctly. When the intensity of effort is reduced, the aerobic energy system takes over. Repetition running, on a track, is ideal to train this quality.

Strength

Gross strength is an essential quality for anyone involved in elite performance, irrespective of their sport. It is the term used for the essential foundation on to which all other aspects of strength are superimposed.

Gross strength is discussed in chapter 3, and athletes looking to develop this quality should refer in particular to the section relating to the systems. Sprinters, middle-distance runners, swimmers and jumpers should consider the simple system, the combination system or the super-set system; golfers and gymnasts only need to consider the simple system; throwers should consider the super-set, tri-set and pyramid systems.

To develop gross strength one must exercise at high intensity and low extent, above the 80 per cent one repetition maximum (*see* page 33). However, this will change according to the training emphasis appropriate to the time of the year, and should strength endurance be required instead of gross strength, then an 'extensive' method should be used whereby the training load is between the 50 per cent and 80 per cent one repetition maximum.

Specific strength

It is in the area of specific strength that the coach/performer can really innovate. Certainly, the individual skills of the heavy field event performer, the swimmer and the golfer lend themselves to a whole host of resistance exercises involving pulleys, resistance pulleys, rope and elastic to simulate a movement made in the particular sport. By securing a pulley or elastic strands to a suitable anchorage point on a gymnasium beam or wall-bars, it can soon be appreciated how the configurations work to produce the right pattern of movement. *See* pages 48–54 and the exercises on page 186.

Power

The term 'power' is frequently used incorrectly. In most cases the word 'powerful' is used to convey a visual impression of a person. But its precise meaning is 'the rate at which work is done', thereby having a force and time component. To be powerful one must be capable of exerting a large force in a very short period of time, and this requires both speed and strength.

As far as the human body is concerned, powerful movements call upon the elastic quality of the muscles. The best way to develop this precise quality is through plyometric exercises. The coach and performer must make full use of bounding, depth jumping, medicine ball work and skill isolation drills, all of which are discussed in chapter 4.

The recent improvements in performance in events such as the heavy throws, jumping and gymnastics, have come about through the modern appreciation of strength training and the related areas of power and plyometrics. An out-of-season period of training which includes a range of plyometric exercises is guaranteed to bring handsome rewards.

Endurance

Although the golfer, gymnast or thrower requires less cardio-vascular efficiency than a long-distance runner, a degree of training in this area is still required as it is the foundation of all fitness. One aerobic session a week spent running at a sustained pace for at least 30 minutes can be sufficient. The speed of the run will vary considerably from person to person and from sport to sport, and with individual experience in this type of training.

Local muscular endurance

While all individual sportsmen and women require a degree of local muscular endurance, it is particularly important for the middle- and distance runner and the swimmer. The requirements for the individual sports athlete are met by 'extensive' weight training and circuit training (*see* pages 67–8).

Anaerobic efficiency

In part, anaerobic efficiency is the same as speed endurance, which has already been discussed. However, for certain sports, particularly middle-distance running, refined anaerobic efficiency is needed. Runners should train by running fast for between 40 and 120 seconds, with a recovery period of about ten times the length of the run, according to the needs of the individual.

Flexibility

Flexibility is often ignored, but, if trained correctly, it will enhance any individual performance. The gymnast and the track and field athlete will probably be the only individuals to pay more than lip service to it, although, as stated in chapter 6, any activity which has power as an essential feature can be enhanced by improved flexibility. A mobile joint is a good insurance against injury.

Individuals must start by using the simple techniques of

callisthenics before progressing to more advanced methods that use joint isolation and the PNF systems.

While a few passive stretching exercises might help to support existing levels of flexibility, they are unlikely to promote any significant improvement in joint dynamics. As part of a general warm-up routine they might stretch a muscle prior to competition and give a degree of improved efficiency, but the elite performer should schedule at least one flexibility session per week lasting a minimum of 30 minutes, to really improve the quality.

Skill

Skill is the key feature of most of the individual-based sports – one has only to think of the intricate skill of the gymnast. Movements which a decade ago were considered impossible are now fairly commonplace.

It is frequently said that 'practice makes perfect'; in fact the word 'controlled' should be inserted at the start of the phrase. It is then up to the coach to provide the degree of control, and make full use of all of the skill acquisition techniques and learning aids detailed in chapter 7. While skill can be broken down into isolated parts and practised in slow motion, true skill can only be trained effectively at competition speed.

Scheduling

It is possible to detail a training schedule with some sports, but not with the individual-based sports. Consider track and field athletics, which involve, in basic terms, the different activities of running, jumping and throwing. Each activity is further subdivided – the sprinter will require a completely different training programme to the marathon runner, yet both are runners. Aside from the running events, which use a very natural skill, the field eventer will need to spend vast amounts of time perfecting the intricate skills of the individual disciplines.

With this in mind, the individual performer has to examine the specificity of fitness, and once the basic foundation of the 'S' factors has been established he or she then has to concentrate on particular forms of fitness. For example, during the out-of-season phase of conditioning the swimmer and the sprinter might use similar methods to develop strength, but as the season approaches the swimmer will use resistant aids for water training and the sprinter will sprint up short, steep inclines.

However, if any of the basic components of fitness are ignored, the ideal of the 'total athlete' cannot be maintained and performance levels will not improve. To make sure that the foundation is secure, it is recommended that the individual uses the unit plan, detailed on page 182. It can be used in conjunction with a yearly plan, as detailed on pages 136–7, and the all-important training diary.

Once a training plan has been adopted for a specific year, it is most unwise to divert from it. Changes should only be made at the end of a year, after a critical analysis of training has been made, in conjunction with the documented training in the diary. Nevertheless, external factors such as illness or injury can force adjustments to the proposed training programme and, indeed, can even necessitate the exclusion of a specific phase or a reduction in the total time spent on developing a component. Unfortunately, emergencies of this nature will have an inevitable effect on fitness, and possibly on performance levels at a later stage.

It is impossible to overemphasise the importance of a planned approach to both conditioning (the preparation of a foundation of fitness) and skill training. Skill has to be continuous; it must be practised 52 weeks of the year so that it is kept in harmony with the development of other components such as strength and flexibility, which in turn will force the modification of a current technique. Likewise, the components of fitness must receive regular, weekly stimulation otherwise they will regress. If a season is too long it might even be advantageous to withdraw from competition for a brief period so as to rebuild the foundations of strength, speed and endurance in order to resume at a higher level.

Recommended reading

Advanced Studies in P.E. and Sport by Paul Beashel and John Taylor
(Nelson, 1997)

Basic Biomechanics by Susan Hall
(Mosby, 1991)

Biomechanics: A Qualitative Approach (4th edition) by Kreighbum and
Barthels
(Allyn, 1996)

The Biophysical Foundations of Human Movement by Bruce Abernethy
et al
(Human Kinetics, 1997)

Exercise Physiology, Energy, Nutrition and Human Performance
(4th edition) by McArdel and Ketch
(Williams and Wilkins, 1996)

Genetics of Fitness and Physical Performance by Bruchard et al
(Human Kinetics, 1977)

Mechanics of Sport Performance by Peter Walder
(Feltham, 1994)

Physical Education and the Study of Sport by Davies et al
(Mosby, 1997)

Physiology of Sport and Exercise by Jack H. Wilmore and
David L. Costill
(Human Kinetics, 1994)

Science of Flexibility (2nd edition) by Michael J. Alter
(Human Kinetics, 1996)

Index